Steve Waugh's
SOUTH AFRICAN TOUR DIARY

IRONBARK

COVER PHOTOGRAPHY

Main photo: Steve Waugh at Stellenbosch during the match against Boland. *Australian Picture Library – Mike Hewitt (All Sport).*
Front cover: Top left, Allan Border with Nelson Mandela during a break in play in the match against the Nicky Oppenheimer XI.
Top right: Merv Hughes and friend, at Soweto.
Bottom left: Shane Warne after having dismissed Peter Kirsten, caught by Mark Taylor, during the second Test at Cape Town. *Australian Picture Library – Thomas Turck (Touchline Media).*
Back cover: Steve Waugh, Mark Taylor, Allan Border and Ian Healy on Table Mountain. *Australian Picture Library – Mike Hewitt (All Sport).*

PHOTOGRAPHS

The following black-and-white photographs that appear in this book were provided by the Australian Picture Library:
Pages 26, 56, 59, 64, 66, 71, 86, 95, 96, 99, 101, 137, 159 – *Mike Hewitt (All Sport).*
Pages 37, 40, 41, 46, 73, 114, 118 – *Tertius Pickard (All Sport/ Touchline Media).*
Pages 58, 112, 119, 121, 139, 140, 143, 145, 147, 153 – *Thomas Turck (All Sport/Touchline Media).*
Thanks also to Mark Ray, for providing the photo on page 72.

First published 1994 in Ironbark by Pan Macmillan Australia Pty Limited
St Martins Tower, 31 Market Street, Sydney

Reprinted 1994

National Library of Australia
cataloguing-in-publication data:

Waugh, Steve, 1965- .
Steve Waugh's South African tour diary.

ISBN 0 330 35625 9

1. Waugh, Steve, 1965- . – Diaries. 2. Cricket players – Australia – Diaries.
3. Test matches (Cricket). I. Title. II. Title: South African tour diary.

796.358092

Typeset and design by Brevier Design
Printed in Australia by McPherson's Printing Group

CONTENTS

DEDICATION

To all those responsible for the end of *apartheid* and the renewal of official sporting links with South Africa.

And to Allan Border, for the great legacy he has left to Australian cricket.

AUTHOR'S THANKS

Special thanks must go to the members of the Australian touring squad – the players, management, coach and physios – for their support and assistance.
Thanks also to Dr Ali Bacher for contributing the foreword to the book and for his assistance during the tour; to Australian journalist Patrick Keane, of AAP, for contributing to the diary; to Jim Tucker for his assistance while we were in South Africa; to Doug Russell, our liaison officer, for his organisational skills during the tour; to Geoff Armstrong, who edited the book and helped bring it all together; to John Mikulcic, of the Australian Picture Library, for his work organising many of the photographs that appear in this book; to the people at *Inside Edge* magazine for their support; and to Ian Russell, for checking the accuracy of the manuscript.

And finally, thanks to the people at Ironbark and Pan Macmillan for giving me the opportunity to write the diary.

FOREWORD

By Dr Ali Bacher

(Managing Director, United Cricket Board of South Africa)

IT IS AN HONOUR and a privilege for me to contribute to Steve Waugh's book about the Australian cricket team's 1994 tour of South Africa.

The matches between the two countries were great encounters, filled with many wonderful moments of cricket – perhaps with none finer than the contribution made by Waugh himself. He was justifiably named Man of the Series (as he had been in the earlier series in Australia), and there is no doubt that on several occasions, as a fielder, bowler and batsman, he provided turning points for his country.

Waugh, by all accounts, is a deep thinker of the game and so it comes as no surprise to me to see that he has gone beyond his contributions on the field and provided this fascinating record of what surely will be regarded as a milestone in world cricket history. This series against Australia also marked for South Africa a special moment in our own history, a moment when all our people cheered as one for our national team and applauded the exploits of our opponents.

With our country on the verge of its first democratic election and our first democractic government, South African cricket could not have chosen a better partner than Australia to make its contribution to the unification and reconciliation process. The Australian team and management went out of their way to be part of this process, and went into violence-torn townships to help in the national bid for peace.

When we were in Soweto, young Shane Warne came and offered his services to our development programme for disadvantaged youngsters and we used him to outstanding effect in several communities. Steve Waugh himself gave advice and encouragement to a Sowetan all-rounder by the name of Jacob Malao and by some great coincidence Malao was chosen a few weeks later to work on the MCC groundstaff at Lord's – exactly the road a much younger Waugh had himself travelled a few years earlier.

The series in South Africa drew huge crowds, and we were able to raise nearly two million Rand from the gates for the establishment of much-needed multi-sports facilities in the black townships.

In world cricket today it is common cause that a country cannot judge its prowess until it has played Australia in a Test series. It is of much pride and gratification to us to have drawn the Test series after such a long period of isolation and against such a talented combination as that which was led by Allan Border.

When it was all over, we knew we had been in a fight. But we knew, too, that we could all have a beer together and mull over all those magical moments that Australian cricket gave South Africa at this momentous time in our history.

INTRODUCTION
By Geoff Armstrong

THE HISTORY of international cricket between Australia and South Africa can now safely be split into two periods. The Old Age represents the 57 years, four months and 27 days between October 11, 1902 and March 10, 1970 – between the opening match of the first Test series involving the two countries and the final Test of the series between Bill Lawry's Australians and Ali Bacher's Springboks in 1969-70. The New Age covers the period from the 1992 World Cup until the day that hopefully will never come – when cricket is no longer a significant international sport.

The lost years between the two ages were a period of great torment and, ultimately, great change. In the Old Age, South African teams were not chosen purely on the basis of merit – many sections of the community were not given the opportunity to represent their country on the cricket field, just as they were not given the opportunities in life that other more privileged and powerful groups took as their God-given right. What made these stark injustices so disgusting and demoralising was that they were determined solely on the basis of race, on the colour of a person's skin. To the outside world, it was all summed up by one word, invariably spat out ... *apartheid*. But, fortunately, by the 1990s, thanks to a long and often bitter battle between power groups located inside and outside South Africa, that dreadful policy was no more, and the current and future generations who represent South Africa in sport and life will serve as a tribute to those who forced the changes.

Australia and South Africa first met in an international cricket contest in 1902. Joe Darling's Australian side, regarded even today as one of greatest of all Test teams, was returning via the Cape from a famous Ashes series in England, and stopped off to play three Test matches, two in Johannesburg and one in Cape Town. The first of these Tests was played at the old Wanderers Ground in Johannesburg, where the visiting team had to battle the impact of high altitude and the vagaries of a matting wicket. Consequently, even though the Australian batting order was littered with legendary names – Trumper, Armstrong, Hill, Duff, Noble, Darling, Gregory, Hopkins, Trumble, Kelly and Jones – they were obliged to follow on, after making only 296 in reply to the home team's 454. History shows that Darling's team of champions recovered to force an honourable draw, with the great left-hander from South Australia, Clem Hill, becoming the first Australian to score a Test century against South Africa. Once acclimatised, the Australians went on to confirm their class with decisive victories in the second and third Tests.

South Africa did not visit Australia until 1910-11, and when they did they had the misfortune to run into the brilliant Victor Trumper at his runscoring best and lost four of the five Tests. The two countries met again in 1912, in an ill-fated 'triangular' tournament in England, with Australia winning two Tests, with the third drawn. In the first of these victories, the Victorian Jimmy Matthews produced something unique in international cricket – a hat trick in each innings, both on the second day of the match. Then came a break of more than nine years, as the horror of World War I was fought out, until Herbert Collins brought the superb 1921 Australian team to South Africa on the way home from England. Collins, who led the side in the absence of Warwick Armstrong (who had been captain during the Ashes series), played an innings of 203 in the second Test in Johannesburg, which remains the only example of an Australian batsman going past 200 in a Test in South Africa. That Test, like the first (in Durban), was drawn, but Australia won easily in Cape Town to clinch the series.

By the time Australia and South Africa next met on the cricket field, in Australia in 1931-32, the home side were captained by the Victorian Bill Woodfull, and included in their number a 23-year-old genius already recognised as the greatest of them all – Don Bradman. In just five innings against South Africa, Bradman smashed 806 runs, including scores of 226, 112, 167 and 299 not out, as Woodfull's team won all five Tests, three by an innings, another by 10 wickets. Four seasons later, while Bradman was unavailable due to illness, Victor Richardson of South Australia took an Australian side to South Africa and won the five-Test series 3-0, with great names such as Stan McCabe, Clarrie Grimmett and Bill O'Reilly dominant. This was the last clash between the two countries until 1949-50, by which time Don Bradman had retired and become Sir Donald Bradman, and the outstanding Victorian batsman Lindsay Hassett was the Australian captain.

The '49-50 Australians included the brilliant left-handed batsmen, Neil Harvey and Arthur Morris, and one of the best of all fast bowlers, Ray Lindwall, but was without the great all-rounder Keith Miller, who had been dropped, apparently because of poor form. However, when the left-hand paceman Bill Johnston was injured in a car crash in Durban early in the tour, Miller was called over as a replacement and ended up playing in all five Tests. Australia won this series 4-0, to take their Test record against South Africa to an imposing 22 wins and just one loss from 29 matches.

The next series between the two countries, in Australia in 1952-53, represented a turning point in the fortunes of the South Africans, who were led in this series by Jack Cheetham and squared the five-Test series two-all, despite the performance of Harvey, who scored 834 runs including four centuries. The visitors' success was built around the off-spinners of Hugh Tayfield, and fielding of a standard unmatched by previous touring sides of any nation. In the fifth Test, one of the batsman facing Tayfield was Ian Craig, who, at the tender age of 17 years 239 days, became the youngest player to wear the baggy green Australian cap.

In 1957-58, Craig was the captain of the fifth Australian team to tour South Africa, and he came back with a 3-0 series win, thanks largely to the heroic efforts of his NSW colleagues, Richie Benaud and Alan Davidson. Benaud took 30 wickets and scored two centuries during the series, while Davidson captured 25 wickets with his left-handed fast-medium bowling. Davidson's new-ball partner in four of the five Tests in this series was the Victorian left-armer Ian Meckiff, and six year's later, in Australia during the next series between the two countries, Meckiff was the pivotal figure in one of the most controversial episodes in the history of the game.

Meckiff had not appeared for Australia since the home series against the West Indies in 1960-61, when he was suddenly brought back for the first Test of the '63-64 South African series, at the Gabba in Brisbane. Throughout his career, Meckiff had been dogged by suspicions over the legality of his bowling action and many had presumed he had been cast aside for those three seasons because of these doubts. However, if his recall was a shock, it was nothing compared with the uproar that came in his first over. Asked by his captain, Benaud, to deliver the second over of South Africa's first innings, Meckiff was sensationally no-balled four times for throwing by the umpire at square-leg, Colin Egar. He never bowled in first-class cricket again.

This was also Benaud's last match as Australia's captain, after more than five highly successful years in the top job. He handed over the reins to the prolific run-scorer Bobby Simpson for the final four Tests, but (after a broken finger had kept him out of the second Test) played in the last three, as the series was tied one-all. However, few could have realised the extra history involved as Benaud waved goodbye to the Test-match scene. Circumstances would see that this was the last Test series played between the two countries in Australia for 30 years.

In 1966-67, Simpson became the first Australian captain to lose a series against South Africa, as the Springboks won 3-1. He was hindered by the absence of his best young batsman, Doug Walters, who had been called up for National Service, while his bowlers had trouble controlling the superb local batting line-up that included such names as Trevor Goddard, Eddie Barlow, Ali Bacher, Graeme Pollock and the star of the series – the outstanding keeper/batsman Denis Lindsay. Three seasons later, Australia, now captained by Bill Lawry, were beaten in South Africa again – this time comprehensively, by four Tests (out of four) to nil. Lawry's team came to South Africa after an arduous five-Test tour on the spinning pitches of India, hardly the ideal preparation for facing such quality fast bowlers as Peter Pollock and Mike Procter. They also had great difficulty coping with the prodigious batting talents of Barry Richards, who made his Test debut in the series opener in Cape Town and scored centuries at Durban and Port Elizabeth. But, even with Richards' brilliance, the innings of the summer was played by the majestic left-hander, Graeme Pollock, who batted for just under seven hours at Durban for 274, the highest score by a South African in Test cricket.

Following Australia's annihilation, most critics regarded Bacher's South African team as the best in the world. Sadly, that status was never challenged. Those Tests against Australia in early 1970 were the last South Africa would play for more than 20 years. Barry Richards' Test career was over almost before it had begun. Throughout the world, governments were becoming increasingly intolerant of the South African government's *apartheid* policy. In 1966, the New Zealand Rugby Board had called off a tour of South Africa after they were told not to include any Maoris in their squad. Two years later, a cricket tour by England of South Africa was cancelled after the South African government objected to the selection of the South African-born Basil D'Oliveira in the England side. D'Oliveira was what the South African regime described as 'coloured' or 'non-white'. In the same year, South Africa's invitation to compete in the Mexico City Olympic Games was withdrawn – after more than 40 countries threatened to boycott the Games if the South Africans competed.

In May 1970, a scheduled cricket tour by South Africa of England was called off – after the British government asked the MCC to do so – on the grounds that to proceed with the tour would impact on relations with other countries, race relations in Britain, and the upcoming Commonwealth Games; and also because the police, having just gone through a tumultuous rugby union series that had featured numerous brawls between protesters and the constabulary, did not like the idea of reliving that nightmare again and again over the 30 days of a Test cricket series.

Over the next 15 months, a similar story was played out in Australia. In 1971-72, the South African cricketers were scheduled to tour Australia. However, a South African rugby tour of Australia in the winter of 1971 developed into an ugly, acrimonious affair, with battles between police and anti-*apartheid* demonstrators as much a part of the tour as tries and goals. Not long after that tour had been completed, on September 8, 1971, Sir Donald Bradman announced that the Australian Cricket Board of Control had accepted the advice of police and politicians, and abandoned the tour. In its place would be a tour by a 'Rest of the World' side. What the Board of Control's announcement in reality meant was that South Africa was, until its government removed its *apartheid* policies, no longer a part of the international cricket world.

South African cricket remained isolated for the next 20 years. In the 1980s, its officials backed a series of 'rebel' tours, by English, West Indian, Sri Lankan and Australian teams, but all the time prayed for the day they might be invited back into the real world. But, as they well knew, the possibility of such an invitation was out of their hands. What was needed was a change in the laws of their country and the philosophy of their government. A major breakthrough came in August 1989, when F. W. de Klerk became South Africa's new President, a change at the top that suggested a possible softening of the government's previous hard line. On February 2, 1990, the African National Congress (ANC) – the most popular 'non-white' liberation movement in the country – was legalised after a 30-year ban. Soon after, as the world watched developments with cautious optimism, the ANC's leader, Nelson Mandela, was released, after nearly more than 27 years in prison. Mandela's incarceration, which had resulted from his work at the forefront of the ANC's campaign against the laws of their land, had been the world's clearest symbol of the supreme injustice of *apartheid.*

From that point, events moved quickly, as Mandela and de Klerk set about creating an atmosphere whereby 'all-race' elections could be held. In June 1991, de Klerk announced that his country's *apartheid* laws had been repealed. Meanwhile, a number of South Africa's sporting bodies, with the United Cricket Board of South Africa, spearheaded by Managing Director Dr Ali Bacher (the same Ali Bacher who had captained his country against Australia in 1969-70), at the forefront, set about establishing merit, rather than race, as the criteria by which representative teams would be chosen.

By October 1991, the Commonwealth Heads of Government Meeting (CHOGM) decided that the time was right for South Africa to be called back into the world of international sport. With the support of the African nations, South Africa was invited to compete in the 1992 Barcelona Olympics, rugby tours to and from South Africa were organised, and the South African cricketers were given the chance to participate in the 1992 cricket World Cup, to be played in February-March in Australia and New Zealand. Before that, India (who had never played a cricket Test against South Africa to this point) invited the South Africans to their country to play three limited-overs internationals. The first of these matches was played, in front of more than 90,000 people in Calcutta, on November 10, 1991, and was won by the Indians by three wickets. Not that anyone really cared about who won or lost.

South Africa had been out of international cricket for exactly 21 years and eight months.

Australia and South Africa finally met again on the cricket field on February 26, 1992 at the Sydney Cricket Ground, in the South Africans' first appearance in the World Cup. The match resulted in a clear-cut win for the visitors, who kept the Australians to 9-170 from their 50 overs and then lost only one wicket in reaching that target with 25 balls to spare. Afterwards, the South Africans received messages of congratulations from both President de Klerk and Nelson Mandela. The South African captain was Kepler Wessels, a tough left-handed batsman who, ironically, had played 24 Tests for Australia between 1982 and 1985. Wessels, seeking an opportunity to play Test cricket, had migrated from South Africa at the height of the sporting ban, before returning home in 1986.

Australia eventually finished fifth in the Cup, while the South Africans survived until the semi-finals, which were played just days before the white South African electorate voted in a crucial referendum asking whether they supported the reforms that would eventually lead to fully democratic elections. This support was gained clearly, and encouraged cricket authorities in Australia and South Africa to continue with plans for twin tours in 1993-94 – South Africa to Australia between November and early February; Australia to South Africa from early February to early April.

In the meantime, South Africa played an official Test in the West Indies and series against Sri Lanka and India. In each case this was the first time the two countries had faced each other in a Test match. In October 1993, Mandela and de Klerk were awarded the Nobel peace prize. Two months later, Australia and South Africa met for the first time in the World Series one-day international series (which in 1993-94 also involved New Zealand), on December 9 at the Melbourne Cricket Ground. The South Africans prevailed once more, this time by seven wickets, but back in Sydney five days later, Australia finally had a win – their first victory over South Africa in a cricket international since the first week of 1967!

The historic first Test between Australia and South Africa since 1970 began on Boxing Day, in Melbourne. The Australians, captained as usual by the great Allan Border, were without Steve Waugh, who 10 days earlier had torn a hamstring in a one-dayer against New Zealand, and also Merv Hughes, who was recovering from knee surgery. In the event, neither was missed, as the Test proved to be a match ruined by rain. Despite the storm clouds, more than 15,000 people attended the first day's play, in which the weather kept Australia to 2-71. The second day was lost completely, and only 69 runs were added on day three. From this point, the Test was doomed to be an anti-climactic draw, although Aussie vice-captain Mark Taylor scored a polished 170 and the South Africans, Wessels (63 not out) and Hansie Cronje (71), batted confidently on the final day.

The second Test began at the SCG on January 2, and, despite a pitch that was slow and below Test standard, the match developed into one of the most exciting ever played on the famous ground. On the first day, the extraordinary 24-year-old Australian leg-spinner Shane Warne was superb – taking 7-56 from 27 fantastic overs as South Africa crashed to 169 all out. On day two and into day three, the home side grafted a lead of 123, thanks to the batting of Michael Slater (92), Steve Waugh's replacement Damien Martyn (59) and Border (49). Warne snared another five wickets in the South African second innings of 239, which left Australia needing a modest 117 for victory, but at stumps on the fourth day they had stumbled to 4-63, after being 1-51. The tireless fast-medium Fanie de Villiers had all four wickets. On the final morning, the tricky run-chase turned difficult in the first over, when Border was bowled by the South Africans' fastest man Allan Donald, and then perilous when the innings crashed to 8-75. But Martyn remained, and number 10 Craig McDermott slammed some brave blows to take Australia within seven of victory. However, Martyn, who had been concentrating totally on defence, suddenly slashed at Donald and was caught at cover. Then, a run later and amid great tension, Glenn McGrath chipped a simple return catch to de Villiers to complete a remarkable triumph.

The third Test was not played until after Australia had won the World Series, defeating South Africa 2-1 in the finals. The Player-of-the-Series trophy was won by Warne, while Mark Waugh (who scored 36, 107 and 60) was the player of the finals, but the performances of even these two players were overshadowed by the emotional tribute the Sydney crowd paid Border on the night of the third final. The future of the Australian captain had been the subject of much media debate throughout the season, as various commentators theorised over whether and when he would retire. For his part, Border gave little away, other than to confirm he had not made up his mind, but this did not stop the fans from cheering and chanting his name, just in case this was the final time their hero would play in an international in the city of his birth.

For the third Test, Cronje replaced Wessels (who had returned home with a knee injury) as South Africa's captain, while Steve Waugh, who had returned to the Australian team before the one-day finals, came back for Martyn. The return of Waugh proved crucial, as he slammed a magnificent 164 in Australia's match-winning first innings of 7 (declared) for 469, which set up an eventual winning margin of 191 runs. However, the Australian victory was overshadowed by controversy over the umpiring, especially that of the country's leading umpire, Darrell Hair from NSW.

On the third day, South Africa's Peter Kirsten was reported and fined following a confrontation with Hair, after the umpire had given lbw decisions against Kirsten's team-mates Brian McMillan and David Richardson. Kirsten was at the non-striker's end when the rulings were made. Then, late on day four with South Africa struggling to save the Test, Hair, in a decision that could have gone either way, ruled dead ball after a leg-bye had been run, which meant Cronje had to return to the batting end, where he was adjudged lbw next ball. And the following day, as South Africa failed to avoid defeat, Kirsten was again clearly unhappy with Hair after the umpire gave him out lbw. There was also much debate over the lbw decision given by umpire Terry Prue that ended the innings of one of the most popular members of the South African team, Jonty Rhodes. Although Cronje later said he had no complaints with the umpiring, and video replays suggested that Hair was probably right with at least most of his controversial decisions, back in South Africa the umpiring created a storm, with a fund being established to pay Kirsten's fine and callers to radio stations suggesting Hair could do worse than purchase a white cane or a seeing-eye dog.

The Australian leg of this '93-94 Australia-South Africa cricket odyssey finished on February 1. Just four days later, Border's men were on a plane bound for Johannesburg, as the eighth Australian team to visit the Republic. The 15-member squad contained no real surprises, and included Hughes, recovered from his injury problems, and the former batting star Dean Jones, who had forced his way back into the Australian one-day team and was threatening, after a sequence of superb performances in the Sheffield Shield and the World Series, to find a place in the Test XI as well. Ian Healy, the wicketkeeper since 1988, was the only keeper chosen. The full squad was (with number of Tests played at February 5, 1994, in brackets):

Allan Border (captain; 153 Tests), Mark Taylor (vice-captain; 52), David Boon (86), Matthew Hayden (0), Ian Healy (59), Merv Hughes (51), Dean Jones (52), Craig McDermott (55), Glenn McGrath (3), Tim May (18), Paul Reiffel (11), Michael Slater (12), Shane Warne (23), Mark Waugh (33), Steve Waugh (62).

On February 2, the day after the third Test ended, President de Klerk formally called South Africa's first non-racial democratic elections, to be held between April 26 and 28. The announcement came amid simmering tension in the Republic, as a number of major power groups, including the *Inkatha* Freedom Party led by Chief Mangosuthu Buthelezi and some 'white' right-wing alliances, stated they would not participate in the vote. Buthelezi, whose party was seen to represent the majority of the Zulu population, told his supporters to prepare for 'casualties and even death' as a result of his election boycott, even though he asked that protests be kept within the law. The ultra right-wing Afrikaner National Front suggested violence was 'unavoidable' unless they were granted an Afrikaner *volkstaat* (homeland), which de Klerk had stated was highly unlikely. Mandela admitted the threat of civil war had to be taken seriously. Meanwhile, in a process that would continue throughout the weeks of the Australian tour, Mandela and de Klerk set out to accommodate *Inkatha* and the other opposition parties, and create an environment in which the elections could go ahead as peacefully and effectively as possible. But all the while there was the threat of bloodshed, and tragically the lead-up to the election would be marred by a series of violent confrontations between the members of the various power groups.

Such was the price of change. It was amid this stormy atmosphere that the first official Australian cricket team to tour South Africa in 24 years arrived at Johannesburg's Jan Smuts Airport on February 6. When the teams of Bill Lawry and Ali Bacher had been fighting for their countries' honour, Shane Warne, Jonty Rhodes and Hansie Cronje had not yet celebrated their first birthdays, while Glenn McGrath and Michael Slater were born while the series was being played and Matthew Hayden's arrival was then still 18 months away. The Republic of South Africa was, in 1994, a nation much different to the one of early 1970, as was recognised and celebrated by the President of the United Cricket Board of South Africa, Krish Mackerdhuj, in the official 1994 tour brochure. Mr Mackerdhuj wrote:

'It is important to note that the relationship between Australian cricket and South African cricket is not a mere extension of what existed in the generally unacceptable past, but one based on the present changes occurring in our country.'

As for the Australian captain, he was clearly very excited to be in South Africa, the only major cricketing nation he had not seen during his long career. After he had battled his way through the cheering crowd that welcomed the Australians at the airport to attend his first press conference of the tour, Allan Border looked out at the assembled throng of reporters and dignitaries and said of the tour: 'This is something I thought would be impossible in my lifetime ...

'It's a dream come true.'

WELCOME TO
SOUTH AFRICA
AUSTRALIA
DIADORA
DIADORA
Enjoy Coca-Cola

DAY 1 *February 5*

THE SIGNAL for a return to life away from home was the arrival of a taxi at the front of our house. Another two-and-a-half months ... but potentially a cricketing experience that everyone in the Australian squad will never forget. Before flying out to begin this historic tour the team was required to congregate at the Airport Park Royal in Sydney to be given our clothing and bags for the tour. All the gear has the logo of the tour sponsor, Coca-Cola, plastered over it. This is the first time the Australian team has been associated with Coke, and the only problem with having a new team sponsor is the amount of gear they provide. On this occasion this amounted to a new bright-red coffin (hard cricket bag), filled to the top with shirts, tracksuits, hats and casual wear – so much, in fact, that I needed another bag to accommodate it all. In total, my touring kit is made up of one coffin, one suitcase, one large carry bag and one small bag (for use on planes and to and from the grounds).

More important than the distribution of the sponsor's gear, however, was a briefing from Graham Halbish (the ACB chief executive) on what we should and shouldn't do while in South Africa. He also gave us a bit of a guide on what to expect in the different cities we will visit. It all seemed pretty common-sense advice, although through it all I kept thinking we may confront certain situations on this tour that we haven't experienced on tours to other parts of the world. To me, the biggest concern is the continuing conflict between the different political groups in the lead-up to the all-race South African elections (which will be held two weeks after our tour ends). The possibility is that we'll see some form of trouble, but hopefully the fact that we're high-profile figures will keep us out of the firing line.

The Australian squad has only two new faces from that of the English tour – Dean Jones and Glenn McGrath. We're being managed by Dr Cam Battersby, who has accompanied Aussie touring sides before and always proved very popular.

During the meeting the roomies for the first two weeks were announced and yours truly claimed the short straw. Big Merv. Actually I tell a lie – Merv is one of the most considerate guys I've roomed with and, believe it or not, has even done my laundry on the odd occasion. Such kindness offsets his bad habits, which strangely seem to happen only after he has drunk too much fizzy drink.

The boarding call came at

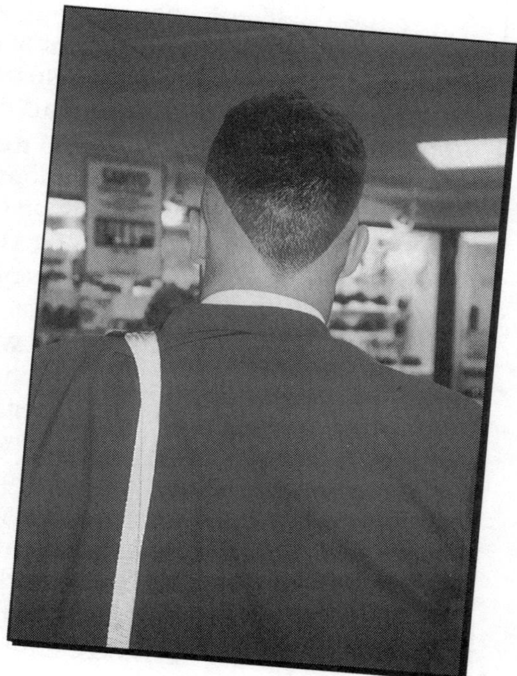

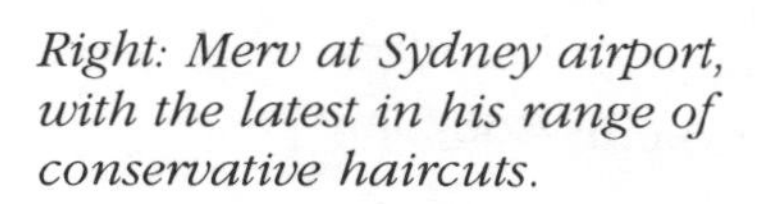

Right: Merv at Sydney airport, with the latest in his range of conservative haircuts.

THE AUSTRALIAN TEAM

Allan Border (c) *AB*
Likes: Mint jelly, XXXX beer, pizza, the Brisbane Broncos RLFC, playing golf, winning the toss

Mark Taylor (v-c) *Tubby*
Likes: Chicken green curries, bourbon and coke, St George RLFC, *Bow River*, by Cold Chisel

David Boon *Babs/Boonie*
Likes: Red wine, collecting Waterford crystal, head-banging music.

Matthew Hayden *Jurassic/Haydos*
Likes: Cricket practice with his brother Gary, Vince Gill, Garth Brooks

Ian Healy *Heals*
Likes: Whitening his boots, the Brisbane Broncos RLFC, ironing his jockstraps, impersonating other team members, McDonald's.

Merv Hughes *Swervin'*
Likes: Freddy Krueger movies, Corona beer, Werribee Aussie Rules, food of any type.

Dean Jones *Lege*
Likes: Buying golf clubs, rottweilers, Carlton FC, blackjack, wine (considers himself something of a connoisseur)

Craig McDermott *Billy*
Likes: Chocolate milkshakes, Southern and coke, sending faxes, training with iron man champion Trevor Hendy.

Glenn McGrath *Norman*
Likes: Talking on phones, hot dogs, shooting pigs, guns of any kind.

Tim May *Maysie*
Likes: Indian food, Sol beer, Norwood FC, reading novels, surviving a week without a major injury, Neil Diamond.

Paul Reiffel *Pistol*
Likes: Sleeping, Richmond FC, relaxing, taking it easy, rain on cricket days.

Michael Slater *Slats/Sybil*
Likes: Bon Jovi, karaoke singing, selling his wedding video, Wagga Wagga, celebrations

Shane Warne *Warney*
Likes: Toasted cheese sandwiches, Boney M, strawberry milkshakes, french fries, midori and lemonade, World Championship Wrestling.

Mark Waugh *Junior*
Likes: Sleeping, horse racing, Southern and coke, gambling.

Steve Waugh *Tugga*
Likes: Movies, Southern and coke, Canterbury RLFC, messy room-mates, sightseeing, Cold Chisel

Manager: Dr Cam Battersby **Coach:** Bob Simpson
Physios: Errol Alcott, Lindsay Tregar

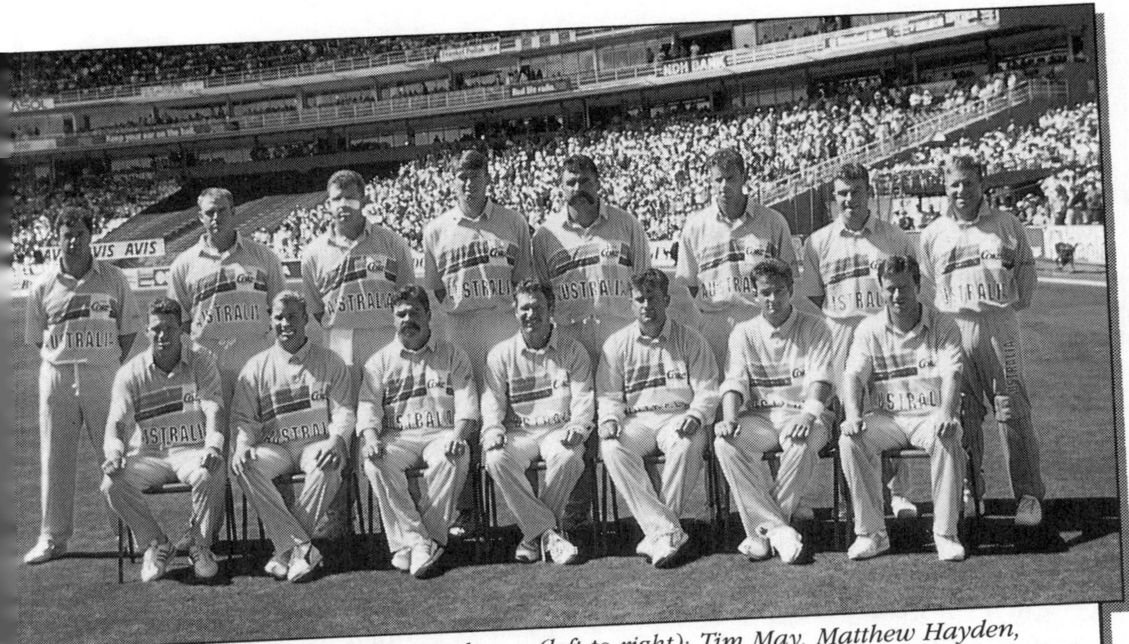

The Australian touring team. Back row (left to right): Tim May, Matthew Hayden, Craig McDermott, Glenn McGrath, Merv Hughes, Paul Reiffel, Michael Slater, Ian Healy. Front row: Dean Jones, Shane Warne, David Boon, Allan Border (captain), Mark Taylor (vice-captain), Mark Waugh, Steve Waugh.

THE ITINERARY

February

10 – v Nicky Oppenheimer XI, at Randjesfontein
12-14 – v Northern Transvaal, at Verwoerdburg
17 – v President's XI, at Potchefstroom
19 – First One-Day International, at Johannesburg
20 – Second One-Day International, at Verwoerdburg
22 – Third One-Day International, at Port Elizabeth
24 – Fourth One-Day International, at Durban
26-Mar 1 – v Orange Free State, at Bloemfontein

March

4-8 – FIRST TEST, at Johannesburg
12-14 – v Boland, at Stellenbosch
17-21 – SECOND TEST, at Cape Town
25-29 – THIRD TEST, at Durban

April

2 – First Day/Night International, at East London
4 – Second Day/Night International, at Port Elizabeth
6 – Third Day/Night International, at Cape Town
8 – Fourth Day/Night International, at Bloemfontein

Note: At the time of the tour, one South African Rand equalled approximately 40 Australian cents.

9.30 pm. Of course, the Sydney players were able to bid farewell to their loved ones, and Glenn McGrath and his girlfriend put on such an enthusiastic show of affection that they had the large crowd in attendance spellbound and provided the camera crews with some steamy footage. Many of the girls ended up in tears. They're left to their own devices while we're away, which makes it much lonelier for them than for the players. We have each other on tour for friendship, but the girls must rely heavily on family for support. The last 18 months, with tours to New Zealand, England and now South Africa, have been particularly tough for our partners and family. We've only had one month off in this period. But that's all part of the deal these days and has to be accepted.

The last-minute shopping was done after we were through customs. Shane Warne and Glenn McGrath purchased cameras, and Warney showed quickly just how much of a novice he is when it comes to photography. This was his instruction to the sales girl: 'I want a camera that takes good pictures without me having to adjust anything. The only thing I want is one of those things that goes in and out.' I think he meant a zoom lens. On the other hand, Glenn impressed all with his knowledge of the caper, though we were soon to find out he possessed a quick bowler's mentality. He decided he needed a tripod to mount his camera – someone had forgotten to tell him he hadn't bought a video camera.

The 14-hour flight, all of it in darkness, saw everyone in the tour party get some sleep ... except for S. Waugh. I can never get comfortable on planes, but fortunately in business class each person has access to unlimited movies, so by the time we touched down in Johannesburg at 5.45 am, I'd seen three movies and a couple of documentaries. But the body was weary and the eyes badly bloodshot.

After making our way through customs we were greeted, unexpectedly, by a crowd of around 500 people. Everyone was wishing us all the best for the tour and were keen for autographs, particularly those of Merv and Warney. It appears Shane has developed a huge fan club – all the cricket in Australia has been shown on television here. We thought our welcome was generous, but apparently the South Africans landed here three days earlier and were met by a crowd of around 7000. That homecoming was followed by a ticker-tape parade through the streets as recognition for their efforts in the Australian summer.

As we boarded the team bus there was a mixture of emotions running through the team, ranging from excitement at the prospects of the tour ... to apprehension of the unknown factors we may encounter during our stay.

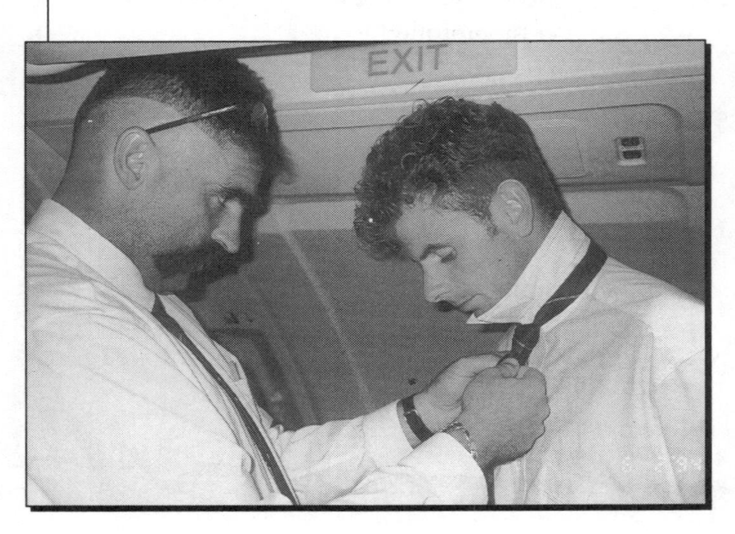

Near the end of a long flight ... and Paul Reiffel needs the assistance of our big fast bowler so he'll look presentable to the fans waiting at Johannesburg's international airport.

DAY 2 *February 6*

AS WE HEADED down the motorway to our destination, the Sandton Sun Hotel, the first surprise for all of us was the inclement weather. We quickly learned that the weather on most days in the past couple of months in Johannesburg has been very miserable. Then, barely five minutes into our journey, we were confronted by a scene of carnage all across the road, after a minibus full of locals had lost control and tumbled across the steel railings separating the oncoming traffic. The top of the van had been ripped open like a can of sardines and the occupants sent sailing through the air onto the bitumen, leaving the horrific sight of dead and badly-injured people strewn over a 100-metre stretch of road. It was a sight I hope I never see again.

Needless to say, the remainder of the journey was a pretty quiet affair. When we finally reached the hotel we were welcomed by a group of Zulu dancers who performed their tribal dances, accompanied by some enthusiastic singing, in a stirring exhibition. After the formalities ended the lads headed enthusiastically for their respective rooms. The thought of sliding between the sheets was a priority for all at this point of time. However, when Merv and I arrived in our room it was obvious some re-adjusting of the furniture was necessary. The two single beds were placed side by side – potentially a nightmare in the making if the big fella was to roll over too far in his sleep. But with the beds a safe distance apart and the curtains drawn, the zeds were being pushed out almost before our heads hit the pillow.

However, within four hours, there were signs of life in room 1507. I felt worse for the sleep, and decided the best strategy to combat the jet lag was to numb the drowsiness with a couple of ales. So, with a few of the lads, I set out in search of a venue and ended up at a bar with a beer-garden type of setting, where a band was playing away from our view. Michael Slater, who was obviously struggling to come to terms with his weariness, commented on the classy singing by the artist who was performing at this particular venue. Slats reckoned he sounded for all the world like Eric Clapton. This wasn't a bad call, except for the fact the band were taking a breather at the time and the CD player was in action, blearing out the tunes via a speaker system.

Hours later, the boys started to come good. It was obvious the fluid replacement plan was paying dividends. Most of the locals were very friendly to us although there was a lot of anger at the perceived biased umpiring in Australia. Some of the umpiring, especially in the Adelaide Test, has upset them, and it is clear Darrell Hair has achieved some sort of celebrity status over here. In fact, the band played a song dedicated to him, although if Darrell was to hear the lyrics, I don't think he'd be rushing out to snap up a copy.

Despite the ribbing we copped, we had an enjoyable time. However, there was one big difference between this beer garden and similar ones in Australia. On entering, the bouncers search each person, looking for guns which apparently are carried as a precaution by many locals. Safety is of paramount importance. The recession is severe and the crime rate is on the increase.

We returned to the hotel to try and catch up on lost sleep. Before I crashed, I called home to tell my wife Lynette we had arrived safely and to find out how younger brother Danny had gone in his first-grade debut for Bankstown. It turned out to be a bit of a let down for him as he wasn't required to bat.

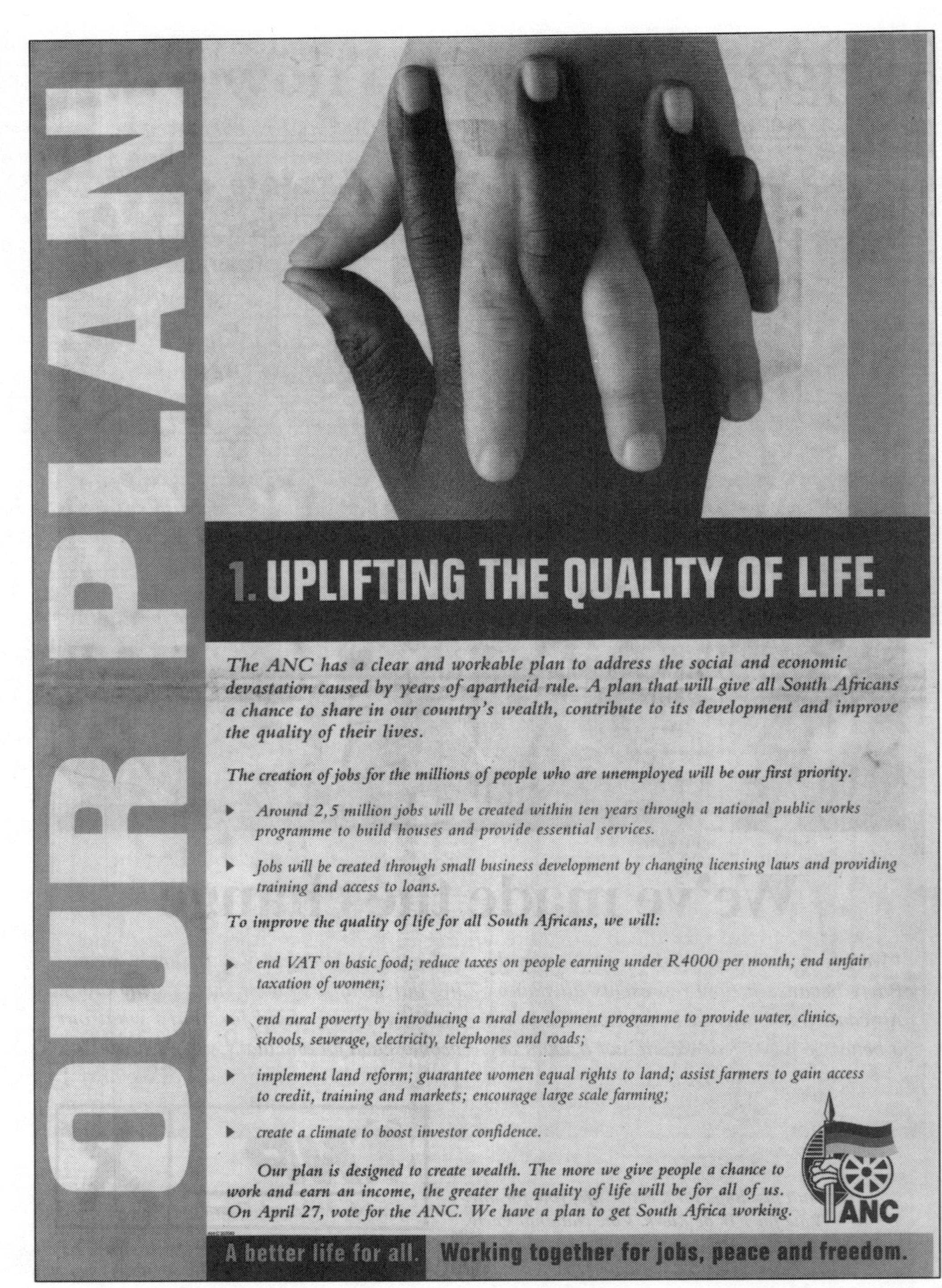

The first local papers we read on tour were, inevitably, dominated by reports, editorials and advertisements concerning the upcoming South African elections. This full-page African National Congress promotion appeared in the Johannesburg Sunday Times *of February 6. The next page of the same broadsheet featured a similar size advertisement for President de Klerk's National Party.*

DAY 3 *February 7*

I MANAGED to get a reasonable night's sleep, although both Merv and I woke up at 3am. We had a chat for 20 minutes to pass the time away, before drifting off to complete a handy 12 hours in the sack. This morning the team had its first look at the Wanderers Ground, and we were all impressed with the surface and the facilities. We can almost sense what type of atmosphere we'll confront when the stadium is full – hostile, very loud and partisan. The stands are positioned very close to the field of play and surround its entirety, thus earning it the name 'the bullring'.

Another rainy night followed by consistent rain during the day earned the boys a reprieve from the nets, but the alternative training arrangements weren't popular. Our physiotherapist, Errol Alcott, decided to try to turn us into Rob De Castellas in one nasty session. Then, after a short routine of catching to let the team get a feel of the playing surface at the Wanderers, our first training run came to an end. All the guys are looking forward to having a bat and a bowl (hopefully) tomorrow.

After the run, the team assembled in the dressing room, where we were informed that, on most occasions during the tour, we will be accompanied by security, especially to and from games. That security is made up of serving police officers, who have undergone intensive training in the form of pistol, assault rifle, shotgun and sub-machine gun use, unarmed combat, identification of explosives, close-quarter protection (for example, surrounding VIP's during parades, in shopping centres and so on) and defensive driving techniques (if, for example, a vehicle is ambushed). We were assured by the leader of this VIP protection unit that there was only a slim chance that their services will be required during our stay, but nevertheless it's comforting to know these guys will be around if we need them.

Our first view of the famous Wanderers Ground included this extraordinary sight of local workers preparing the square ... one blade of grass at a time.

With the weather deteriorating once again, our proposed goodwill coaching session in the township of Soweto has been postponed to a later date. But it wasn't quite bad enough to deter most of the lads from an outing on the golf course. My afternoon was spent in the gym with Ian Healy, Glenn McGrath and Errol Alcott. I concentrated on a few strengthening exercises for a troublesome shin splint which has caused me a few problems of late. Later on, back in the hotel room, I was surprised to see Merv checking out a map of South Africa. I could see the concern on the big fella's face, and was wondering what had caused his problem. I was soon to find out.

Merv asked of me: 'Have you seen how far we'd have to travel to get to that coaching clinic in Swaziland?'

I assured him the camp was in Soweto, and that Soweto was actually only 10 minutes away.

I found a copy of an afternoon paper which featured many cricket articles. In one, the former Australian 'rebel' tourist Mike Haysman put his two bob's worth in, saying the South Africans had nothing to worry about and should win the series. However, the quote of the day, without doubt, belonged to our captain, Allan Border. When asked: 'Do you know much about South Africa?' he replied ...

'I've read a few Wilbur Smith novels.'

DAY 4 *February 8*

ONE COULD be forgiven for thinking we were back in England again. The rain continued to tumble down, and there was no sign of a breakthrough in the thick bank of cloud hovering over and around Johannesburg. Consequently, yet another nets session was cancelled, but we were in dire need of some exercise and an appropriate venue, in the form of an indoor sports centre, was located. The choice of our physio was indoor soccer and European handball, which had quite a few of the lads fearing for their safety – it's common knowledge the big fella (Merv) is a renowned thug in confined venues and doubly dangerous when a ball is involved. A bookie would have offered no more than even money about a stretcher coming into play. However, despite the fears of a serious injury, the games did go on and the Nerds versus Julios rivalry was revived.

In England, on the '93 Ashes tour, the team was divided into the Nerds and the Julios, with which group you qualified for being based on how much attention you paid to your appearance. At different stages during the tour the two teams entered a variety of sporting challenges, with the honours evenly shared. Unfortunately, in South Africa, the Julios are missing a couple of key players from the English tour and, as a consequence, Glenn McGrath (an unlikely replacement!) was drafted in. But he couldn't help his new comrades and the Nerds ran amok, scoring decisive victories in both events. Merv was unstoppable in his assigned role of the enforcer, entrusted upon him by our very astute and tactically brilliant captain, Tim May.

With the official contests over, the lure of the gymnastics equipment and training pit full of foam rubber pieces proved irresistible for quite a few members of the team. Matt Hayden attempted a manoeuvre on the rings that would surely have seen him walk away with the gold medal at the next Olympics – if only he could have completed it successfully. But, unfortunately, he was a little rusty on the technical side of things and nearly dislocated both shoulders in a clumsy exhibition. Meanwhile, in the pit a nasty scuffle was developing between Craig McDermott and Glenn McGrath. We heard sounds of muffled agony emanating from deep beneath the foam pieces and realised Glenn was in a spot of bother. I made the foolish mistake of attempting a rescue mission and within seconds was fighting for survival as more bodies entered the arena. After checking myself for bite marks and grazes, it was back on the bus and back to the safety of our hotel. A later walk to a hairdressing salon adjoining our hotel resulted in a trade-off by the manager, who offered Ian Healy and myself a free facial in return for a couple of tickets to the one-dayers.

Having never experienced a facial before, and knowing that it couldn't do any more damage than presently existed, we agreed to give it a try. The sight of Ian Healy with a mudpack on his face, eyes covered by cotton wool, and a towel wrapped around his head, was priceless to all who witnessed it. However, the anticipated miracle of a fresh, smooth face didn't come to fruition and we both felt slightly cheated when we caught a glimpse of a mirror and saw no obvious improvement.

The first of our many functions on this long awaited tour took the form of a dinner, with former Australian Prime Minister Bob Hawke the special guest speaker. The bad news for the lads was that we were each assigned to separate tables, which was not a popular move by the authorities, but despite this most of the team enjoyed themselves because Bob Hawke held the audience captive with his emotional speech. However, arguably the highlight of the night came not during Mr Hawke's address but during Simmo's speech and in particular our coach's comment relating to an earlier story the former PM had told the audience about his (Hawke's) days carting manure around as a handyman at university in Western Australia. Simmo suggested Mr Hawke had had the perfect training for a career in politics, which brought the house down ... with the possible exception of the former Prime Minister.

DAY 5 *February 9*

PERSISTENT overnight rain and constant drizzle this morning once again led to the abandonment of turf cricket practice. An alternative, in the form an indoor practice, was found – a poor substitute, but at least it was a chance for the batsmen to put bat to ball and the bowlers to get rid of the stiffness that resulted from the flight over. Probably the greatest benefit from these sessions comes from the catching routines that get your feet moving and reflexes going.

Not long after arriving in Johannesburg we'd received an invitation to play golf at the exclusive River Club, and today we took advantage. When we arrived, we discovered a tremendous layout of lush fairways and quality-looking greens. The course was built around 20 years ago by a section of the wealthy white population who were sick of having to wait around to play a round of golf and consequently decided to build their own course. There are currently only 200 members, and the only way to join them is by invitation. If accepted, a new member needs to part with a 29,000-Rand fee, and then an annual subscription of 5500 Rand to maintain the facilities.

An indication of the enormous interest in this tour was the appearance of a German television station, who interviewed AB before he was due to tee off. My partner for today was an employee of the South African billionaire diamond magnate, Nicky Oppenheimer, who told us to expect some trouble leading up to the election. Apparently, there are at least five or six radical parties who will go out of their way to cause trouble. Only yesterday a representative of one of these parties approached Mr Oppenheimer for some funds, but once it was revealed their policy was 'one bullet for one settler', as in 'white' settler, their request was refused.

By the end of the day the lads had managed to collectively record a victory over the members. It was a relaxing afternoon, most notable for the first appearance of the sun while we've been on tour.

Tonight's dinner, not for the first time since we arrived in Johannesburg, was at the Sports Cafe. It's proving a popular venue, with sporting videos being played continuously on monitors located on every table and on most of the walls.

DAY 6 February 10

TODAY MARKED the first serious day of cricket on tour, but before the bus pulled out of the hotel an amusing incident took place featuring one of our bodyguards and Tim May. The man in question is a former South African heavyweight boxing champion by the name of Pierre Coetzer who only last year lost to the American, Riddick Bowe, for the right to fight for the Heavyweight Championship of the World.

The story began two days ago when the team was introduced to our security guards, one of whom was Pierre. Upon seeing him for the first time, and being taken aback by his outstanding physique, Maysie couldn't resist a jibe at the expense of the ex-champ and managed to send him a bright shade of red, which apparently had never been achieved before. Sensing an opportunity to put the wind up Maysie, a quiet word was had to Pierre by a few of the guys. The plan involved Pierre informing Tim that he didn't appreciate the ridicule he'd copped and that, because of it, he'd fix Maysie up at some stage when no-one was around. The last 48 hours have seen the boys adding fuel to the fire at every opportunity. When Pierre boarded the bus to check that everything was in order this morning, someone said to Maysie that Pierre was looking for him. Maysie, who was sitting down the back of the bus and was unaware the boxing champ had just boarded, yelled out: 'Get the weak so-and-so on the bus.' It was at that precise moment that he caught the eye of Pierre in the aisle walking

A historic moment for the Australian cricket team during our first match of the tour, against Nicky Oppenheimer's XI. Allan Border (with his back to the camera) introduces us to the leader of the African National Congress, Nelson Mandela – the man destined to become the President of South Africa after the April 27 elections. To my right in our line-up is our physiotherapist, Errol Alcott; to my left Ian Healy and Matthew Hayden.

his way, which sent our courageous off-spinner as white as a ghost and ducking for cover under the nearest seat.

Today's fixture was played on the private grounds of Nicky Oppenheimer, heir to a billionaire empire established as a result of diamond mining by his grandfather Ernest. The pavilion and surrounding facilities cost six million Rand to complete but the result is a picturesque ground similar to one you might find in England. The game provided an opportunity for some much-needed practice and Jones (60) and Hayden (40) found some reasonable touch on a slow pitch not conducive to strokemaking.

The undoubted highlight of our innings was the lunch-time meeting with African National Congress leader Nelson Mandela, a man most expect to be the next President of South Africa. We were all introduced to Mr Mandela, who had a brief word for each of us. It was an opportunity that would never have come about if we weren't part of the Australian cricket team, and we were all extremely grateful to be part of the occasion.

At the end of our innings we had totalled 223, with my contribution a short innings of 11. But I wasn't worried, as this type of game is mainly a goodwill gesture – in this case we were raising money for the promotion of cricket in the townships. The game's second half allowed our bowlers to gain some rhythm, especially Hughes and McGrath, who haven't had a lot of bowling recently.

Once again the highlight of the afternoon session didn't come from the cricket. As is usual at these type of games, a carnival atmosphere prevailed and a ground announcer was on hand to add information between breaks in play when necessary. Our reserves couldn't let this opportunity pass them by and proceeded to feed the commentator numerous pieces of information intended to take the mickey out of, you guess it ... Maysie. The first barrage came as Tim chased a ball unsuccessfully to the fence. The commentator called it as: 'Look at him go, the former schoolboy sprint star!' This is somewhat of an exaggeration, as it is common knowledge Maysie couldn't run out of sight in a dark night. More was to follow. Each time Maysie went near a ball a comment was passed on to the crowd along the lines of: 'There he is again, ladies and gentlemen, the best ring fieldsman in the world.' The barbs continued during his bowling spell when the crowd was told his hobbies included orienteering, origami and stamp collecting.

No wonder he's captain of the Nerds!

Oppenheimer's XI needed around 100 runs to win with six wickets left when a nasty thunderstorm put paid to any further chance of play. The most impressive aspect of the game was the success of Jacob Malao, the first player to come through the talent identification scheme from Soweto. He justified his backing with a haul of 3-59.

At these type of games we're inevitably obliged to stay for a drink or two, which sometimes can be a bit of a chore. However, on this occasion it was extremely enjoyable because of the presence of one of the opposition players, Roy Pienaar, who has a talent for magic. He ran the lads through his routines and had them spellbound with his array of tricks and illusions. Warney and I ended up pestering him to the point where he finally succumbed to the pressure and let us in on a few secrets – which we immediately began practising on the 40-minute bus ride back to the hotel. Warney, of course, is already considered by many to be a magician with the ball, and he looks like he has the necessary skill to be on stage as well. He'd mastered more than a few of Pienaar's skills by the time we arrived back at the Sandton Sun.

A square cut during my brief innings against the Oppenheimer XI.

Waiting for me at the hotel was a fax, addressed to Mark and I, from two young cricket fans, Felix and Burick van Schalkwyk, which read:

Dear Steve and Mark Waugh,

We were very surprised to read in our cricket souvenir collection album that your birthdays are on the second of June. We are also twins and our birthdays are also on the second of June, but we are 11 years old. You must then be good guys. We are also interested in cricket and hope to be as good as you guys.

I (Felix) hope you Aussies win.

I (Burick) hope the Springboks win.

Good luck!

The team's now regular haunt, the Sports Cafe, gained our patronage once more for dinner. The cafe has, among its many attractions, a computerised racing bike and up until tonight, Slats had sustained an unbeaten record. But now he was confronted by the unbeaten local champ who, to our amazement, took Slats on the last bend to record a popular victory. Our man was left a shattered mess, hunched over the handle bars, trying to find out where he went wrong.

DAY 7 *February 11*

THE DAY BEGAN with a totally unexpected and shattering piece of information – our coach informed us that last night's decision to cancel practice had been reversed. This was a nasty blow considering the poor state of health I was in. My roomie was equally unimpressed, as he had a day in the sheets on his agenda. But we somehow managed to motivate ourselves and a short time later boarded the bus and headed for the Wanderers Ground.

This was our first fair dinkum training run, and it saw all the players in pretty good form. This was not a real surprise, as we've played a lot of cricket recently and the break we've had was not enough to allow any rust to set in. I'm hitting the ball as well as I have ever done and am looking forward to this tour as a chance to cement my position in the side.

An unusual factor comes into play here in Johannesburg. As we are over 1600 metres above sea level, there is less oxygen in the air which causes a couple of problems. We've found our energy being sapped very quickly, and that the cricket ball travels further through the air (which means we have to make slight adjustments when judging catches). By the end of the session, everyone realised we are going to have to work hard to adjust to these very unusual conditions if we are going to compete successfully.

After practice we returned to our hotel for a quick change of outfit and bite to eat, before heading off to a coaching session in Soweto. The 40-minute drive there took us through a remarkable contrast in housing, which began with the millionaire residences close to our hotel, all of which have extensive security featuring alarms and razor-mesh fencing. We passed by the central business district of Johannesburg, which is similar in size to Sydney, but we've been advised to avoid going there, especially after dark, as it is considered unsafe. Once past the city centre, and as we got closer to Soweto, the standard of living became increasingly poorer. There were pockets of housing, that could be best described as shacks, scattered as far as you could see. In among these were houses that must be owned by slightly more wealthy people, as the dwellings were brick and consisted of probably one or two bedrooms. As I looked at the environment these people lived in, I must admit I had visions of the squalor I have encountered in parts of Pakistan, India and the West Indies.

Somewhere in the middle of this scrum of young cricket fans in Soweto is Craig McDermott.

Allan Border congratulates me after I had taken the wicket of Allan Donald on the final morning of the second Test, at Cape Town.

Australian Picture Library — Mike Hewitt (All Sport)

Australian Picture Librar
Tertius Pickard (Touchline Me

Above: The Wanderers Cricket Ground in Johannesburg, during the first of the one-day internationals.

Below: One of the early highlights of our tour was our trip to Soweto, where we hosted a coaching clinic for a group of keen young cricketers. What struck me most about the children we met was their passion for the game and their natural talent.

Craig McDermott (left), Shane Warne (centre) and Mark Waugh limber up before the start of the one-day internationals.

Australian Picture Library — Tertius Pickard (Touchline Media)

David Boon, during his innings of 58 in the opening one-day international, at the Wanderers.

Australian Picture Library — Tertius Pickard (Touchline Media)

*he Australian vice-
aptain, Mark Taylor,
'ho played in three of
ıe four early one-day
ıternationals, but
ıissed the first Test
ırough illness.*

stralian Picture Library — Thomas Turck (Touchline Media)

***Above:* Mark Waugh bowling during the first Test, at the Wanderers, which South Africa won comfortably by 197 runs.**

Australian Picture Library
Mike Hewitt (All Spo

***Below:* A pull shot late in the day during my innings in the first one-day international, at the Wanderers. I finished with 46 not out.**

Australian Picture Library
Tertius Pickard (Touchline Med

Allan Border leads his Australian team down the controversial players' tunnel at the Wanderers during the first Test. The 'fans' who lined the tunnel weren't slow to tell you what they thought. Directly behind AB is David Boon. Australian Picture Library — Mike Hewitt (All Sport)

Australian Picture Library -
Mike Hewitt (All Spo

Two of the key members of the Australian team.
Above: David Boon, for so long a mainstay of the batting order.
Below: Shane Warne, who the local media were quick to criticise in the early days of the tour. However, by the end of the series the South Africans had come to realise just how devastating his bowling can be.

Australian Picture Library -
Mike Hewitt (All Spo

Shane Warne (left) and Mark Taylor with a new legion of fans.

Most of the locals in Soweto must have heard we were coming because when we arrived their welcome was very friendly. So many people were waving to us from the streets. When we left the team bus, we ventured to a playing field with a pretty ordinary surface, on which about 200 black kids were playing a form of cricket similar to the 'Kanga' cricket the Australian cricket authorities have introduced so successfully at junior levels. This style of cricket allows every player a chance to have a go at batting and bowling and to learn the basics of the game.

Our coaching session with the kids lasted for about an hour and a half. The thing that struck us, above anything else, was the natural talent these kids possess. No doubt, some of that skill will filter through to the national side at some stage in the future, now that opportunities are available to them. Cricket is a sport that hasn't really held an interest in the townships previously because there haven't been any playing fields, equipment is too expensive and there has been no coaching and very little attention given by the media. But this is all changing through the dreams and hard work of Dr Ali Bacher and his colleagues. The gathering was addressed by Dr Bacher, who revealed plans to create a new sporting complex on the ground where we had conducted the clinic, including new change rooms, three turf wickets and facilities for the whole community. When you see the poor state of the grounds and realise just how restricted their lives have been, you realise the extent of the tragedy that has been their inability to show off their skills. But now it will happen and happen very quickly.

Allan Border also spoke to the kids. He held them spellbound because, thanks to the recent coverage on television and in the papers, they all know how great a cricketer he is. He told them he was wondering which one of the present group would be the first person from Soweto to play cricket for South Africa, something which I'm sure is enough motivation for all of them to practise hard and achieve the ultimate. The experience for all in the Australian team was very satisfying and humbling. At home we take all the opportunities given to us for granted. In Soweto they're a luxury.

As soon as the presentation was over, the kids raced back to their cricket games, all dreaming that playing for South Africa is not an impossibility ... but a reality.

DAY 8 *February 12*

A SEVEN O'CLOCK wake-up call is, in my opinion, far too early when the reason behind it is a cricket match, but this morning it was necessary because the game against Northern Transvaal was scheduled to commence at 10am and the ground is in Pretoria, which is 30 minutes away. The four players sitting this fixture out are AB, Warney, Billy and myself, a tough choice as tours these days don't include many fixtures outside Tests and one-day internationals. It can be cruel on players who miss out on the 'warm-up' games, but at the same time you have to try and get the all players in good form. Consequently, players who have niggling injuries or are in very good form miss out.

On an excellent playing surface the Australians were sent in to bat, a strange decision considering the wicket was a batsman's paradise. Slater and Taylor set off at a steady pace and posted a 50-run partnership, enhancing their reputation as the best opening combination going around.

A poor crowd was in attendance, so it felt somewhat strange to have two security guards sitting in among us in the players' balcony, and to have one of them carrying a gun just in case something out of the ordinary occurred. As the day progressed most of the batsman found some valuable touch while spending time in the middle. The reserves also spent one and a half hours over in the nets adjoining the ground, on what we all agreed were practice wickets as good as anywhere in the world.

By the time bad light and rain stopped play we were 5-274 with Dean Jones on 75 not out. Deano was back to his most confident and arrogant best, and will push hard for a position in the Test line-up, especially after his twin hundreds in his last Shield game in Australia.

At the end of play a function was slipped into our program. Drinks and food were served in the committee's room, a bit of a pain in the neck for the players but important as a goodwill gesture. While the boys were pillaging the savouries a huge electrical storm swept over, and the ground was turned into a lake within minutes. On the way home, Warney, AB, and I practised a few matchstick tricks Roy Pienaar had shown us. The results, surprisingly, weren't too bad.

I called Lynette tonight, and discovered she had twisted her ankle taking Chester (our cocker spaniel) for a walk. I couldn't help but laugh. I miss her as always but we have both (sort of) accepted that being away from home is part of the job and one of the few negatives of being an international cricketer.

DAY 9 *February 13*

THIS MORNING at 8 o'clock Merv pulled open the curtains to reveal another overcast morning. While my roomie readied himself for the day's cricket, I pored over the papers, which seem to be all bad news, with stories of massacres, civil wars, murders, burglaries and the like. The prospect of the elections in April is clearly causing problems, with some parties causing trouble and rival groups beginning to antagonise each other. One gets the feeling that this situation will get much worse before too long.

Down at the ground I gave the boys a dose of the John Williamson song *True Blue* on the ghetto blaster, a game move considering the poor response it had received yesterday. However, I'm sure I'll have them all loving it by next week – even Warney, who has taken a sharp dislike to the tune, probably because it doesn't sound like Boney M or Abba (two of his favourites). A long day was ahead for the reserves, as the practice wickets weren't covered overnight and as a result are waterlogged and out of action until tomorrow afternoon. This meant we spent the entire day watching the cricket.

In the morning session, the remainder of our batting collapsed somewhat, to be all out for 363, with Jones falling 15 runs short of a century. Then the 12th man's nightmare materialised, as Jonesy informed us his sore and swollen knee wouldn't allow him to take his place in the field. The continued excellent food and service were evident once again. Lunch went down very well with the boys, except Errol Alcott, who wanted the refrigerator emptied of all the soft drinks, which to that point had proved very popular.

When play ended at 6.12pm, with 19 overs still scheduled to be bowled, the Australians were 0-2 in their second innings. The opposition had been bowled out for 209, a somewhat flattering total from our point of view as the bowling and fielding was below our accepted standard. On the positive side was the bowling of Paul Reiffel, who settled into a great rhythm, and to a lesser extent Glenn McGrath. Merv, who is still really on the comeback trail, struggled to get it together and looked well short of a bowl. He desperately needs the match practice to help him iron out his problems before the big games begin. In saying this, we all know what a great player he is and no-one in our team would bet against him being a major force in the upcoming series. The other front-line bowler to be used was Tim May who I thought was reasonably impressive even if his statistics didn't read all that well. This is something he is currently experiencing, but as we all know at this level, if you are doing the basics right the results will eventually come. I'm positive this is going to be the case for Maysie, even though at the time it can be very frustrating and disappointing when you think you deserve better.

One very unusual statistic to come from today's play was that three wickets were taken on no-balls, which is something in the normal course of events you might not see in a whole season's cricket. At the end of the day the wickets had been shared by Reiffel (four), McGrath (three) and Hughes (three), the beginning of what will become a tight battle for positions in the international matches.

Opposite page: Another photo from our trip to Soweto.
Mark Waugh give some batting tips to a potential top-liner.

DAY 10 *February 14*

AT THE resumption of play this morning, our tactics were for our boys to bat for 50 to 60 overs and achieve a lead of somewhere near 400 and then hopefully bowl this weak Northern Transvaal batting line-up out in the day and a half that remained. By mid-afternoon, Plan A was going along like clockwork with Tubs in great touch making 75, but more importantly, playing the pull shot with authority, a sign he's struck some good form. With cricket being such a mental game, a little thing like playing a favourite shot well can be very important for one's confidence. The same could be said of Junior, who waltzed his way to 134 with his big shots coming off, especially the drive through midwicket and the shots over the infield against the spinners. Heals also found some batting form and, more importantly for him, had some quality time in the middle, something he must take advantage of as he won't get many chances before the big games come around.

By mid-afternoon, the practice facilities had finally dried out and we reserves took the chance to burn off a few calories and gain some form and fitness. Meanwhile, back in the centre, the Northern Transvaal batsmen were hopelessly outclassed. They gave an inadequate display, to the point where it was almost too easy for our lads. In saying this, our bowlers looked impressive with Reiffel backing up his good work in the first innings with four more wickets, and Hughes starting to find some more rhythm (although he is still a long way from his best). McGrath and May also had their moments and the fielding looked much better this time around. In the end the opposition's total of 186 flattered them and only came because their tail hit out lustily. But by that stage it was a lost cause, and the boys were able to win with a day to spare.

One official record that was achieved during the game was Heals' 10 catches and one stumping, which were the most dismissals ever completed by a wicket keeper in South Africa. This is a fine achievement, which adds to his already formidable record.

A valuable and conclusive win was just what the team needed – we all know both winning and losing can become habit. The more you succeed the easier it gets and, conversely, the more you lose the less confident you become. We were a happy squad as the bus made its trek home, with the team spirit bubbling and the boys looking for bigger prizes and, as always, great friendships to be made from our times together.

Right: Our wicketkeeper, Ian Healy, who finished the match against Northern Transvaal with 10 catches and a stumping, a new record for keepers in South Africa.

DAY 11 *February 15*

DESPITE THE fact the game against Northern Transvaal was over, we decided to venture back to Centurion Park because, as the practice facilities are first rate, it was decided a practice session was the best way to spend the morning. An added bonus was the availability of the centre wicket, which was put to good use, particularly by the quick bowlers who took the opportunity to come off their full run-ups – something they can't normally do in the confines of the nets. However, bad news was just around the corner ...

After bowling only four balls, Merv broke down complaining of a sharp pain in the mid to lower region of his back. If this turns out to be more than just a spasm, it will create problems not just for the big bloke but for the entire team. Inevitably, the press contingent got wind of the story and were clamouring all over our management for some details, but it will be 24 hours before the full extent of an injury of this type is really known. The session ended after two and a half hours, and for everyone bar Merv it was a thorough and pleasing workout.

Merv looked in a sorry state back in the dressing room, with sticking plaster all over his back. As the boys see it, the muscle damage isn't the main problem. What's of more concern is the extensive hair loss the big fella's going to suffer when the bandages are torn off. When we asked Errol why he was so sadistic as to not shave Merv's back before he whacked the plaster on, he defended himself by saying he didn't have enough blades to do the job. But, then one of Merv's more caring team-mates asked why our physio didn't ask the groundsman if he could borrow a lawn-mower. Even though it was obviously a traumatic time for him, Merv still managed a laugh. Needless to say, we're all hopeful he'll pull up okay tomorrow.

I spent the afternoon in the gym, to make up for the last couple of days which have been lazy ones for me. Also there was my roomie, and even at this early stage, he appears to be on the road to recovery. His workout in the pool gave Errol the indication the injury isn't as serious as was originally thought.

During our travels around the cricket world, the Australian cricket team has regularly run into rock bands and this was the case again today. Mark Waugh and AB caught up with a few of the roadies who are touring with the English group Depeche Mode and invited us to a concert tonight. I'm always keen to see a gig, and set out for the centre of Johannesburg with Mark, Pistol, Heals and our security guard, Rory, who is a great guy and already part of the team. As usual, we were searched for weapons before entering the entertainment centre, but the check was a shocker. Our man Rory didn't have his 'bum bag' scrutinised, so they didn't find the 9mm hand gun tucked inside. As for the concert – I thought it was disappointing. All their music sounded very similar and they relied too much on their props, especially a large screen behind them, to create an atmosphere. I must admit, however, that most of the audience (obviously loyal fans) had a great time. Perhaps I just don't enjoy their type of music. Afterwards, back at the hotel, Pistol and Heals joined Merv and myself in our room, and the big fella ran us through his repertoire of jokes, which lasted upwards of two hours. Having had treatment on his back for most of the day, he is clearly in better spirits and hopeful his injury isn't too severe.

JOHANNESBURG

Beeld

Gestig in 1974 — WOENSDAG, 16 FEBRUARIE 1994 — R1.00 (BTW ingesluit)

TOWERBINGO 5

U het steeds 'n kans om 'n klomp pryse in **Towerbingo 5** los te slaan. Wat van 'n splinternuwe yskas ter waarde van R3 300, of videokameras, ook ter waarde van R3 300? En moenie vergeet van die handige kontantprys van R250 wat vandag gewen kan word nie. Trek sommer dadelik u kaart nader en kyk of u bingo-nommers en gelukkige nommers u dalk vandag 'n prys in die sak besorg. Die nommers is binne.

Mark (links) en Steve Waugh (28) van Sydney, Australië, is seker die bekendste tweeling in krieketkringe. Hier is hulle op Centurionpark saam met mej. Tarryn Jordaan (18), dogter van mnr. Alan Jordaan, president van die Noord-Transvaalse Krieketunie. Foto: CHRISTIAAN KOTZE

SAP vang nege ná aanval op nagklub

Ma van vier kinders doodgeskiet

Johan de Waal

NEGE mans is gister in hegtenis geneem en beslag is gelê op 'n groot hoeveelheid wapens ná die koelbloedige aanval oergisteraand op 'n nagklub op Newcastle waarin 'n ma van vier kinders doodgeskiet en 'n man gewond is.

Volgens maj. Balz Naidoo, skakeloffisier van die Polisie in Durban, het die Polisie gister beslag gelê op drie R4-gewere, een R5-geweer, vier M26-handgranate en 'n groot hoeveelheid ammunisie. Die verdagtes is gister op Madadeni en Osizweni naby Newcastle in hegtenis geneem.

Die aanvallers het Maandagaand omstreeks elfuur tot voor die oop deur van die Crazy Beat Disco in Sutherlandstraat gestap en met outomatiese gewere op die sowat 25 dskogangers losgebrand. Minstens twee van die aanvallers het klapmusse gedra, het maj. Naidoo gesê.

Mev. Gerda van Wyk (31) van Drakensbergrylaan 78, Newcastle, is doodgeskiet en mnr. Chris Malone (40) van Ladysmith is in die bobeen gewond.

Volgens mnr. Hans Swanepoel (30), wat saam met mev. Van Wyk by die nagklub was, is dit net 'n wonderwerk dat nie nog mense in die aanval doodgeskiet is nie.

Mev. Gerda van Wyk

aan haar regterhand gesien en haar gevra of sy seergekry het. Sy het probeer antwoord, maar kon niks sê nie."

Volgens mnr. Swanepoel het hy bloed aan haar bors gesien. "Ek het haar klere afgetrek en die enkele koeëlwond bokant haar hart gesien."

Hy het noodbehandeling toegepas, maar mev. Van Wyk is 'n paar minute later dood.

Mnr. Malone is na die Newcastle-Hospitaal gebring. Sy toestand is bevredigend, het 'n hospitaalwoordvoerder gesê.

Die aanvallers het kort ná die voorval in 'n wit Toyota Cressidamotor gevlug. Die Polisie het dié motor ook teruggevind.

Mev. Van Wyk word oorleef deur twee dogters uit haar eerste huwelik, Marinda (13) en Kathy van Rooyen (11), en twee seuns uit 'n tweede huwelik, Neville (8) en Dawie van Wyk (3).

Sy word waarskynlik Vrydagoggend op Newcastle begrawe.

Dit is onbekend wanneer die verdagtes in die hof sal verskyn, het maj. Naidoo gesê. Foto's op bl. 4.

Boekewêreld vandag binne

Waugh-tweeling weet hoe om 'n bal te woer

Lorette Grobler

VERGEET maar van die Wright-broers; dis deesdae die Waugh-broers van Australië wat weer die vliegkuns uitgevind het.

Ramp eis 22 lewens

PORT ELIZABETH. – Lyke en beseerdes is gistermiddag nog uit trekkers na 'n bus wat gisteroggend omgeslaan het... Lees volledige berig op bl. 4.

Vinnige Fanie de Villiers

ONTMOET VINNIGE FANIE!

– kans vir Beeld se jong lesers

Zoeloe-vrese word aangepak, sê FW

Die wil moet egter daar wees vir 'n kompromis

Peet Kruger, Politieke Beriggewer

DIE Regering en die ANC werk aan voorstelle om die Zoeloe-koning se vrese en kommer oor die toekoms van die Zoeloe-monargie te hanteer.

Krugerrande: boere (met nog baie skuld) koop nou vir 'n vale

Curt von Keyserlingk

Mej. Christina Estrada

Sol verloof aan nuwe dol – 6.

Man byt hond dood wat hom wou aanval

DNEPROPETROVSK (Oekraïne). – 'n Man wat 'n hond doodbyt?

Bel Beeld: Jhb: (011) 402-1460 Pta: (012) 325-2878 tot 2894

Sterk opswaai verstom ekonome – S1

The front page of the February 16 edition of the local Johannesburg paper, Beeld, *which is published in* Afrikaans.

DAY 12 *February 16*

OUR FIRST appointment of the day was an 8.30am fitting for our one-day clothes from Benson and Hedges. This, the players thought, was a trifle early but it couldn't be changed. Our next engagement promised to be much more exciting – the removal, in room 1108 at 9.30am by our physio Hooter, of the elastoplast from Merv's back. The boys, sensing the potential unpleasantness of the operation, turned out in good numbers and weren't disappointed. When the first strip was removed it took with it a thick layer of black hairs. If the screams of agony were anything to go by, I think this might have hurt. Beads of sweat formed on the brow of the big fella, and then he was told there were only seven more strips to go. Fortunately, Paul Reiffel was capturing these torturous events on his video camera and by the time the last strip was ripped off, Merv was minus a large portion of his mohair rug. He was also in a fair amount of discomfort, with a few spots of blood trickling down his back. But he was okay. Upon surveying the damage in the mirror, he muttered: 'I'd better give Greg Matthews a ring at Advanced Hair Studio to arrange for the replacement of the hair I've lost on my back.'

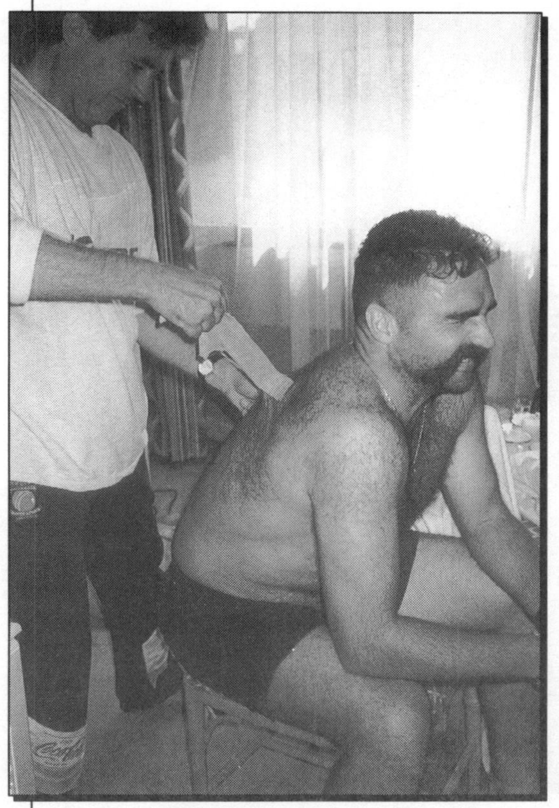

The operation that left Merv minus most of the hair that had once been on his back.

As our management had allowed us the privilege of a day off today, a bus trip was organised to visit a lion park and then on to Gold Reef City, a former gold mine which is now an amusement park. The Leeupark Lion Park, which is 30 minutes from our hotel, was the scene of a horrific accident two months ago. The one strict rule of the park is to stay within your car at all times, but a group from Taiwan decided to try and get the photograph of a lifetime in front of a pride of 11 lions. Unfortunately, the lions perceived them as a threat and proceeded to maul them to death in only 30 seconds. Consequently, there was no chance of us bending any of the rules, especially when we had the chance to watch the lions at feed time devouring the dead horses and donkeys that are given to the park for the animals to eat.

After watching these imposing animals roam around, and then getting the opportunity to handle the lion cubs that are raised here, it is hard to imagine people wanting to wipe the species out. For us they are a symbol of Africa.

We spent the afternoon at Gold Reef City, where we had the run of the park and enjoyed whatever rides we wanted to go on, and also took a trip down a gold mine shaft to see how this precious metal was once extracted from the ground. The 200-metre drop in darkness down the shaft was an ideal time for Merv to start skylarking, and he began jumping up and down, and shaking the lift, which he seemed to find even more enjoyable when the other passengers became more anxious.

At the park we came across a shop inviting people to sample a local drink which consists of 58 per cent alcohol. The lads gave it the thumbs up, but were less keen on another (supposed) delicacy called *Moepani*, a worm similar to a witchetty grub, which had been cooked and was firm in texture. The only cricketers silly enough to give it a tasting were country boys McGrath and Slater, who described the flavour as 'wood-like'. Even so, they were quite keen for the other lads to sample the taste, but we were all put off by the locals, who had previously turned their heads away in shock and disgust when an earlier sampling had taken place.

We spent this evening at a Portuguese Restaurant called 'Villamora', which put on an excellent feed. It also provided our first sighting of vegetables since we hopped off Qantas flight QF63 last week.

Two of the best-looking inhabitants at the Leeupark Lion Park.

DAY 13 *February 17*

THIS MORNING'S six o'clock wake-up call failed to entice either Merv or myself out of the sheets, but the back-up call half an hour later managed to coax us out of the comfort and warmth of our beds. We faced a two-hour trip to Potchefstroom, for a match against a President's XI in what would serve as our final hit out before the one-day internationals, which begin on Saturday.

Within the first five minutes of our journey most of the team were pushing the zeds out, so that by the time the bus arrived at the ground the lads were rested up well and keen for a game. The match, to be played in the heart of right-wing (Afrikaner) territory in Western Transvaal, had attracted a capacity crowd, who, having been starved of high-class cricket for so long, were eager to mix with our team. Everyone, it seemed, had an autograph book to be signed or a camera at the ready.

As is protocol in these games, we had first use of the wicket but, unfortunately, we got off to a shaky start and both Taylor and Jones had been dismissed by the time the boys located the hot dog stand and brought some breakfast back to the dressing room. Fortunately, Boon and M. Waugh put together a handy partnership, which gave me enough time to devour my hot dog before I was called into action. While I spent my first couple of overs trying to adjust to the slow-paced wicket, Mark decided it was time to give the crowd some fielding practice, and the score began to race along until his luck ran out and he was caught on the fence attempting yet another journey ball (six). Ten minutes later, a storm hit the ground with such ferocity that no turf was visible within minutes. The arena resembled a lake, with pieces of temporary fencing, umbrellas and debris floating across the surface. As the rain teemed down, atmosphere in the Australian dressing room quickly changed to one of frivolity and fun, and eventually it was decided no further play could be achieved.

Glenn McGrath, standing amid the 'floodwaters' after a torrential downpour had curtailed our match against a President's XI at Potchefstroom.

The spectators had obviously looked forward to today's outing and a torrential downpour wasn't about to put them off. So, even while the rain continued to tumble down, they began sliding along the wicket area and started up their own ball games in the outfield. Meanwhile, a small ceremony, hosted by the local Mayor in a room overlooking the ground was our last appointment for the day. This proved to be a very entertaining event for the crowd, especially when, in full view of the gathering and to the delight of the schoolgirls present, Merv caught Warney by surprise and 'dacked' him.

The journey home turned out to be a nightmare. Our driver had only three gears (the other was lost due to mechanical failure) and therefore what should have been a two-hour trip became a three-and-a-half-hour ordeal. By the time we made it back to the Sandton Sun we all felt like we were suffering from jet lag and most definitely lacking in match fitness, which is a bit of a worry when we thought of the altitude and the fast-approaching one-dayers. Another cause for concern in the camp was an asthma attack AB had suffered today, which prevented him from taking part in the game and will require some tests tomorrow morning to pinpoint the cause. However, even with these minor setbacks, the squad is in excellent spirits, and the lack of cricket practice might even turn out to be a blessing in disguise because a few of the guys are still carrying niggling injuries from the recent heavy schedule. Hopefully, the rest will recharge the batteries.

Cricketers can be creatures of habit, especially when touring, so if we stumble across a good venue to eat or drink we usually spend a great deal of time there. So, after being impressed by Villamora last evening, we went back for more. After dinner, I returned to our room to watch some highlights from the recent Winter Olympics which prompted more than a little dreaming. It must just about be the ultimate in sport to stand on a podium with a gold medal around your neck and your own national anthem playing in the background.

The bus-trip back from Potchefstroom to our hotel in Johannesburg developed into a tedious three-and-a-half hour ordeal. All the guys could do was try to find some sleep. The four men in sunglasses are (left to right) Allan Border, Michael Slater, Tim May and Craig McDermott. In the back row, at right, is Glenn McGrath.

DAY 14 *February 18*

AS EACH morning passes, our wake-up calls are coming later and later, as our keenness to get to the breakfast buffet diminishes and our eagerness to stay in the cot increases. Our humble abode in the Sandton Sun is now in a total state of disarray, with clothes scattered to all corners of the room, bags piled on top of each other and furniture rumoured to be lurking somewhere. In among this rubble we have managed to misplace eight sets of room keycards (the plastic-card type that open the room door) which, to the dismay of the staff at reception, must be close to some sort of record.

The scheduled pre-match practice session at the Wanderers Ground, our last before the first of the one-dayers, turned out to be a shambles as the Australian and South African teams arrived at the same time. This was in itself a problem, as you have to share the nets, but was made even worse by the fact that the practice wickets were still damp from the persistent rain that has fallen during the past couple of days. To cap this off, the Northern Transvaal Cricket Manager (and former Springbok cricketer), Eddie Barlow, wouldn't allow either side onto the main ground as he feared we would damage the surface, which is holding a lot of moisture.

Despite these handicaps, we turned in a solid workout and in the process managed to lighten Simmo's cricket ball bag. At least a dozen balls went missing as they sailed into the adjoining corporate tents which have been erected for the upcoming game. The quality of the workout, plus the news that Merv's back is continuing to improve after the treatment from Errol Alcott, is good for the morale and the structure of the team.

Glenn McGrath, with a group of autograph hunters ... and 'Chips' the doll, which our young fast bowler 'won' after a series of temperamental outbursts.

As the appointed social director, it was my job to find a restaurant for tonight's pre-game dinner. Because the town centre is 25 minutes away from our hotel the options were few, so I decided the much-frequented Portuguese restaurant downstairs would be a good choice. We didn't want a late night as the bus is leaving for the ground at eight o'clock tomorrow morning.

Before dinner, the newly appointed fines committee of Reiffel (chairman), McGrath (new tourist) and Healy detailed their first series of accusations at their colleagues. A typical fine is for lateness on buses (the charge: one Rand – about 40 cents Australian – per minute late) which left Junior and Matt Hayden 15 Rand the worse off. Going out to dinner without letting your room-mate know where you're going brings a two-Rand fine, and for foolish acts, such as Boonie wearing in a new pair of batting gloves for two days before realising they were a left-handed pair (and consequently of no use to him), the penalty is two Rand.

Before the meeting ended, a new team member was introduced. A few days ago, while in a local toy store, I came across a large baby doll called 'Carry Chips', which I think is very appropriate for the 'spit the dummy' award for the week. The doll sucks its thumb and has a nappy, and should prove a great embarrassment to the recipient, which is the most important thing. The inaugural winner, and a popular choice, was Glenn McGrath ... for his continued temper tantrums when he gets out, which normally lead to gear finding its way to all parts of the dressing room.

Everyone agreed the dinner went well, especially after word filtered around that the Australian Cricket Board would be paying the bill. The guys quickly reconsidered their orders (there was a rush on the seafood platters at 92 Rand a pop), and a few bottles of the better quality wines were sampled.

THE ONE-DAY INTERNATIONALS

DAY 15 *February 19*

THE DAY began with a fairly light breakfast of toast and vegemite (a few of the guys always take this precious little jar away with them), tea, cereal and orange juice and then it was onto the bus for a police escort to help ensure a speedy trip to the ground. We quickly realised just how handy that escort was, as the traffic and queues around the ground were chaotic.

As we had expected, the welcome by the crowd was quite boisterous. The team bore the full brunt of the crowds emotions and in particular a barrage of sheep jokes Australians normally associate with Kiwis. We found it almost amusing that they were now directed at us. To keep the crowds under control, and to stop them from entering the field during the games, security guards with Alsatian dogs were placed around the boundary, inside the fence, which nearly caused a casualty among our ranks before play began. Boonie safely held a skied catch of Simmo during the warm-up, but ended up only inches from a snarling canine who seemed to fancy our little champion's calf muscle as a breakfast snack.

The Australian starting XI was pretty much as expected. Taylor was preferred to Hayden and Slater at the top of the order, while Glenn McGrath beat Hughes and May for the final bowling spot. The full side was: Taylor, Boon, Jones, M. Waugh, S. Waugh, Border (c), Healy, Reiffel, Warne, McDermott, McGrath. The South African team that opposed us was: Peter Kirsten, Gary Kirsten, Hansie Cronje, Jonty Rhodes, Kepler Wessels (c), Adrian Kuiper, David Richardson, Richard Snell, Eric Simons, Fanie de Villiers, Allan Donald.

Allan Border (left) and Kepler Wessels prepare for the toss before the start of the first Australia-South Africa one-day international on South African soil.

Before a capacity crowd of 30,000 people, Wessels won the toss and elected to let his batsmen have first use of a good-looking batting wicket. However, despite the friendliness of the pitch, in the early overs we managed to pin the locals down, thanks to some consistently tight and accurate bowling from Reiffel and McGrath. But then the two danger men – Cronje and Rhodes –

changed the game with some energetic running between the wickets and improvised batting strokes. After having restricted them to 2-100 off 30 overs, South Africa managed to end up on 3-232. Cronje batted elegantly and superbly for 112 and Rhodes gave the impetus at the business end of the innings with 47 well-crafted runs.

From our point of view, the end total was a little disappointing. We work on a formula for calculating the opposition's final total that works like this: you double what their score was after 30 overs, and add an extra 10 or 20 runs if they have lost only one or two wickets at that 30-over stage. So, when we kept the locals to 2-100 after 30, we were expecting to be chasing between 200 and 220 – not 232. Overall we were reasonably happy with our efforts, although our fielding wasn't as sharp as it could have been and probably cost us 10 runs. But we all believed that the total was very gettable.

However, after a tremendous start which produced 100 runs off 23 overs for the loss of only Taylor, we self-destructed in the crucial middle section of the innings. We seemed to have the game under control, but lost three wickets (Boon, Jones and M. Waugh) and fell fatally behind the required run-rate. This was surprising, especially as it was at the hands of a couple of medium pacers, but we tried to bamboozle them with fancy shots that ended up being our downfall. By the time AB and I managed to steady the ship a little we needed 66 from the last 10 overs, a solid rate but very achievable in this rarefied atmosphere that allows balls to travel far greater distances than normal. However, every time we got within striking distance of the target they would bowl a good over, and in the end their five-run victory was probably a fair result.

We weren't quite good enough to take our chances today. In saying that, I must give credit to the opposition, especially the batting of Cronje and Rhodes and the coolness of Fanie de Villiers, who produced two magnificent overs late in our innings to keep the game in their favour.

A losing dressing room, such as the Australian room at the Wanderers this evening, has an eerie feeling about it. Hardly a word was spoken as each player tried to work out what went wrong in the team's and their own performance. Everyone knows losing is a part of sport. But it's important that you can take some positives out of each game so hopefully this unwanted feeling will not keep occurring in the future. On this occasion Simmo thought we needed a bit of a blast and demanded we work out where we can improve for the next game. He also asked for a more disciplined approach.

Back on the bus, the boys tried to put the loss behind us. We can't wait to claim some pride and revenge in tomorrow's encounter.

Bouncing back after three losses good for morale

IT IS always nice to get a win under your belt and it's great for us to take an early lead in the series. It was important for us, because we went into yesterday on the back of three defeats against the Australians — the two World Series finals and the Adelaide Test.

We always had a good chance having batted first and scored 232. Anything over 225, even on a good batting wicket always puts you in a position of strength and although there were one or two tense moments out there at the end, our guys did very well under pressure.

The much-maligned theory of having a guy who bats through the innings also seemed to work pretty well. When you have somebody getting a 90 or a hundred, you're bound to have a good chance of making a 220-230 sort of total.

Hansie's innings was really tops. When he and Jonty came together they made a crucial stand which enabled us to get that winning total.

Fanie de Villiers was also worth his weight in gold once again and likewise Jonty's fielding. I reckon it's worth 20-30 runs to us in these sort of games.

I also thought the two guys coming into the side — Adrian Kuiper and Eric Simons — did extremely well under pressure. Obviously, they were both pretty keyed-up but they came through with flying colours.

Once Dean Jones and Mark Waugh had got out, I think we held the upper hand. It was a tough, tight finish, though, which was great cricket for what was a great crowd.

Having rejoined the guys after a month at home with my knee injury, I noticed how teed up the squad has been. I know how tired everyone was after what was a demanding tour to India and Australia and, of course, it's far from over with another tough series just begun.

By the end of this season most of us will be pretty exhausted. (My knee, by the way, came through yesterday very well.)

The Australians will be a bit stung by yesterday's defeat but they have a pretty balanced attitude to one-day cricket. There's a lot of cricket to come and they are a very good team.

KEPLER WESSELS
SA captain

Cricket

Vice-captain's debut 100 in the limited overs game helps set up a five-run margin for magnificence

Cronje king of the Wanderers

Colin Bryden
at the Wanderers

HANSIE Cronje's effortless mastery made the difference in the first one-day international yesterday, although until late in the afternoon it seemed that it might not be enough.

The eventual margin was just five runs and the match was only put beyond reach of Australia in Fanie de Villiers' penultimate over, the 49th of the innings.

With a frenzied crowd chanting "Fanie, Fanie", De Villiers bowled three balls from which Steve Waugh could not score, grudgingly conceded a single and then bowled Allan Border as the Australian captain, with desperate measures necessary, stepped towards square leg and swished in vain as his legstump was knocked out of the ground. Finally, the crowd could celebrate, with an improbable 24 runs needed off the last two overs.

Deeds in one-day cricket are quickly overtaken by events. The series continues today at Centurion Park and by Thursday the teams will have met four times. Few games, however, have provided as much excitement and good cricket as was served up to a capacity crowd yesterday.

Cronje's innings was studded with strokes so pure that they would have graced any Test match, while his bludgeoning destruction of Shane Warne was the very stuff of one-day cricket, sending the crowd into ecstasy as he twice lifted the leg-spinner over midwicket for six.

The South African vice-captain shared a thrilling third wicket partnership of 106 off just 94 balls with Jonty Rhodes — close to eight runs an over — as South Africa reached 232/3 off 50 overs.

South Africa's total, however, owed almost everything to the two 24-year-olds. Before he was joined by Rhodes, Cronje had taken the initiative away from the Australian bowlers, of whom Reiffel and McGrath were impeccable.

There had been times when it seemed South Africa's innings would subside into a strangulation imposed by accurate bowling and cautious batting. Kirsten, despite some cracking offside strokes early on, found it progressively more difficult to beat the field but Cronje went down the wicket, driving firmly in the V between mid-off and mid-on. A six over mid-off against Steve Waugh heralded the start of the second 25 overs of the innings in which the score more than trebled.

Later, Australia were to make a much brisker start, reaching 103/1 midway through their innings, 32 ahead of the South African total at the same stage.

The partnership between Cronje and Rhodes was breathtaking. If fitter and faster men between wickets emerge anywhere in the world, then in-fielders may as well go out to pasture. Rhodes in particular turned noughts into ones, ones into twos and even a nought into a two when a scampered single forced an error from the field.

Cronje's first 50 was impressive enough, scored off 69 balls. His second 50 required a mere 39 deliveries and it was only after reaching his maiden one-day international hundred that he showed signs of tiredness, twice scooping the ball into the air before falling, two balls from the end of the innings. His 112 equalled Gary Kirsten's record for South Africa, set in the first match of the World Series finals in Melbourne last month.

Batting had been the only option for Kepler Wessels after winning the toss. It was a pitch of such perfection for batsmen that most bowlers would have been happy to hand over their duties to the bowling machine, with the odds utterly against them.

The prevailing weather pattern equally made it sensible to have runs on the board in case interruptions made the task of the team batting second more difficult. As it happened, for the first time in many days the scudding clouds over Johannesburg did not herald a downfall.

Warne was clouted for 56 runs off 10 overs. His shoulder may well be troubling him but those who say he could turn the ball sharply on glass were not proved right on a surface as unhelpful to spin as any he is likely to bowl on.

On this splendid batting surface the powerful Australian batting line-up always stood a good chance and Allan Donald's second over was disastrous for SA. Every ball yielded runs and the last two were hit to the boundary with effortless timing by David Boon, momentarily silencing those spectators who had picked up on the first three letters of his name to taunt him mercilessly.

Boon played an innings that threatened to be a match-winner but having offered one half-chance to Rhodes at backward point off Kuiper, he made the mistake of giving Rhodes an opportunity to make amends just seven runs later.

Eric Simons, making his official international debut at 31, was introduced into the attack at a crucial stage and conceded nine runs off his second over. He then proved his credentials by conceding just 28 runs off his next eight overs, including a match-turning second spell in which he took 2/13, the vital wickets of Mark Waugh and Dean Jones.

Steve Waugh and Border put on 54 at almost a run a ball but the task grew ever more difficult and finally impossible.

CENTURION ... Hansie Cronje acknowledges the crowd after reaching his century against Australia at the Wanderers yesterday. Cronje went on to make 112 before being caught by Paul Reiffel — Picture: JOHN HOGG

FIRST ONE-DAY INTERNATIONAL, WANDERERS

(South Africa won the toss)

SOUTH AFRICA

P N Kirsten c Reiffel b McGrath (143min, 114 balls, 3x4, 0x6) ... 47
(driven to mid-off)
G Kirsten c Healy b Reiffel (82-31-1-0) ... 13
(cutting close to body, edged to keeper)
W J Cronje c Reiffel b McDermott (146-120-7-3) ... 112
(mistimed on-drive to mid-off)
J N Rhodes not out (90-39-4-0) ... 47
A P Kuiper not out (2-1-0-0) ... 2
Extras (lb, 2w, 5nb) ... 12
TOTAL (3 wickets, 50 overs) ... 232
FALL OF WICKETS: 1/28 (G Kirsten), 2/123 (P Kirsten), 3/226 (Cronje).
K C Wessels, E O Simons, † D J Richardson, R P Snell, P S de Villiers, A A Donald did not bat.
BOWLING: McDermott (8-0-20-0) (5-0-16-0) (2-0-18-1) 10-0-62-1 (1w, 5nb); Reiffel (7-1-18-1) (3-0-20-0) 10-1-28-1 (1w, 3nb); McGrath (7-1-15-0) (3-0-14-1) 10-1-28-1; S Waugh (7-0-31-0) (3-0-23-0) 10-0-54-0 (1nb); Warne 10-0-56-0.

AUSTRALIA

M A Taylor c Snell (58min, 48 balls, 3x4, 0x6) ... 30
(top out back, inside edge)
D C Boon c Rhodes b Kuiper (104-81-7-0) ... 58
(forcing stroke, diving catch backward point)
D M Jones c Cronje b Simons (92-62-2-0) ... 42
(lofted to deep mid-wicket)
M E Waugh c Richardson b Simons (32-20-0-1) ... 14
(top-edged hook high to wicketkeeper)
S R Waugh not out (72-62-3-0) ... 46
*A R Border b de Villiers (41-27-2-0) ... 38
(stepping away to leg, miss)
† I A Healy not out (9-4-0-0) ... 4
Extras (lb, 2w, 1nb) ... 8
TOTAL (five wickets, 50 overs) ... 227
FALL OF WICKETS: 1/61 (Taylor), 2/109 (Boon), 3/143 (M Waugh), 4/155 (Jones), 5/209 (Border).
BOWLING: Donald (5-1-22-0) (3-0-16-0) (1-0-9-0) 9-0-48-0 (1nb); De Villiers (8-0-24-0) (2-0-8-0) (3-0-10-1) 10-0-42-1 (1w); Snell (6-0-30-1) (2-0-3-0) (2-0-15-0) 10-0-48-1 (1w); Simons (3-0-16-0) (6-0-13-2) 10-0-29-2; Kuiper (6-0-22-1) (1-0-8-0) 7-0-28-1 (1w); Cronje 4-0-20-0.
Result: South Africa won by five runs. Man of the match: Hansie Cronje.
Umpires: B Lambson and C Mitchley. Third umpire: W Diedricks.
Conditions: Hot, good batting pitch, fast outfield.
Attendance: 30 212.
† denotes wicketkeeper * denotes captain

Away from the helm, but still leading as a batsman

No longer the captain, Hansie Cronje showed his huge value to the SA side, writes **Ian Hawkey**.

HANSIE Cronje, somewhat uncharacteristically, cancelled his appointments earlier this week. It seems he had a bad case of 'flu, which had kept him even from the nets, although yesterday's century was hardly the work of a man under the weather.

The previous appointment Cronje had cancelled — or, rather, postponed — was the captaincy of South Africa, announcing on his return from three months on tour that the pressure of leadership had taken the edge off his batting. To his credit, he had foreseen in early January that it might and he, perhaps before anybody else, reached the conclusion that it had.

"It is always nice to be able to concentrate solely on your batting," said Cronje last night. In his previous seven one-day internationals as national captain during the tour to Australia, Cronje scored two 40s, one 28, was out three times in the teens and finally a duck. When that duck was joined by another in his next innings, in the third Test at Adelaide, and followed by a three, he was moved to see causes beyond the caprice of umpire Darrell Hair.

At home in Bloemfontein four days after Adelaide, Cronje scored 120 in close to even time for Free State against Western Province. Forty-eight hours later, he finished the task, captaining his province to the night series final. Some homecoming.

But no time to dwell on it. Back to Johannesburg, from where Cronje and his father had driven overnight a week earlier so that Free State could reinstate their skipper for the B & H semi-final.

This time, the Castle Cup against Transvaal. Another four days with the same character as most of the previous 48: more brinkmanship from the skipper. Victory, and only victory would leave Free State with a chance of retaining the trophy.

Cronje's Free Staters won in the last hour of four rather helter-skelter days at the Wanderers, but the captain's own contribution as a batsman had been just 16 runs spread across his two innings.

Back to Bloemfontein, and bed. Down with influenza, Cronje had still time to seek influence, notably from Grey College headmaster Johann Volsteedt, who he looked up at his *alma mater*.

Yes, he might have told Volsteedt, it *had* been a busy two weeks since he first spoke of relinquishing the captaincy. And a remarkable month before that. Was he exhausted? Burnt out? Cronje ran 66 of his 112 runs yesterday, as well as 59 of his two partners'. No shortage of fitness nor stamina there.

Cronje's century has begun the SA challenge in this one-day series with the same pugnacity and purpose as he did in their last. It was in Melbourne in December that the vice-captain had recorded his previous highest limited-overs international score, the 91 not out with which he guided SA to a seven-wicket win over the Australians. Then, as yesterday, he dominated his individual battle with Shane Warne.

"In Australia," said Cronje, "Shane Warne did a lot of damage in the one-day games by picking up two or three wickets at crucial times in the innings and then he'd end up giving away only about three or four runs an over. Yesterday, we just didn't let him do that."

UP AND OVER ... Jonty Rhodes watches one that got away. The Natal captain ended the day unbeaten after having 47 runs — Picture: JOHN HOGG

Nothing in a name as Kepler leads with cautious courage

When selective extracts from an article by **Peter Roebuck**, former Somerset captain and now a leading journalist, were published in SA this week, he was in his own words "miffed, actually livid"

NOW comes a chance to correct the impression given by the dismembered chunks quoted this week. South Africa has played extremely well on its return to international cricket. India and Sri Lanka have been beaten, a draw secured on the notoriously demanding tour of Australia and a valiant World Cup campaign fought. Astonishingly, the first ever Test in the West Indies was nearly won. They have done it all without a single great cricketer in their ranks, not one player who could be certain of commanding a place in the Australian team.

It has been done, moreover, under the shadow of a celebrated past from which it will take time to break free. Allan Border's team has only just escaped from the censuring recollections of the heroes of '75.

Most encouraging of all, the Afrikaners have taken to the game. To see De Villiers, Hansie Cronje and Kepler Wessels at work is to know that Afrikaners can bring courage, tenacity, collectivity and a certain nobility to their endeavours. Cricket is not reserved for the Salty Dicks, as Englishmen are apparently called, one leg being in Africa, one in England and their private parts dangling in the ocean between. No longer can cricket be dismissed as a game for the pampered and privileged few.

To see thousands of Afrikaners cheering their team at Potchefstroom was to sense what could be in a country of extremes striving to find a middle way. And they watched a coloured man strike with his first ball, and a Xhosa keeping wicket capably.

The other side of what might be had been experienced in Bloemfontein on Wednesday, listening to the spellbinding oratory of Mr Terreblanche, whose roars and whispers echoed across a packed hall silent until near the end, as the struggling, scared folk heard of visions and compared them to their meagre lot.

That more Afrikaners are playing is great, because the game must be held in common. Slower advances will be made amongst those born with darker skins for it can take 20 years to produce a Test cricketer, and so many cultural, educational and economic challenges must be faced. Impatience is the enemy, for 20 years is a long time. Meanwhile nets must be built, coaches helped and kit provided, even into areas far away from the glare of publicity. No money can be wasted, and it was surprising to hear that all the selectors had been flown to Durban to announce their team. Better to ring Mr Pollock and to buy a few more bats.

Eventually, cricket broadcasts will be in English, Afrikaans and all the township languages, as with soccer, the people's game. Unfortunately few blacks attended the match in Potch, though rather more than were at Mr Terreblanche's meeting.

Not that everything is hunky dory in South African cricket. Pace is too dominant and I stand by the observation that Shane Warne might not have made it here or in England. Also the 18-25s may not be a vintage crop.

As regards the captaincy, it is a little known fact that it was a German physicist called Kepler who introduced the word "inertia" into the language. But I will not join the ageing critics from Transvaal. To my mind Wessels and Cronje have done splendidly, leading by example. Their caution has been unsurprising, for their team is extremely inexperienced and lacks depth. Cronje did lose his way a little in Australia, though had he called correctly in two of the three Final matches it might not have mattered.

Wessels should play for two or three more years, if his knees can take it. Certainly he should rise above such incompatibilities as inevitably occur behind the scenes. Cronje then would have time to mature as a batsman.

But, really, the problem is not with the present, it is with the future, whose challenges are formidable. South Africa must appreciate all of its peoples, the flamboyant and the solemn, and must in particular find some top-class spinners. It can be done and it will be if everyone involved concentrates on the years as well as the minutes.

THE INSIDE EDGE

PLANS for the Sunday Times to provide the best possible coverage of the South African team at the Winter Olympics in Lillehammer have been frustrated by bureaucracy. Our correspondent has been told she cannot send reports because she is a member of the official delegation. The decision does nothing to dispel the impression that the Olympic movement is secretive and over-protective.

THE umpiring of Darrell Hair in Australia this summer must have impressed someone. The Australian has been nominated to stand as an independent umpire in the current series between West Indies and England. Hair approaches the task with confidence. "I give myself 10 out of 10 but some other people wouldn't." Peter Kirsten might just be one of those other people.

WHILE the Winter Olympics in Lillehammer captivates those able to watch M-Net it is sobering to think that 10 years ago the Olympics were held in Sarajevo, now a living hell in a crippling civil war. The rink where Torvill and Dean won fame to the strains of Bolero has been destroyed by shelling and overlooks a makeshift graveyard.

WHO'D be a figure skating judge at Lillehammer, should Tonya Harding complete the perfect round in the Winter Olympics? Can human judges be unaware of the scandal surrounding the attack on her rival, Nancy Kerrigan?

NOW and again we have no choice but to "Edge" ourselves. Golf writer Dan Retief, playing in a Transvaal Golf Union day, was partnered by Emfuleni's Danny Kinnear. Retief lamented the slide from prominence of amateur golf.

"If you had to ask me the name of the current SA strokeplay champion I wouldn't know it," said Retief. "I am," smiled Kinnear.

THE press release from Sun International arrived in the Sunday Times office on Friday marked "Exclusive" and "Urgent". Amos Mansdorf would play in the SA Open tennis at Sun City. Good story. Only problem was it had been all over the daily newspapers on Thursday after a release by Tennis South Africa on Wednesday.

DESPITE the most assiduous proof-reading, errors are an almost unavoidable part of the printing business. Sue Doull, having produced a splendid Australian cricket tour brochure, was mortified to find a picture of Peter Kirsten had been transposed so that he appears batting left-handed. The Weekly Mail lifted the picture this week to accompany their self-styled world-class coverage of the tour — still batting left-handed.

It is possible, of course, that in the desperate quest to find another Graeme Pollock, Kirsten has been practising left-handed strokes in preparation for the coming Tests ...

ALTHOUGH in general we support the glasshouse principle in drawing attention to other newspapers, it has been difficult to avoid a touch of cynicism after surveying headlines this week. "Wessels glad to be back in charge." "Kuiper, Simons believe they can do the job." "Wessels sê SA kan wen." Now, if Kuiper and Simons said they were horrified at the prospect of playing for SA or Wessels thought his team would lose, THAT would be news.

The back page of the sports section of the Johannesburg Sunday Times *of February 20 tells the story of the previous day's hometown triumph.*

DAY 16 *February 20*

WE HAD to wear another very early wake-up call this morning (7am), because today's match, at Centurion Park, is 25 minutes away in Pretoria. When we did arrive at the ground the queues at each entrance point were outrageously long – people were joining lines stretching back 500 metres – in yet another vote of approval by the spectators for one-day cricket.

Both teams remained unchanged from yesterday and, with the coin once again landing correctly for the home team, South Africa batted first on another great-looking strip. The most popular theme among the crowd's banners today was that man Darrell Hair, who has almost reached cult status over here and is more talked about than Nelson Mandela. It has reached a stage where they are selling Darrell Hair T-shirts with the umpire raising his middle finger in the air, and there were Darrell Hair banners, none of them complimentary, in the crowd as well.

Centurion Park is another top-quality playing surface. It has a hill surrounding the ground that allows the spectators to have a barbecue while they watch the game – a great idea for everyone except the players who can pick up the scent of the steak and onions. It made me feel homesick. Almost from ball one the South Africans had their noses slightly in front, with Cronje and Rhodes doing the damage once again. But if we had been able to grab a couple of quick wickets we would have been on top. Both these batsmen are held in high esteem by the people of South Africa, as both cricketers and men, with

A handshake with South African paceman Richard Snell after the locals had gone two-up in the one-day series. In the background is Kepler Wessels.

Paul Reiffel, during South Africa's innings at Centurion Park.

Rhodes' popularity being along the same lines as Warney in Australia. The pressure of captaincy affected Cronje in Australia, but now that Wessels is back in charge it appears a huge weight has been lifted from his shoulders and he is playing exceptionally well.

Neither side gave a centimetre in the first 40 overs, but the whole nature of the game changed dramatically from that point, when Cronje and Rhodes picked up the tempo in much the same way they did yesterday. Rhodes was eventually out for a classy 44, full of great running and deft footwork, while Cronje's knock didn't end until the 47th over, when he became yet another victim of the man who possesses without doubt the most deadly throwing arm inside 25 metres in world cricket – Allan Border. Cronje was on 97 when AB shattered the stumps from side on to cruelly prevent a second consecutive century. Even though Rhodes and Cronje had been superb, at this stage we were quite happy with our progress, as a score of 240 looked the likely total and that was a total we fancied making. The ground is small, the outfield quick and the wicket was a batsman's paradise. But if you relax for a minute in limited-overs cricket you can get stung, and today was a perfect example. Adrian Kuiper pummelled 47 off 22 balls, including an astonishing 26 off McDermott's last over. That 26 included three monstrous sixes (off the last three balls) that dislodged a few snags off the hotplates and turned a good total into an excellent one of 265.

Our game plan was to try and reach 0-50 or 0-60 off the first 15 overs, but instead we collapsed dramatically to 4-34. Taylor, Boon, Jones and M. Waugh all fell to some aggressive bowling backed up by a fielding side pumped up for victory. When AB joined me in the centre, his instructions were to play some shots, be aggressive, and give it a real go. If we were to go down, then we'd go down swinging.

Following this strategy, my own game began to flourish, as did AB's, and we added 107 runs in 15 overs to get us into a position where we could challenge for a victory. Luck, however, wasn't on our side and Allan was run out at the bowler's end after the most sweetly timed shot of my entire innings was deflected by the bowler back onto the stumps. All the bowler was trying to do was get out of the way. That was the beginning of the end. Our required run-rate keep hovering between 6.5 and 8 per over, which was not impossible but was very hard with so few wickets in hand. In the end, in the 43rd over, I was last man out (for 86). We were still 56 runs adrift.

I really thought we would bounce back today and level the series, but full credit to the South Africans, who I don't think can play much better than they are at the moment. Australia, on the other hand, have a fair bit of improving to do. But even though the scoreline is 2-0 the mood of the team is optimistic and very determined. We've always considered our ability to fight back to be probably our best asset.

On a brighter note, tonight we helped Slats celebrate his 24th birthday with a couple of quiet ones at the Sports Cafe – a tough ask for the little bloke as we all know much he hates a celebration. But then, most of us are partial to a celebratory ale.

DAY 17 *February 21*

AT 9.30 this morning, we boarded a South African Airways flight to Port Elizabeth for the third match in the one-day series, which begins tomorrow. Any internal flight is guaranteed to have the over-six-foot (180cm) row of McGrath, McDermott and Reiffel seized up by the time we arrive, as the seats have very little leg room, and this was no different.

Management has decided on a complete change of roomies for this section of the tour, with yours truly teaming up with Matt Hayden. Merv's new partner is Glenn McGrath, which has set up a potential nightmare. We all recognise Merv as the team's big kid, but McGrath has aspirations to take over the mantle and in many ways is already a greater menace and nuisance to his fellow team members.

After yesterday's batting I can't believe how sore I pulled up. I put it down to all the sudden movements of turning and stopping that are required in the one-day form of the game. As a result I probably turned in one of my worst training sessions for a while today, but hopefully a good night's sleep tonight will do the trick. During our fielding session it was soon very apparent that, as we are now back to sea level, the ball doesn't travel nearly as far through the air as it did in Johannesburg. And it's a lot slower as well. I know that sounds strange but it's very true.

On a tour of this nature the team receives many invitations to restaurants and clubs, and tonight we had the opportunity to dine at one of the top restaurants in Port Elizabeth. The place was called 'The Ranch' and it didn't let us down. Merv was in fine form again and his array of jokes held the whole restaurant captive and the team spellbound – even though we've all heard them many times before.

David Boon, with an ice pack on his bung left knee and a supply of imported anaesthetic at the ready.

DAY 18 *February 22*

MY NEW roomie, being a keen surfie and beach bum at heart, decided to get a 5am wake-up call this morning so he could, in his words, 'catch a few tubes as there were some good right-handers coming in'. The beach is directly across the road and, as both he and Slats knew they wouldn't be playing today, they chose to get some exercise in before settling down to watch the day's cricket.

This was an especially vital game for Australia, as we couldn't afford to go 0-3 down. By the time we arrived at the ground, another huge crowd had gathered, which we have come to expect at one-day internationals anywhere in the world. The people over here are as keen as the Australian crowds for cricket. In fact they may even be keener, probably as a result of being starved of top-level sport for so much of the past 23 years. Our whole team is recognised wherever we go, thanks to the recent coverage of the South Africans' tour of Australia. Here in Port Elizabeth, the sheep jokes and banners once again were out in full force, with one sign reading 'Shane Loves Merv Ewes'.

This time, after losing the first two tosses, AB called correctly and not surprisingly elected to bat on what looked like another batting paradise, complete with relatively small boundaries.

After a watchful start and the early loss of Taylor, Jones and Boon began to lift the tempo. By the time 20 overs had been bowled the scoreboard read 1-90 and a platform had been established for us to achieve a big total. In the next 15 overs we seized the initiative, with Jones and M. Waugh finding the boundary boards regularly and setting us up for a final onslaught. When Jones was out for 67, McDermott was sent in as a pinch hitter. This is a position he has been used in with moderate success in the past, but today he came off and 15 runs came from the nine deliveries he faced. Then things got even better. In the last 10 overs we managed to smash 91 runs, with Border, who adopted a stance and swing reminiscent of his baseball days, playing a great cameo of 40 off 17 balls. The end product of all this good work was a record one-day international total in this country of 6-281. But while it may have been a record, we knew it didn't automatically guarantee us a victory, as the ground is small and the South Africans have been on a roll.

However, thanks to a great opening burst from McGrath and McDermott, the opposition were immediately in trouble and the required run-rate was beyond seven an over by the time 10 overs had passed. From this position we gradually squeezed the life out of their challenge. They kept losing wickets at vital stages in their quest to stay up with the required rate, until they were eventually all out, 88 runs adrift.

The biggest difference in our game today was our intensity in the field and our desire to win. We have been just been a little too relaxed of late, perhaps as a result of the abundance of one-day games we have played in recent times. Too much cricket could be a danger to the future of one-day cricket, as there is a certain amount of sameness about each game, especially when the opposition is the same. It may still be great entertainment for the crowd, but the players' motivation can relax if they know exactly how their opponents will approach the game and how each player will perform every time they meet in combat.

After the win it was great to be part of a smiling, happy dressing room, with

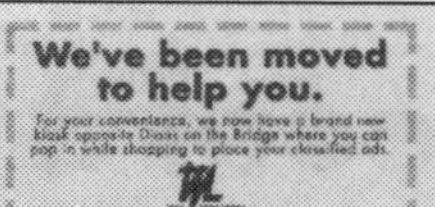

SPORT

INSIDE:
- Trials for SA racehorses?
- Neale Emslie's cricket column
- EP primary schools' swim team

18 ★ PORT ELIZABETH, TUESDAY, FEBRUARY 22, 1994

Avengers of Oz!

By GUY HAWTHORNE

AUSTRALIA will be seeking revenge when they take on South Africa in the third one-day international at St George's Park today.

It is not often that Allan Border's team suffer two defeats in a row and they will obviously be going flat out to redeem their pride and reputation as one of the leading teams in world cricket.

But it won't be easy as Kepler Wessels's team are riding the crest of the wave following their convincing victories at the Wanderers and Centurion Park over the past few days.

The string of injuries and illnesses which dogged the SA squad on its recent tour of Australia reared its ugly head again yesterday when livewire Jonty Rhodes was hurt during the afternoon's net session and key fast bowler Fanie de Villiers stood down due to a bout of flu.

Rhodes' injury was reminiscent of those to the Kirsten brothers, Peter and Gary, in Australia. This time, however, it did not occur in a match situation but in practice.

Rhodes took a knock on the helmet from a fiery delivery from Allan Donald. The Natal captain was badly shaken and sported a fair-sized lump high on the left side of his head. Thankfully there was no bleeding, but he was still rushed off to see a doctor.

However, it will probably not prevent Rhodes from taking his place in the side.

He, along with Peter Kirsten and Hansie Cronje, have tamed the Aussie attack in the first two internationals and they will once again be key men in South Africa's bid for victory.

De Villiers spent yesterday in his hotel bedroom after coming down with the flu, but the SA management said it was nothing too serious and the illness was not expected to keep him out of action for long.

De Villiers has also proved a key figure in South Africa's attack and the excellent line and length he has maintained has kept a tight hold on the Aussie batsmen.

Australia may well include Tim May in today's lineup, but whether he has the ability to contain a rampant and in-form Cronje or the powerful strokemaking of Adriaan Kuiper remains to be seen.

The match is again likely to go down to the wire and it is the team who makes best use of their chances that will likely come out on top.

South Africa are seeking a hat-trick of victories and, if they manage this, they will certainly be in the driving seat for the rest of the one-day series.

But the likes of the David Boon, the Waugh twins, Dean Jones and Border will not take defeat lightly.

Spinners may play in today's encounter

SOUTH Africa yesterday left out Andrew Hudson and Richard Snell from their 14-man squad for today's third Benson & Hedges limited-overs international cricket match against Australia at St George's Park, writes Guy Hawthorne.

The final 11 will be named shortly before the start of the match.

Australia will also only name their starting lineup this morning, but have already surprised by calling up spinner Tim May to the squad beaten in the first two internationals.

Matthew Hayden and Michael Slater are two members of the touring team who must be wondering what they must do to get into the squad.

On a St George's Park track that has never been of much assistance to fast bowlers, one of the SA quickies will probably make way for Natal off-spinner Pat Symcox to play his first match of the tour.

Allan Donald, who was dropped for Sunday's match after some disappointing one-day performances, will probably carry the drinks, leaving Craig Matthews, Fanie de Villiers, Eric Simons, Adrian Kuiper and Hansie Cronje to supply SA's pace attack.

Kuiper's success on Sunday, when he smashed 47 not out off just 22 balls, and Simons' impressive bowling performance at the Wanderers on Saturday should ensure they retain their spots in the side.

With Hudson not in the squad, Gary and Peter Kirsten will once again open the innings, with in-form Hansie Cronje at three and Jonty Rhodes, who is reported to be fit despite being hit on the helmet by a Donald delivery at nets yesterday, at four.

That would leave skipper Kepler Wessels at five, Kuiper at six, Simons at seven and hard-hitting Symcox at eight, with wicketkeeper Dave Richardson, Matthews and De Villiers completing the lineup.

The inclusion of May in the Aussie squad was probably influenced by the state of the St George's Park pitch which has always favoured the spinners in the past.

The Aussies may even consider playing May instead of Shane Warne, who has taken a pasting from the South African batsmen in the opening two encounters.

The match starts at 10am.

The teams are:

SA (from): Peter Kirsten, Gary Kirsten, Hansie Cronje, Jonty Rhodes, Kepler Wessels (capt), Adrian Kuiper, Eric Simons, Pat Symcox, Dave Richardson, Craig Matthews, Fanie de Villiers, Allan Donald.

AUSTRALIA (from): David Boon, Mark Taylor, Dean Jones, Mark Waugh, Allan Border (capt), Steve Waugh, Ian Healy, Paul Reiffel, Shane Warne, Craig McDermott, Glenn McGrath, Tim May.

Umpires: Cyril Mitchley, Rudi Koertzen and Karl Liebenberg (TV).

TV SPORT

SUBJECT to change, the scheduled sport on television today is:

Cricket: Third one-day international, SA v Australia at St George's Park (TV1, 9.45am to 6pm).

Cycling: Rapport Tour second day (CCV, 9.40pm).

Winter Olympics: Ninth day highlights (M-Net, 9pm).

Rugby League: Stone Bitters league (NNTV, 8pm).

Baseball: Niteball series (NNTV, 6.30pm).

Ultra Man: Iron Man competition (NNTV, 6.45pm).

Has this hand lost its magic?

Aussie spinner Shane Warne shows the fingers that has tied up many batsmen all over the world — except, it seems, in South Africa.

AT HOME they call him the Wizard of Oz because of the magic he spins with his tricky balls. But in South Africa, Shane Warne has failed so far to mesmerise our top batsmen the way he did in Australia.

In the first two one-day games his figures were 4/36 and 1/41. Warne will be hoping to restore his reputation at St George's Park today — if he plays.

Aussie captain Allan Border has said he would not like to overexpose Warne by bowling him in too much limited-overs cricket.

Border also defended the talented leg spinner after Sunday's match. "I thought he bowled quite well," said Border.

"Hansie Cronje gave him the long handle and that turned what could have been a good spell into one that was just so-so. Hansie is the only player who is getting after him at the moment."

Picture: MIKE HOLMES

Willie is surprise leader

By MARK BEER

WILLIE Engelbrecht, South Africa's greatest all-round cyclist in recent times, surprised even himself on the opening day of the 1994 Rapport Tour yesterday afternoon.

Engelbrecht, a former winner of South Africa's premier stage race, won the opening prologue and the right to wear the leader's yellow jersey in today's 152km first stage between Port Elizabeth and Humansdorp.

The leader of the powerful Peaceforce Security team — the only professional squad on tour — covered the 2,1km around St George's Park in three minutes and two seconds to achieve his aim of "gaining publicity for our new sponsor".

"I'm really surprised that I managed to win the time trial," he said. "It's a real boost to my morale and I'm really happy.

"To grab the main jersey so early in a field of this magnitude is really surprising."

The world's leading amateur riders are in the Cape for a race which is the first of 20 worldwide making up the World Cup of cycling.

Engelbrecht, who won the tour in 1986, beat Australian Dean Jones — no, not the cricketer — by five seconds, with Malcolm Lange of the South African amateur A team third in 3:08.

With 1 456km left to race on this gruelling tour, which ends in Paarl on March 5, Engelbrecht said he was keen to get rid of the yellow jersey "as soon as possible".

"We don't really need the pressure at this early stage," he said. "It was good exposure to get onto the podium this early, but now we have to consolidate and get working together as a team."

Engelbrecht said it was his eventual aim to get team mate Andrew McLean into yellow, but only on the second week of this 14-day trek along the garden route.

"Andrew is the man who is going to win this tour for us," he predicted. "He has never won it and is so hungry for success right now."

With 13 overseas teams in the race, Engelbrecht's ultimate goal of overall honours for his "rookie" squad appears far-fetched.

Germany, the defending champions with current world road champion Jan Ullrich and two Olympic gold medalists in their A team, are still the ones to beat in the race for R190 000 in prize money.

If the going gets tough later next week, there is no question that the two German squads will "team up" to make things difficult for the South Africans — just as they did last year, when McLean was left as the sole local survivor against a German "blitz".

Talk here is that Engelbrecht and company — including the two local amateur squads — may have to join forces later to prevent a European sweep. — Sapa

See picture Page 17.

Russia lead way

LILLEHAMMER, Norway — A record-tying sixth gold medal did not dull the thrill of Olympic triumph for Lyubov Egorova yesterday, and Pernilla Wiberg raised Sweden from the depths of despair, earning royal kisses for her Alpine skiing gold medal.

Also on the 10th day of ...

Emese Hunyady, silver medalist in the 3 000, upset the favourite in the women's 1 500-meter speedskating race. Her gold was Austria's first-ever in speedskating.

With six days left in competition, Russia had a total of 17 medals, followed by Norway with 16 and Italy with ...

Doll and dummy for Aussie pace bowler

... member of the Australian cricket team has embarrassing consequences, as young fast bowler Glenn McGrath discovered yesterday.

McGrath, who played for Australia in Sunday's limited-overs defeat by SA at Centurion Park in Verwoerdburg, yesterday boarded the flight to Port Elizabeth carrying a big doll, complete with dummy, under one arm.

The lanky Australian was singled out by his teammates after an outburst during Sunday's match, when he buried the ball into the turf in a fit of anger, and it was decided the "offence" was deserving of the "Spit the dummy award".

He is now obliged to carry the doll for as long as his teammates decide, or until another of the Australians is guilty of a similar transgression during a tour match.

Four EP schoolboys in SA touring rugby team

By STAN TERBLANCHE

FOUR Eastern Province players have been included in the South African U-19 Junior Academy team for the Junior Rugby World Champions in Lyon, France from March 28 to April 4.

Included in the squad of 24 are Jean-Pierre van der Mescht, Roelof Viljoen, Ivor Motali and Nardus Coope.

Van der Mescht was selected last week to play in the EP sevens trials, but was forced to withdraw following a decision of the EP High Schools Rugby Association.

The rest of the touring party consists of 16 Western Province players, four from Northern Transvaal, and one each from Boland, Free State, Griqualand West, Northern Free State, Eastern and South Eastern Transvaal.

The equivalent of the SA U-19 Development team, they will wear white jerseys with a green and gold stripe.

The team will be managed by Spiere van Rensburg and the coach is Andre Spies.

The full squad is: Full-backs: Y Manuel (WP), F Petersen (WP — also fly-half, centre). Wings: S Adams (Boland), J P van der Mescht (EP). Centres: S le Roux (N Tvl), D van Schalkwyk (E Tvl). Flyhalves: L Koen (WP), E Diedericks (WP). Scrumhalves: G Daniels (WP), R Viljoen (EP). Loose forwards: C Krige (WP — captain), F Booysen (WP), N Coope (EP), J Fredericks (WP), N van der Walt (S E Tvl). Props: J Breedt (N Tvl), B Makhetta (Griq W), F Rautenbach (N OFS). Locks: G Jacobs (WP), I Motali (EP), L Muller (N Tvl), S Temple (N Tvl). Hookers: C Dercksen (OFS), T Noati (WP).

WI in command against England

KINGSTON, Jamaica — Jimmy Adams guided West Indies to a first innings lead of 173 in the first Test at Sabina Park yesterday as England again discovered the harsh facts of cricketing life in the Caribbean.

The home side were finally dismissed for 407 just before tea on the third day with the left-handed Adams unbeaten on 95, tantalisingly short of a first Test century.

England managed to capture the last four West Indies wickets for 18 runs, but still face a long, hard slog to save the match over the final two days.

Keith Arthurton was able to add only only 13 to his overnight score of 113 before falling to a brilliant gully catch by Lewis off Malcolm.

England's misfortune continued when Graham Thorpe was taken to hospital for an X-ray on his right hand after he spilled a slip catch offered by Winston Benjamin.

His absence forced England to reshuffle their batting order with Robin Smith expected to bat at number three.

Scores: England 234; West Indies 407 (Arthurton 126, Lara 83, Adams 95no). — Sapa-Reuter

EP delay sevens team until tomorrow

THE Eastern Province sevens rugby team for the Winfield interprovincial tournament in Stellenbosch on Friday and Saturday will only be named tomorrow night.

The decision to delay the naming of the nine-man squad was taken after last night's trials at the Boet Erasmus Stadium.

However, the squad has been reduced to 18 players from which the final team will be selected.

The squad is:

Forwards: J Kirsten, A Missie, B Pinnock, B Liebenberg, B Hutchinson.

Backs: D Human, G Miller, R Potgieter, F Langenberg, M Koester, T Markow, F Crous, M van Vuuren, A Fourie, A Coetzee.

Several leading players were not considered due to injuries, but EP should still be able to field a strong combination.

Among the newcomers included in the squad is the former Natal No 8 Ben Liebenberg.

The provincial selectors have also named a President squad to take part in trials on the UPE B field on Saturday morning at 10am.

The players are: L Abdul, F Louis, G Wakeford, S Nkweni, T Koyler, C Ellis, H Pedro, C Breda, L Joseph, R Swartz.

All the players — sevens and those taking part in the trials at UPE — must report to the Boet Erasmus Stadium tomorrow at 5.30pm.

All clubs are reminded that nominations for next Tuesday's trials for the 15-man game must be in by noon on Thursday. The trials will be held on the Police field and players must report at 5.30pm.

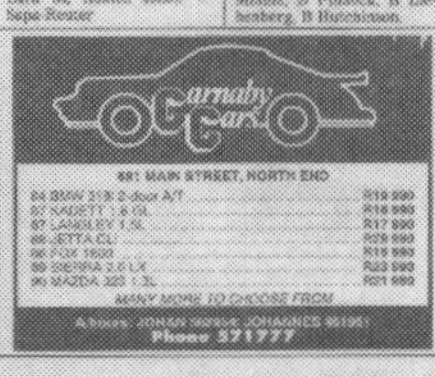

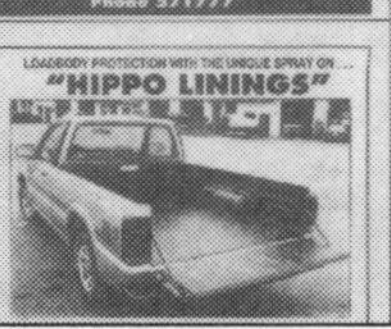

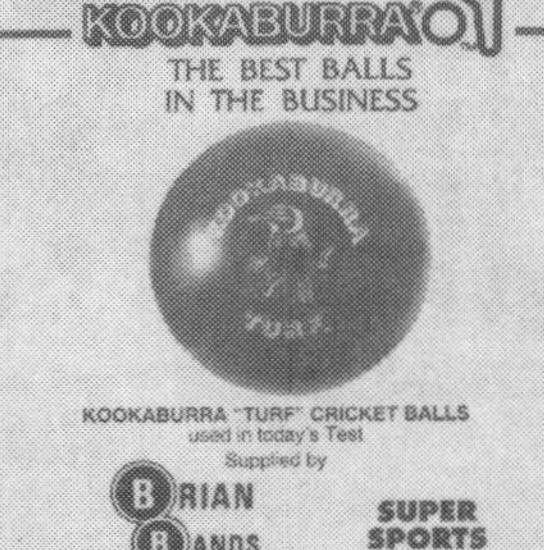

The back page of the Eastern Province Herald *carried the headline 'Avengers of Oz!', but what caught our attention was the article which asked 'Has this hand lost its magic?'. Shane was soon to prove that any obituary concerning his spin-bowling genius was more than a little premature.*

the beers flowing and the boys in good spirits. When people say it doesn't matter who wins but how you play the game they obviously haven't played at this level, because I can assure you it is no fun at all to lose. On the presentation dais, AB received the envelope with the winner's cheque for the first time and for some reason actually opened it. This is an unusual thing to do, because in Australia the envelopes are always empty and just for show. AB was shocked to actually find a real cheque and instantly panicked, as he realised he'd thrown the loser's cheques for the first two one-dayers into the garbage bin.

When we got back to the hotel, I gave Lynette a call. This was the first time I had managed to co-ordinate the times right so it wasn't one or two o'clock in the morning in Sydney. It's always great to be able to catch up on all the news at home, as everyone is always a little bit homesick even though we are lucky enough to have some great mates alongside us during our travels.

Allan Border, who hit for such effect in the third limited-overs international that he finished with 40 from just 17 balls, as Australia smashed 6-281 from their 50 overs. AB's imposing form in the early one-dayers had quickly silenced those critics who had questioned his right to stay as captain of the Australian team.

DAY 19 *February 23*

WE FACED another early morning flight, this time to Durban, but thankfully it was only a short trip so there were not as many of the usual arguments among the boys over who gets the prime window seats, which are, of course, the ones that allow you to sleep that little bit easier. Not for the first time, we received another friendly welcome, this time in the form of Zulu dancers who performed a tribal dance that was quite intimidating at first sight but was, we were assured, a friendly gesture.

Our hotel room had to have its appearance altered quite dramatically, with furniture making way for luggage because it is easily the smallest room we've encountered so far on tour. Then we had to make our way to another training session, which had all the boys jumping with joy as we're all a little tired and sore after three games in four days. But, then again, our success since Bob Simpson took over has been based around hard work – especially in training sessions.

Michael Slater was clearly keen to impress and struck the ball superbly in the nets. He must be a good chance to play tomorrow. After the batting and bowling sessions were over, our fielding session started sedately with a few friendly catches, but turned nasty soon afterwards as Simmo warmed to the task. I'm sure I saw a smile begin to appear on his face, as he had the boys gasping for air and straining to take that miraculous catch ... followed by two or three more. Those who survived the coach's drills then inspected the match wicket and saw a very grassy strip that will obviously suit the seam bowlers more so than the spinners.

While we were gathered around the wicket, Dean Jones asked the groundsman: 'Are you going to leave all this grass on or mow some off by tomorrow?'

To which the friendly curator replied: 'I'll see what Kepler wants.'

This seems a rather strange situation – our captain has no say in the make up of our wickets in Australia and I can't see why it should happen over here.

Maysie has been suffering withdrawal symptoms because he hasn't had the chance to devour his favourite cuisine of Indian. Since arriving in South Africa he has made many enquiries as to the locations of the country's finest Indian restaurants, and finally here in Durban (which has a large Indian population) he had his chance. However, after sampling most of the entree dishes and examining each spice and sauce on offer, Maysie felt he had been let down by his contacts and came away feeling slightly deflated by the whole experience. But, later on, he did admit that his voracious appetite had been partly satisfied.

DAY 20 *February 24*

THE FAMILIAR sight of huge queues waiting for the gates to open greeted the team bus when we arrived at the ground this morning. What was very apparent was the large numbers of cricket fans of Indian descent among them. During our warm-ups we copped our usual dose of abuse, but I must admit it was less than what some touring sides have had dished out to them in Melbourne and Sydney.

For the first time in this one-day series both captains were uncertain as to whether they should bat first or not. The wicket looked like it was going to suit the bowlers, which didn't happen in the first three contests, and when AB won the toss (which he had hoped to lose) he reluctantly chose to bat. Normally there is a distinct advantage if you can post a good score when batting first, because you can then put pressure on the team chasing.

Unfortunately our hopes for a big total were shattered by a diabolical start. Persistent bowling and some lazy batting had us in dire straits at 4-23. From that low point, Boon and Border began to restore the balance until Boonie departed with the score on 91, which was the signal for another collapse. We were eventually all out for 154. Only AB played anywhere near his best, for 69 not out. There is a distinct possibility that this will be AB's last tour and, if it is, the way he is playing at the moment, he'll be going out with a highly successful tour under his belt. Knowing his determination, a hundred in his farewell Test is more than possible.

These fans had clearly been impressed by Adrian Kuiper's unbeaten 47 in the second one-dayer.

Our batting performance was our worst in a long time. There was a lack of application evident which will have to be corrected before the Test matches begin. When we bowled, our quest for early wickets was thwarted by a couple of very close lbw shouts that didn't go our way. The scoreline got away from us until Pistol chimed in with two quick wickets, and then Warney had Rhodes lbw to make them 3-69. But, once again, Cronje proved to be the thorn in our side and remained unbeaten on 50, while Wessels was 40 not out when they reached their convincing seven-wicket victory.

This defeat will force us to have a good look at not only our own games but also their batsmen, especially Cronje who is full of confidence at the moment. Even though the one-day internationals scoreline now shows Australia 1-3 down (with four more matches to be decided after the Test series), we are all still very confident we have their measure in the five-day game. We're looking forward to correcting the balance of the results between the two sides when we meet again in a week's time in the first Test. As for tonight – a quiet evening was had by the lads. We had no reason to celebrate after such a comprehensive hiding.

HANSIE VERSUS THE AUSTRALIANS

DAY 21 *February 25*

IT APPEARS our manager, Cam Battersby, will have to delve into his pockets to pay fines (on behalf of the Australian Cricket Board) for the nightmare programme that faced us today. We began with a 6.30am wake-up call, to make sure we made our 8am flight to Johannesburg. Once there, we had to change planes, which meant we were waiting around for three-quarters of an hour. When we finally took off, there was barely time for the plane to level out before we were descending into our next stop, the town of Kimberley, where a 25-minute delay awaited us. Kimberley is well known for its diamond mining – but not much else. The last section of our day's trip was another short flight, this time to Bloemfontein, where we were greeted by 2,300 kids who had been given half a day off from school to collect some autographs, which was exactly what we needed after our marathon trip.

Our team manager, Dr Cam Battersby.

When we arrived at our hotel, another welcoming ceremony greeted us – this time a group of marching girls thrilled us with a baton twirling routine. When the show ended, we finally reached the safety and comfort of our rooms, and almost immediately the beds had two new occupants fast asleep, although I was frustrated for a short time by a tune Matty was able to punch out due to his newly acquired head cold.

Four hours later a phone call disturbed the silence, and we were made aware the lads were about to dine at the Hard Rock Cafe. This caused problems. After searching in vain for a clean outfit, an iron was summoned for. The end result was not very pleasing to the eye, but that was soon forgotten when I heard of an extremely rare happening that had occurred this afternoon. It was almost unbelievable to think that Merv had complained to management about his room-mate (McGrath) being a nuisance and making too much noise when he wanted to sleep. This is something Merv has subjected all of us to at one time or another.

There is a feeling among the team that the Hughes/McGrath combination may have been an absolute masterstroke by our men in charge, as the two quicks can annoy each other and leave the rest of us in peace. Merv has told me he's getting a little concerned about his roomie's love of guns and weapons but they are part of life on the farm, which is where McGrath was brought up in north-west NSW. Just recently, when each team-member was given a Swiss Army pocket knife as a gift, McGrath eyes lit up with excitement at the prospect of experimenting with his new toy. The big fella feels he might be part of that first experiment and is not feeling at all comfortable about being locked away in the same four walls as his roomie.

An enjoyable night was had by all at the Hard Rock Cafe. The boys gave the menu a good nudge, and then washed down their meals with a few cleansing ales.

DAY 22 *February 26*

ANOTHER IMPRESSIVE venue greeted the side when we arrived to joust with the local Orange Free State side in what will be our final hit out before the first Test. The people of Bloemfontein have developed a reputation for friendliness, but the place is probably best known as the home of Zola Budd, the long-distance bare-foot runner.

Border and McDermott were again rested for this match, along with McGrath and Jones, although not much can be read into the latter two selections as the whole 15 members of the squad have a good chance of playing in the Test series. Stand-in skipper Mark Taylor called correctly and elected to bat on yet another feather-bed (great batting wicket) strip, and both he and Slater found some good touch in a fine opening stand. However, by lunch we'd stumbled slightly to be 2-100. Taylor reached 35 before getting a fine delivery which he was good enough to edge to the keeper and Boonie made a rare failure. Then Slats went soon after lunch, which brought me to the crease to join up with Junior.

For the first 15 minutes of my innings I felt as if I was half asleep, a problem that can happen quite often in these type of games, where there is no crowd or atmosphere to fire me up. But with these early difficulties overcome, I knuckled down to the task. I realised I might not get another opportunity before the Test and time in the middle is precious to a batsman. The end result was a fourth-wicket partnership of 242 runs in 155 minutes, which was a new Australian record partnership in South Africa. Junior played superbly for his 154, a welcome return to form after some indifferent shots in the one-dayers. I was also pleased to reach 102 but, more importantly, to feel in total control for most of the innings and find the gaps in the field fairly regularly – a good sign for a batsman.

Healy and Hayden played out the last hour without any signs of trouble, to leave us at 5-415 at the end of a great day's play for Australia. With a few of the guys not participating in today's proceedings and nearby tennis courts available, Warney couldn't resist the chance to put his John McEnroe antics to use. I then received a challenge, as Warney was still smarting from a hiding I handed to him in Perth during the Test against New Zealand last year. He was keen for revenge, but unfortunately his game hasn't improved sharply enough to warrant a serious hit out and the first set went my way 6-0. However because there was a small crowd in attendance, the customary 'dak dropping' ceremony (for not winning a game in the set) was postponed. However. those lucky few who were there were treated to some colourful language from my 'opponent' and also an attempt to launch a tennis ball to the moon. But there was some light at the end of the tunnel for my leg-spinning colleague, and he only went down 6-4 in the second set. Now he is vowing to inflict a defeat upon me before the tour is over. The only certainty to come out of the match is that, thanks to Warney's theatrics on court, Chips will have a new owner.

Heals, AB and I took the opportunity to see the movie *Mrs Doubtfire* tonight and we didn't come away disappointed. It's a great show full of good one-liners. After the show we caught up with the other lads at the Hard Rock Cafe where I couldn't resist the Chicken Fahitas once again, even though I over-indulged last night and promised not to repeat the performance. But I weakened and will no doubt pay for it when the fat-measuring callipers are brought out at next week's weight check-ins.

Donald will come bouncing back in Test series

THREE-one up in the one-day matches has given us a good start to our contests against the Australians. I've been very happy with the way we've done it, too.

It was also very important for us to get back into winning mode — by the end of our tour of Australia, they had beaten us three times and were on a bit of a high. If we'd gone away from this week's one-day internationals behind, it might have been demoralising.

The balance of our sides during this week has been very good. Obviously Hansie Cronje's contribution has been outstanding and Adrian Kuiper's form has made a big difference to our batting.

Our attack also performed very well, especially in Durban, where Craig Matthews was outstanding. With him and Fanie de Villiers taking the new ball, it was also very effective to have Eric Simons coming in and bowling with such discipline afterwards. Eric has responded well to coming into the national team.

The one experiment that didn't come off was having Allan Donald at first change. He's going through a difficult period in the one-day games but it would be very short-sighted to write him off. I certainly don't think that he can't do it in the one-day games. He remains a great fast bowler who will be crucial in the Tests.

Limited overs cricket and Test matches are totally different games. The first Test starts on Friday and the hard work starts now.

There are one or two question marks about the make-up of the Test team which the selectors will have to look at, notably Brian McMillan's fitness, but this weekend's Castle Cup games should sort out those final decisions. Selection is never easy.

In any series, the first Test match is always very important and in this one, particularly so. I can see each of the three Tests — Johannesburg, Cape Town and Durban — producing a result so it will be crucial to try to gain an upper hand.

The conditions will be very different to those at Adelaide for our last Test meeting with Australia and we've recovered well from that defeat.

KEPLER WESSELS
SA captain

Cricket

Twins hammer magnificent centuries

Savagery as Waughs cane OFS

Ian Hawkey
at Springbok Park

THE Australians made light of their first day in Bloemfontein yesterday. For all but David Boon it was batting practice against gentle bowling. By the close they had amassed 416 runs for the loss of five wickets and were pondering declaration.

Mark Taylor, captaining the side, won the toss and asked Free State to field. Taylor and Micheal Slater put on an untroubled 66 before Taylor edged one outside off stump and the next man, Boon, top-edged soon afterwards. From then on, however, another tempo took hold for the rest of the day.

Slater, leaning into easy drives, hit a neat 65 from 105 deliveries, sharing in an appealing partnership with Mark Waugh falling to an outstanding slip catch by Gerhardus Liebenberg. The fielder leapt early and quickly to gather low and one-handed to his right. It was the best thing that happened to Free State all day.

Thereafter it was all Waugh. With his 154, Mark Waugh made it two centuries in his two first-class matches on this tour.

Both Waughs were savage against the spinners. Kosie Venter, the off-spinner, and Nicky Boje, the 20-year-old slow left-armer, have contributed much to another good Free State summer but neither of them have been taxed by class such as this before.

For their Free State colleagues it was a long day in a field that frequently seemed impossible to police.

The Waughs took two and half hours for their mammoth partnership of 232, facing 284 balls between them, 26 of them banished to the boundary.

Can they ever have batted better together?

Yes, exactly twice as well. Four years ago, they put on 464 for New South Wales in Perth.

They might well have gone on to exceed that yesterday, had not each Waugh reached his milestone and then almost wilfully sacrificed his place at the crease for other men wanting innings ahead of the Wanderers Test.

Mark Waugh reached his 150 moments before his brother reached 100, cutting Bradley Player for four. He repeated the shot next ball but then, looking to go over the top, mistimed and spooned high over mid on. Mickey Arthur took the catch.

Fifteen minutes later Steve Waugh completed his 31st first-class century and almost as promptly sliced a Herman Bakkes delivery to third man, where Player caught. His contribution included 44 runs from boundaries and took 171 minutes and 182 balls. If Steve Waugh's innings was always marginally lower-key than his brother's, it wanted nothing in authority.

Mark Waugh batted with his trademark fluency, punishing the bad ball and finding gaps on both sides of the wicket. His driving was all exquisite synchronicity and he accumulated his boundaries at will: four sixes and 15 fours at a run per ball. His century was the 47th of his career and not one of his more difficult ones, either.

There was little to trouble any of the Australian batsmen within hundreds of kilometres of Bloemfontein in the sunshine yesterday. Allan Donald was in Cape Town for rest and recuperation and Franklyn Stephenson was at home in Barbados on leave.

Beyond that the Castle Cup champions have sound support bowlers in Player and Corrie van Zyl but on a true pitch, the only delivery to scare the Australians was one from Player that clipped the peak of Mark Waugh's helmet as soon as he took guard.

"It wasn't quite as short as I thought it would be," explained the batsman afterwards, "and it was just before lunch so I was half asleep." Well, the next 154 balls were dreamy.

Player took the best of the meagre rewards but at some expense and Van Zyl bowled sensibly enough. Bakkes provided too much short stuff to convince anybody that he is Free State's new White Lightning. Venter suffered likewise on a day when the home side had not much to do but chase.

SCOREBOARD

AUSTRALIA first innings

M Slater c Liebenberg b Player	65
M Taylor c [illegible] b Van Zyl	35
D Boon c [illegible] b Van Zyl	8
M Waugh c Arthur b Player	154
S Waugh c Player b Bakkes	102
[illegible] not out	[illegible]
[illegible] not out	[illegible]
Extras	[illegible]
TOTAL for 5 wkts	416

FALL: 1/66, 2/80, 3/136, 4/367, 5/382.
BOWLING: [illegible]

Time make-up provision aids results

Colin Bryden

THE chances of the Tests between South Africa and Australia reaching outright conclusions have been enhanced by a provision to make up lost time by up to an hour each day.

In theory, if the first five hours were washed out, all the time could be made up by playing an extra hour on the first day and adding an hour to each of the remaining four days.

In Australia, where the first three days of the Melbourne Test were decimated by rain, play could be made up on the same day only. If the South Africans rule was in force an extra hour would have been played on both the last two days, although it is unlikely the match would have ended in anything other than a draw.

Dr Ali Bacher, MD of the United Cricket Board, claimed it would be the first time in any series that so much time could be made up.

South Africa go into the first Test on Friday with a 2-1 lead in matches against Australia at the Wanderers Stadium. SA were within two wickets of victory when the last two hours of the rain-hit fourth Test in 1966/67 were washed out. The teams have only met at the ground five times.

SA v AUSTRALIA at Wanderers
[illegible]

THE MOMENT OF TRUTH ... Australia's Shane Warne at the point of delivery. The picture shows his stock leg-break delivery, distinguishable by the position of the hand as the ball leaves it and a devastating weapon in Test cricket. Warne has kept the best of himself back from the first fortnight of the tour — notably his flipper — but possibly the greatest match-winner in world cricket will be preparing this week for the first Test at the Wanderers, beginning on Friday. Picture: Danie Coetzer/PicSA

When this man is spinning, all of SA will hold its breath

Ian Hawkey

WHEN South Africa's selectors meet on Tuesday to finalise their side for the first home Test match against Australia for 24 years, they will find the case for pace compelling. The Wanderers conditions and the drought of alternatives mean that likeliest match-winners for the home side on Friday will be its fast bowlers.

For their opponents, however, the key figure is still a leg-spinner. Australia's Shane Warne will be more encouraged by the recent history of Tests at the stadium than his own record there. Warne's 0/36 from ten overs in last Saturday's one-day international is a far less significant guide, perhaps, than Anil Kumble's 6/53 for India there last year.

Kumble's leg-spin, neither as varied nor adventurous as Warne's, was as decisive a contribution as any in last year's drawn Johannesburg Test. Warne has yet to display his art to its fullest in this country but on Friday he will be back in his favourite, five-day arena.

Allan Border, the Australian captain, this week spoke in defence of his bowler after four one-day internationals in which he only once finished with figures that do justice to the International Cricketer of the Year. "He's been limiting the ball well and it's only really Hansie Cronje who's taken to him at all. He's still bowling exceptionally well."

Cronje, relieved of the distractions of captaincy, will play a key role for South Africa and must be expected to do so from the position he has crafted as his own, number three, despite the return of Kepler Wessels to the batting order. Assuming the selectors keep faith with Hudson and Gary Kirsten as openers and Peter Kirsten at four, Wessels would come in next, with Jonty Rhodes at six to give the batting a greater look of steel than at almost any time in the last three years.

The candidacy for the lower order will provide the selectors with longer debate. The continued absence with knee injuries of Brett Schultz and probably Brian McMillan are problems to which they are now probably reconciled, Allan Donald's foot injury less so.

Donald is not taking part in Free State's match against the tourists but is instead in Cape Town, seeking the attention of physiotherapist Craig Smith for a problem on his right foot. A preliminary bone scan has, however, been encouraging.

In Donald's case, one-day form will be considered no guide to what he might achieve in the Test series. In the cases of Craig Matthews, Richard Snell and even Eric Simons, successes and failures in a competition so different from a Test match may yet play a part.

Matthews' destructive 4/10 on Thursday has suggested his recall (he was dropped for the Adelaide Test) and Simons might easily find himself in the 12 as an all-rounder to replace McMillan, his bowling being preferred to, say, Adrian Kuiper. Snell, by contrast, did not have one of his better weeks but leaving him out on a home ground where he bowled with considerable pace and success a fortnight ago seems unlikely.

Unlike their opponents, the South Africans will be reluctant to invest heavily in spin during this series. Pat Symcox's place in the squad appears increasingly tenuous and Clive Eksteen's chances with the national side seem biennial. Eksteen perhaps ought to get one in three weeks' time at Newlands, where he has a fine record.

The Australians are in the happy position of being able to name a full-strength side for the first time since August last year, although they would be still happier if Merv Hughes was to complete his return to Test readiness with the aggression and the averages of old against Free State over the next three days.

Likewise, off-spinner Tim May is yet to rediscover the form that gave him 25 wickets in last winter's Ashes series. Much as they would like to see May and Warne operating in tandem, the four selectors — Border, coach Bobby Simpson, Mark Taylor and David Boon — may decide that the Wanderers offers better opportunities for a third seamer, Paul Reiffel.

THE INSIDE EDGE

RUGBY's post-unity progress has not been untroubled. Schalk Burger, MC at the M-Nite Series announcement, related the story of a player in the Eastern Cape who turned up at a disciplinary hearing and removed his shirt to reveal evidence of ugly bite marks.

To which revelation, in all seriousness, replied the representative of the offending club: "Mr Chairman, I've always said that the unity process would not be without its teething problems."

WITH serious, five-day cricket starting this week, we can look forward to a break from the artificially jolly Benson and Hedges advertisement which has South African cricketers supposedly ready to "whack every Aussie ball." Ugh.

JOHANNESBURG may have lost the chance to bid for the 2004 Olympics but they are front-runners for the 1994 Bad Losers award. At a media conference to announce plans for the wildly expensive white elephant of an athletics stadium that they are planning, even without the Olympics, they handed out gifts to the media — Johannesburg 2004 T-shirts.

ALSO in bad taste was Radio 702's phone-in to collect money for Peter Kirsten after the Darrell Hair incident. However much sympathy there may have been for Kirsten, he transgressed a code of conduct and there do have to be rules. The whip-round and a succession of sheep jokes on a radio station not known for the quality of its wit had a sequel when Australian captain Allan Border refused to be interviewed on 702.

After appeals which went all the way to the Australian Embassy, Border will be talking to 702. Hopefully he will not be interrupted by the trademark guffaws which are so irritating in the middle of bulletins on the station.

The announcement of the umpires for this week's first Test at the Wanderers had Australian journalists wary. "Another sheep joke?" asked one when he saw the name of Barry LAMB-son.

WITH New Zealand taking a pounding from Pakistan's fearsome fast bowlers, Wasim Akram and Waqar Younis, it is not surprising that there are renewed whispers about the way they achieve reverse swing. "No one has come up with a satisfactory explanation," said Kiwi coach Geoff Howarth. Another ball-tampering row?

MORE bleating about fast bowlers comes from Jamaica where England's tailenders took a merciless pounding from Courtney Walsh and Curtly Ambrose. Under the one-bumper-an-over rule, rising deliveries into the chest area are unpunished, although in theory umpires could invoke ungentlemanly play provisions. West Indian captain Richie Richardson says laconically: "If you can't stand the heat don't go into the kitchen."

GREG Chappell relates a story of the umpire striking back. Going in to bat for Somerset on a murky evening the young Chappell immediately appealed against the light. Tommy Spencer, the umpire, scornfully rejected his request, telling Chappell: "If we went off for light like this we'd never finish a game in this country."

Some time later Chappell plucked up courage to make another appeal. This exasperated Spencer. He pointed skywards. "What's that?" he asked. "The moon," said Greg. "Well, if tha' can see that far there can't be much wrong with the bloody light," said Spencer.

SO you thought the tennis tournament at Sun City at the end of next month was the South African Open? Wrong, according to advertisements for the "Standard Bank Open" which is billed as the premier event in "southern Africa." Perhaps the subterfuge is still necessary, although by next year the farcically created, "independent state" of Bophuthatswana will surely be back in South Africa.

THERE'S nothing like a human drama to boost interest in sport. The Nancy Kerrigan-Tonya Harding showdown on ice attracted record TV viewership figures in the US. How many understood the complexities of the judging system is another matter.

Winter Olympics

Atlanta is priority as skaters fail

Colin Bryden

THE numbers may be smaller but the results are all too depressingly similar to those achieved by South Africans at the Barcelona Olympics in 1992.

Neither of SA's skaters at the Winter Olympics in Lillehammer performed up to the standards that earned them qualification.

Dino Quattrocecere suffered a figure skater's nightmare when he fell four times, finishing last.

Cindy Meyer was keeping pace with the leaders in her heat of the 500m speed skating elimination series until she hit a dislodged track-marking block midway through the race and slid into the barriers. She got up and finished a distant 30 seconds behind the other skaters. It was small consolation that the skaters who qualified from the four-woman heat went on to win silver and bronze.

Facing up to the poor results, team leader Sam Ramsamy said yesterday: "I have been gathering information from the successful teams and I will report to my executive that we must implement Operation Atlanta immediately to ensure the best possible preparation for the 1996 Summer Games."

END OF THE DRAMA ... silver medallist Nancy Kerrigan (right) hugs gold medal winner Oksana Baiul Picture: AP

After the Kerrigan–Harding show, orphan takes the glory

IN different circumstances, 16-year-old Oksana Baiul would have been much more the focus of the Winter Olympics, rather than a coda to the weeks of controversy and sensation.

If there had been no nightstick, no Nancy and Tonya, no indictments, no shouting headlines, the sad story of the young orphan girl from the Ukraine would have provided more than enough of the drama and metaphor that the sports opera hungers for.

And it would have had the added ingredients of inspiration and joy. A young girl who skates through an injury, dissolves into tears and then recovers with a gold medal and a playful craving for a chocolate bar.

Three years ago, Oksana Baiul was a teenager who had seen more pain in her short life than those twice her age should have to suffer. Her father faded from her life when she was two. The grandparents who helped raise her had died within an year of each other.

Then her mother became ill; three weeks later she was dead of cancer.

At Thursday's practice, Baiul and Tanja Szewczenko of Germany skated backwards into each other at nearly full speed. Baiul had a long gash in her right shin, requiring three stitches. The collision injured her back. Her coach Galina Zmievskaya, who took Baiul in after her mother died was near tears.

"I thought it was another streak of bad luck," said Zmievskaya, a short, solid woman who watches over Baiul with the fierceness of a mother grizzly.

It was clear the pain was still there as Oksana warmed up. The tall, willowy skater, moved tentatively at first, holding the small of her back and grimacing.

Nancy Kerrigan went on before Baiul, skating a nearly flawless performance that left the ice covered with bouquets. Oksana had to wait for stray petals to be cleared away.

Although denied gold by a wafer-thin margin, Kerrigan came of age, joining Peggy Fleming, Dorothy Hamill and Kristi Yamaguchi as the newest US skating sweetheart.

Kerrigan, 24, produced the best free skating performance of her life and thrilled a massive television audience at home. Her one mistake — she did a double flip instead of triple on her opening jump — almost went unnoticed.

The judges were split 4-4. But German Jan Hoffman gave winner Baiul 5.9 for artistry and 5.8 for Kerrigan after awarding the American 5.8 for technique to 5.7 for Baiul. The higher artistic marks put Baiul at the top.

For Kerrigan it all came just seven weeks after a man intent on foiling her ambitions attacked her backstage with a black retractable police baton after practice at the US championships in Detroit.

☐ Vreni Schneider of Switzerland raced into the Olympic record books yesterday, winning her fifth career Alpine medal and third gold in the women's slalom.

Fifth after the first run, she had to beat archrival Pernilla Wiberg of Sweden, who also was going for her third career gold, as well as up-and-coming slalom skiers Gabriela Zingre of Switzerland, Elfriede Eder of Austria and 18-year-old first-round leader Katja Koren of Slovenia.

Schneider flashed through the 60 gates of the second run in 56.33, the fastest time of the day, for a two-run total of 1 min 56.01 sec, 0.34 faster than Eder's 1:56.35.

Koren, usually more comfortable in the speed races, held on for the bronze in 1:56.61.

The 29-year-old Schneider already had two medals in these Games — silver in the combined and bronze in the giant slalom — but the glory of Calgary had eluded her. In 1988, she became only the third woman to win two Alpine gold in a single Games, capturing the giant slalom and slalom.

Four years later, she fell in the giant slalom and managed a pitiful seventh in the slalom at the Albertville Games. — Sapa-Reuter-AP

The back page of the sports section of the Johannesburg Sunday Times *of February 27 relates the story of a very productive day for the Australians at Bloemfontein.*

DAY 23 *February 27*

SIMMO IS obviously very keen to have us match conditioned before the Test begins next week, and this morning he put us through some pretty demanding fielding drills, one of which resulted in Junior misjudging a catch and tearing his thumb-nail off. This might only be a small injury, but it's a worrying one as it affects every facet of the game.

While we were out in the field, back in the dressing sheds the bomb disposal unit had been called in after a threat had been received at the ground. The sniffer dogs were there to check all our cricket coffins, and were happily going about their work until one Alsatian approached Merv's kit, had a quick bo-peep, and then recoiled in horror after he came across some rigid looking socks and mouldy shirts that were obviously too much for the poor, yelping animal to take. We all prayed the bomb hadn't been planted in the big fella's bag as there seemed little chance of any other animal wanting to stick its dial into such a nasty concoction of stained and sweated articles.

On a more serious note, we were all assured there was no trace of trouble. It had turned out to be a hoax. When play resumed, Tails decided to give our remaining batsmen a chance to gain some form, and Healy and Hayden made 30 odd each before the declaration came at 8-450. Then, a much improved burst from Merv almost certainly guaranteed him selection in the first Test. He once again struggled a little for rhythm in his first spell, but it became clear during the day that he's on the improve and not too far away from his best.

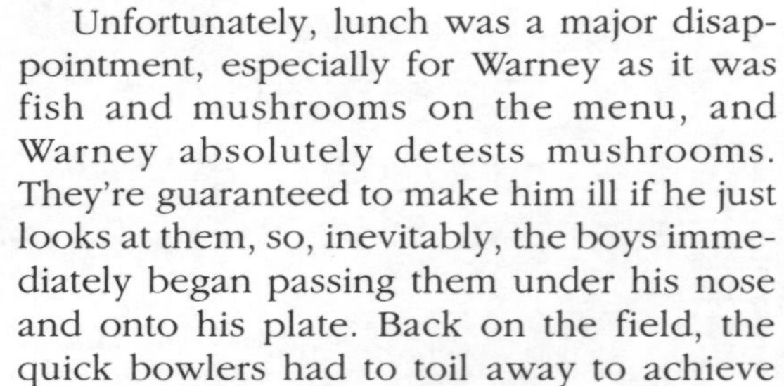

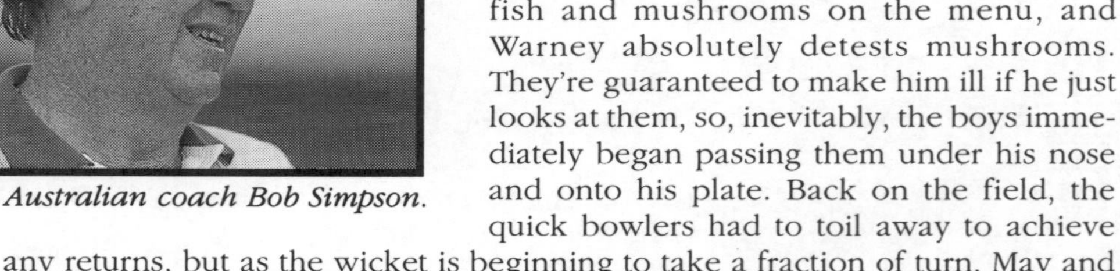

Australian coach Bob Simpson.

Unfortunately, lunch was a major disappointment, especially for Warney as it was fish and mushrooms on the menu, and Warney absolutely detests mushrooms. They're guaranteed to make him ill if he just looks at them, so, inevitably, the boys immediately began passing them under his nose and onto his plate. Back on the field, the quick bowlers had to toil away to achieve any returns, but as the wicket is beginning to take a fraction of turn, May and Warne settled down into some long spells of bowling. Maysie looked the goods, claiming five victims, and his spin twin took three.

In the main, the opposition's batting effort was poor, but the one exception was another fine effort from Cronje, who again looked very comfortable against our attack and especially aggressive against our spinners. More than once he lofted them out of the park, which prompted Maysie to ask if his name, Hansie Cronje (pronounced 'Kronjay'), was in fact Hansie Longway. During the past 18 months Cronje has been the one batsman who has looked assured against Warney's bowling. He is obviously the danger man in the South African line-up, because if he continues to score runs in such a manner, his confidence will be infectious among his team-mates.

During a long day in the field the players often have to amuse themselves to make the time pass quickly, and Heals, being a clever imitator of accents, put

Shane Warne, bowling on the fourth afternoon of the second Test, in Cape Town, when he and I, with more than a little help from some superb fielding and shrewd captaincy, combined to shatter the South Africans' second innings.

Australian Picture Library — Mike Hewitt (All Sport)

Australian Picture Libra
Mike Hewitt (All S

Two of the key men in the South African line-up.
Above: Jonty Rhodes sweeps Warne during the second Test.
Below: Andrew Hudson hammers Glenn McGrath during his century in the first innings at Cape Town.

Australian Picture Libra
Mike Hewitt (All S

Shane Warne makes a spectacular attempt to catch Brian McMillan during the second Test.

Australian Picture Library — Mike Hewitt (All Sport)

My bowling figures in theSouth Africans' second innings of the second Test – 5-28 from 22.3 overs – were the best of my Test career.

Australian Picture Library — Mike Hewitt (All Sport)

shot to the
f-side
oundary
uring my
nings of 86
Australia's
rst innings
Cape Town.

stralian Picture Library — Thomas Turck (Touchline Media)

Craig McDermott, who bravely ignored injury to lead Australia's attack during the Test series.

Australian Picture Library — Mike Hewitt (All Sport)

Ian Healy, after reaching a typically aggressive half-century in the second Test. Healy's innings, which ended on 61, helped establish a crucial first-innings lead for Australia of 74.

Australian Picture Library — Mike Hewitt (All Sport)

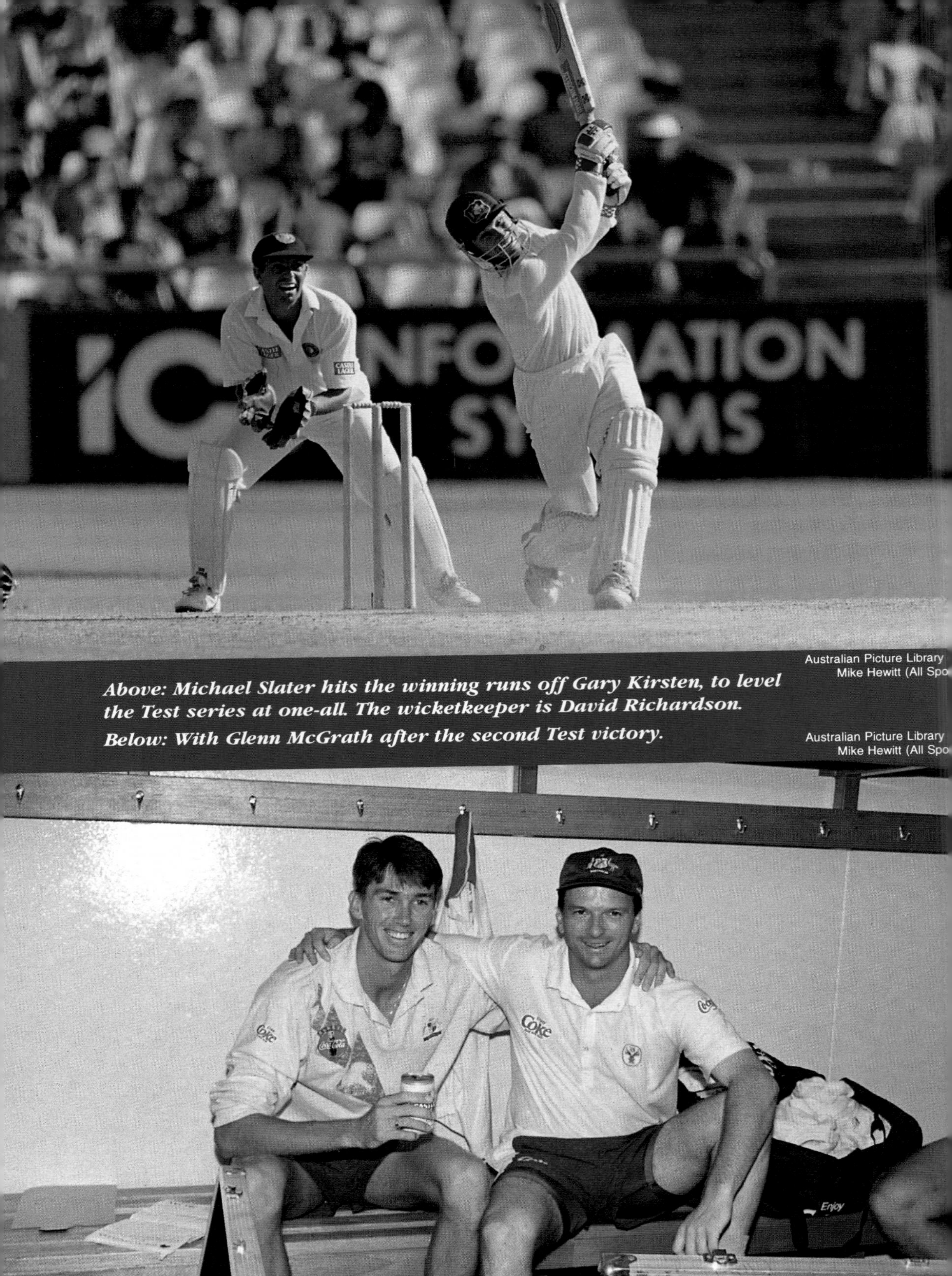

Australian Picture Library
Mike Hewitt (All Spo

Above:* *Michael Slater hits the winning runs off Gary Kirsten, to level the Test series at one-all. The wicketkeeper is David Richardson.

Below:* *With Glenn McGrath after the second Test victory.

Australian Picture Library
Mike Hewitt (All Spo

his three weeks of observations to use by using a strong Afrikaans accent when encouraging our bowlers throughout the day. It must have worked because five minutes from time, Orange Free State were all out for 264. It was another satisfying day's work out for our frontline bowlers, who have all displayed glimpses of form at one stage or another. The only complaint for us during the day was the unwillingness of our reserves to play a part in the game by actually watching the action in case they were needed. What was also frustrating was their tardiness in bringing out the drinks when required. Arguably the worst effort was turned in yesterday by Glenn McGrath who, with temperatures in the mid-thirties, greeted both Mark and I during our long partnership bereft of water, suncream or dry towels, all essential items for a 12th man at a drinks break.

Afterwards the media was keen to find out how Merv was progressing, and it was during one interview that the quote of the day was delivered. A reporter wanted to know why Merv had bowled 18 overs in three separate spells of six overs (6,6,6), and Merv replied, straight-faced: 'Because Mark Taylor worships the devil.'

Tonight we grabbed another quick feed at the Hard Rock Cafe, which has turned into a home away from home. Its good menu, friendly atmosphere, close location and pinball machines are the main attractions.

DAY 24 *February 28*

ON A TOUR of this length there is a danger the team's routines may become a little boring. So, in order to stop this, one of the players will occasionally have a turn leading the warm-ups. This morning's designated leader was Ian Healy, a trained physical education expert, who relished the chance to show off organisational skills learned at college. He marshalled the troops as if he were undergoing a practical exam, first putting us through a military-like stretching routine and then following up with a game of touch football that saw him pick up every infringement imaginable. The penalty-ridden encounter was finally settled by the fleet-footed May, who miraculously snared an intercept pass and streaked away from the opposition to score. However, his joy was short lived as he didn't realise Merv was hot on his heels. After scoring Maysie slowed to a jog, whereupon the frustrated Victorian fast bowler swooped on him like a lion attacking its prey and applied a nasty facial massage plus a string of body blows. The assault continued long after the rest of the two teams had vanished from view. Fortunately, Maysie was able to take part in the day's cricket, but only after a couple of Panadols and a few visits to the toilet helped ease the suffering caused by nausea and a bleeding nose.

Our batting order was altered slightly to give the men at the top of the innings another dig, and then the lower-order batsmen an opportunity for some time in the middle. Slats made the most of the good wicket, against a steady but not dangerous attack, to post a well-struck century, but at the other end of the scale Boonie failed again, a rarity for probably the most consistent batsman in the world today.

All the other lads looked in good touch with Warney, Heals, Tubs and Jurassic all having a reasonable hit out. As our total grew, plans were made to tie up our captain to prevent him from declaring but Tubby slipped through the net and halted proceedings. Our chance to wrap the game up began straight after tea, with the opposition requiring 465 to win, an almost impossible ask. However, things weren't looking all that flash at the close of play. Cronje is unbeaten on 42, his side well placed at 1-102, and the prospect of an exciting day's play exists for tomorrow.

Another invitation to dinner, at a popular local restaurant called 'Characters', was accepted and, as usual, Merv stole the show with his repertoire of jokes. As I've explained, we've heard them all before, but he still gets a laugh because of his ability to deliver the punchlines perfectly. Afterwards, and not for the first time, my roomie Matt H. and I began talking about cricket, and the conversation didn't end until 1am. Matt's quest for insight into the game is voracious. He's very level-headed, which will undoubtedly hold him in good stead during a career which is bound to be a long and successful one.

Day 25 *March 1*

WITH THE prospect of a long day ahead in the field, team warm-ups were abandoned this morning. Instead the pre-match preparation was left to the individual and most of us settled for a light stretch followed by a bit of catching. Some of these fielding exercises were with a tennis ball, a technique that helps promote 'soft' hands when catching the ball, which are essential to prevent the ball from popping out.

However, when Hansie Cronje was at the batsman's end today that catching practise seemed totally useless. As soon as play resumed he took control, while all his team-mates stumbled around him. His century was reached with ease and the only resemblance of a chance resulted in a diving one-handed effort by Tubs at first slip which jarred our captain's thumb and prevented him from taking any further part in the action for the day.

While Cronje was mauling our attack unmercifully during the afternoon session, Heals came out with a one-liner so funny that play could not continue for a good two minutes. Among the opposition was a player who was rather portly in appearance (in fact he was the spitting image of an Oompa-Loompa in Willy Wonka's Chocolate Factory). After being frustrated for a fair length of time, and with the lads desperate for a breakthrough, Heals called out to Maysie (the bowler at the time) that it might be a good idea to put a Mars Bar on the wicket, just short of a good length, to entice the batsman out of his crease and create the chance for a stumping. All the players, including the two batsmen, lost control. But, to the recipient's credit, he took it on the chin and even managed to reply: 'Don't worry about a Mars Bar – give me a pizza and you'll get me.'

However, later on, the batsman admitted he doesn't mind chocolates ... but if we'd gone through with Heals' plan he reckoned Boonie at short-leg might have got to the Mars Bar first!

After a lengthy delay, the next ball found the edge and made its way to me at first slip. But I was still laughing, and barely managed to co-ordinate my hands and spilt a regulation catch. So the chuckling continued. At the other end, Cronje was growing in status to the point where he was unstoppable, hitting fours and sixes almost at will. His 200 was passed with ease and then 250. Three hundred was within reach, but Cronje possibly sensed this and fell one run later – caught in the outfield to end a stupendous innings that featured immaculate concentration and superb stroke-play. But we wondered whether he should have batted for so long with a Test match starting only two days from now. After such a long innings, the mental tiredness can affect you for days. I guess only he knows how fit he is and whether or not he will be able to handle it.

The Orange Free State eventually fell 60 runs short after a gallant effort. We were relieved to be on the winning side even though we had been made to work hard of the victory. The work of Merv was our most impressive aspect to come out of today's play – a four-wicket haul was his reward for a consistent effort. I took my 200th first-class wicket, a milestone I thought I would never achieve when I began my career nine years ago mainly as a batsman who could bowl a bit.

During my spell I was warned for bowling two bouncers in one over at an opposition batsman who probably stood only 155cm. I thought it a bit harsh as the first short ball was only shoulder height. Maysie obviously agreed, and chipped to the umpire: 'We can't help it if he was fed experimental food at birth.' Next ball, Maysie in an attempt to fire me up had the opposite effect when he yelled out: 'C'mon, Tugga, let's send him gnome.'

The most annoying part of touring is, without a doubt, packing up after a game. It always seems your clothes have multiplied during the previous four days, to the point where there's no way they'll fit in your bag. Because we're leaving early in the morning, I decided to pack tonight, and the experience was even worse than ever. My traveller's cheques were nowhere to be found, until, on 25th check of the carry bag, they chose to come out from underneath the lining at the bottom of the bag. Despite the heartache they'd put me through, I was pretty pleased to see them.

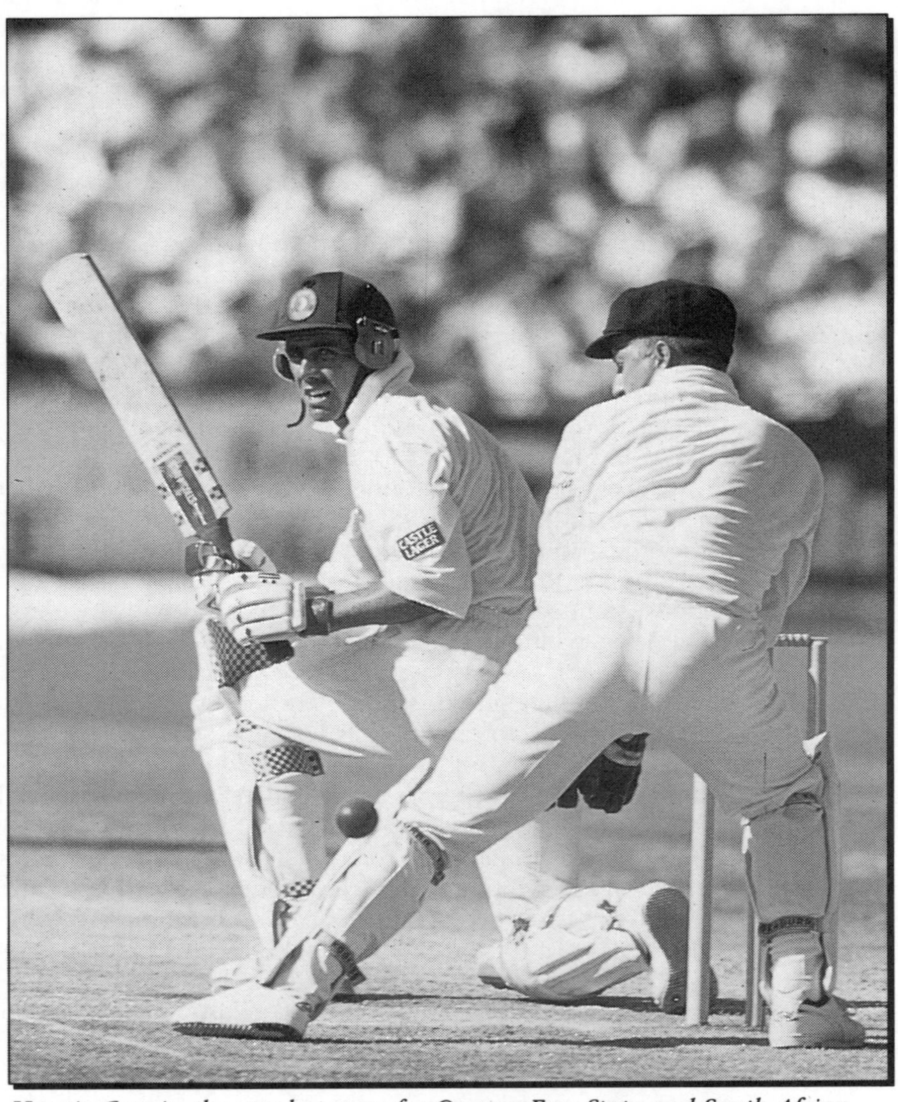

Hansie Cronje, the star batsman for Orange Free State and South Africa.

DAY 26 *March 2*

THIS MORNING'S flight was just a short 45-minute journey back to Jo'burg – a relatively comfortable exercise unless you get stuck next to a 140kg woman, which was the unfortunate (but amusing) seat allocation bestowed upon Matt Hayden. Our arrival back at the Sandton Sun Hotel came as somewhat of a surprise to the staff there, who had no knowledge of our arrival time. Consequently, there were no rooms available for the next two hours. With time to kill, Merv (my roomie again!!) and I set off for a bite to eat, which was postponed when we stumbled across a cinema complex inside the shopping arcade which was showing *Robin Hood – Men In Tights.* This particular flick was obviously not the flavour of the month. The entire audience totalled four, our two comrades being an elderly couple who made the mistake of sitting in the row immediately in front of us and paid the price by having to continually avoid flying maltesers and jelly babies. This wasn't the greatest movie we'd ever seen. Probably the most humorous moment came when, during a moment of boredom, a malteser put a dent in the middle of the screen.

After the film reached its merciful end, the following few hours were spent motionless in bed. The only signs of life came with the occasional use of the index finger to operate the remote control of the television. A 6pm departure was scheduled for the dreaded cocktail party at the Australian High Commission, which unfortunately for us was 45 minutes away in Pretoria. But, surprisingly, the affair wasn't as torturous as expected, with edible food being provided instead of the usual ghastly selection of hors d'oeuvres – items such as smoked oysters, caviar and pate that don't go down too well when you're accustomed to McDonald's and KFC. The whole affair only lasted 90 minutes, and the obligatory photo with all the dignitaries was the highlight of the evening. Somehow, all the staff (and there were plenty of them) managed to squeeze into the snap.

David Boon, at fielding practice at the Wanderers the day before the first Test.

DAY 27 *March 3*

I WOKE this morning feeling refreshed after our day away from cricket, and I think most of the blokes must have felt the same, because we produced a tremendous training session. We weren't out there that long, but what we did was of high quality – a much better way of training than a long drawn-out session at a lower standard.

I'm feeling as confident about my game as I've ever felt and can't wait for the series to begin. This optimism is reflected through the squad – we're all desperate to win the series. Our keenness has been exacerbated by all the debate over Australian umpiring we've heard since arriving here. According to the South African press and public, that was the only reason we were victorious in the third Test in Adelaide.

The Test wicket has an unexpected look about it. There is much less grass on it than we'd anticipated and some surface cracks are visible already, which suggests that, unless the wicket is affected by overnight rain, we will be going in with two spinners rather than three quicks. The square was one of the main topics for discussion at tonight's pre-Test team dinner. As the team's social director, one of my duties is to organise these dinners, and my criteria for the choice of venues revolves around three important elements – a nice variety of food, a relaxed setting, and, most importantly, an expensive menu as the ACB has to settle the account. For tonight, I chose a place called 'Turtle Creek', which gained the approval of the boys. Billy really cashed in with 18 oysters as a starter, a gesture that didn't go unnoticed, and the lads congratulated him on such a fine selection.

The only bad news to come from the evening was that Tubs has gone down with a bad dose of the flu and might struggle to be fit for tomorrow's match.

Maysie, once again, had the lads in fits of laughter with his recollection of the eight broken arms he has suffered in his lifetime ... and how they were achieved. The causes included a collision with an apple tree while playing footie in the backyard; tripping over while attempting a Michael Jordan-type manoeuvre on the basketball court; his sister unwittingly removing a ladder from underneath him while he was climbing the backyard tree; and, perhaps the most ridiculous of all, the victory leap over the net after winning a grade-four tennis final. Unfortunately, his jump was only high enough to catch the top of the tape with the Volley OC's ... and down he went.

The extent of the damage to the ACB coffers was a somewhat disappointing 1900 Rand, but this was more than compensated by an enjoyable evening. All the guys are in good spirits and excited about the challenge ahead. Afterwards, back at the hotel, we met up with our replacement physio, Lindsay Tregar, who has arrived following the unexpected departure of our regular physio, Errol Alcott. Lindsay will remain with us for the rest of the tour.

THE
FIRST TEST
LAZER
LAZER
LAZER

DAY 28 *March 4*

THE ATMOSPHERE on the bus while travelling down to the ground was tense, which is normal for the first morning of a Test match as everyone is keyed up for a big performance. Unfortunately, we did have problems – Tubs remained in serious doubt with his dose of flu, while Junior was in trouble with a finger injury. In both cases we waited until after our warm-up before making a decision, which in the case of our vice-captain was bad news. After being advised by a doctor, Tubs decided he wouldn't be able to do himself or the team justice by playing, so Matt Hayden won his first Test cap – an opportunity he's been desperate to get for the past 12 months. Junior, although probably not 100 per cent right for the game but having had a brief chat with AB, elected to play.

South Africa chose a side consisting of four quick bowlers and no spinner, while we went the other way, with two quicks and two spinners. This left Reiffel, McGrath and Jones (and, of course, the sick Taylor) on the outer.

Kepler Wessels called correctly when the coin landed on a dry looking wicket and elected to bat first, which was a little surprising considering they had gone in with a pace attack that may have extracted some life out of the first-day wicket. The crowd was only moderate, and they witnessed an entertaining morning session that had the match evenly poised at lunch, at 3-103. I thought our bowling was reasonable and our fielding was back to its best, with a lot of hustling and good chat to help each other out and support the bowlers.

A feature at the Wanderers Ground is the electronic scoreboard, which has among its many features various cartoon-like characters flashing up on its screen when an exciting event takes place. For example, when a six is hit, a man is seen on the screen devouring six hot dogs, or six dancing hippos doing the can-can is shown to entertain the crowd.

The crowd didn't need the cartoons to keep them interested in the middle session, as the cricket provided great entertainment. Another 100 runs were added for the loss of four wickets, which left us in a commanding position. Jonty Rhodes was the only stumbling block remaining; if we could have snared him we would have had a great first day. But Rhodes continued to impress after the interval, until he top-edged an attempted pull shot and was out for a valuable 69 – a knock that came when his team needed a substantial innings to hold the side together. The South Africans were eventually all out for 251, which still leaves us with the chance to put the match out of their reach if we can build up a big first-innings lead.

As I mentioned earlier, the feature of our performance today was our superb fielding. Not a chance was missed and a real buzz was always present in the air – a feeling that doesn't go unnoticed by the batting team and puts them under extra pressure.

Our day was capped off by a sparkling, unbeaten 34-run partnership in seven overs by Slater and Hayden, surely one of the youngest first-wicket combinations Australia has ever fielded. Judging by the amount of extravagant shots coming from his flashing blade, Slats looked as if he wanted a first-innings lead by stumps. At the other end, Jurassic copped the traditional welcome to Test-match cricket – a searing bouncer from Allan Donald that wrapped him on the knuckles first ball. It was an initiation he won't forget in a hurry.

A quick after-stumps shower was required as Slats, Heals, Maysie and I had taken up an invitation to go and watch the Australian women's hockey side take on South Africa in the third of a four Test-match series. Australia went into the game leading the series 2-0. Unfortunately, our presence didn't inspire much confidence, as our girls went down 2-1 in a game they probably should have won.

Shane Warne, during South Africa's first innings at the Wanderers.

DAY 29 *March 5*

THE CROWD that built up this morning was much larger than yesterday, and thankfully had an Australian contingent in it. A few tour groups had flown in before the start of the match to add some Aussie flavour to an otherwise partisan and somewhat arrogant crowd. What was quickly obvious was the fact that Darrell Hair's popularity hasn't diminished over the past few weeks – there were banners all around the ground ridiculing and chastising him for what the locals perceived as a poor performance in the last Test in Australia. The most popular effort of the day was: 'Darrell Hair for the electric chair'.

Disappointingly, our quest for a game-winning day began badly when Slats was caught at deep third man, of all places, in the first over of the day. This is the sort of freakish dismissal that tends to lift the opposition. Then, both Hayden and Boon fell after getting a start to leave us, at 3-70, in a similar position to what South Africa had been in yesterday. However, Junior and AB began to look comfortable, although in the period before lunch a personal battle between Brian McMillan and AB got a bit warm. There were quite a few exchanges between balls, as both men refused to yield an inch. At lunch, with the score at 3-120, full baby chickens were on the menu (Merv was rumoured to have taken three down) and things were looking okay ... until the arrival of McMillan at our table. Brandishing a pistol, he warned AB not to mess with him any more or our captain would be paying the consequences. Fortunately, the gesture was made with tongue firmly in cheek and ensured that what might have been said in the heat of the battle wasn't taken too seriously.

When play resumed disaster struck disappointingly quickly, as Junior was run out just when he and AB looked like they were gaining the upper hand. It was one of those run outs that comes from nowhere, with a comparatively easy looking single being turned into chaos through some indecision and unsure calling. Worse was to follow – 10 balls later the captain was run out as well, after I'd made a poor call. This dismissal was a lot tighter than the first run out, and the third umpire was needed to confirm Allan's fate. Suddenly the balance of the game had shifted back to the South Africans. They were brimming with enthusiasm, while the shock at having two batsmen run out so quickly (a very rare occurrence in Test matches) saw us crumble under pressure to be 8-201. I was still there on 31 with Craig McDermott when we went to the tea interval two runs later.

The wicket was beginning to show signs that it will deteriorate and be difficult to bat on in the last couple of days. It was obvious we needed a healthy first-innings advantage, and I was determined to try and help the team post a decent total. The costly run out of AB, for which I was responsible, had made me even more single-minded in my approach. Disconcertingly, Billy (who it appears has picked up the symptoms of Tubby's virus) spent the entire 20 minutes of the tea break on his hands and knees driving the white porcelain. While the Test was at a crucial point, there was one of the not out batsman, in his creams, wearing his pads and with his spiked shoes protruding from under the cubicle door, begging for no more.

After managing to stomach some medication, Billy proceeded to bat like a genius out in the middle, mauling the opposition's attack to the tune of 31 runs in 23 balls before he was lbw to an Allan Donald slower ball. That was just

Allan Border, during his innings of 34 in Australia's first innings.

about the end, as Maysie's elegant technique couldn't delay the inevitable and we were all out three runs short of South Africa's total. I was left a frustrating 45 not out.

By the time stumps were drawn, South Africa had progressed to 42 without loss. All up, it had been a disastrous day for Australia, especially when you consider that at the start of play things had looked so promising. We certainly have a lot of work to do.

Before I conclude today's entry, I must mention the Johannesburg crowd. It was very evident throughout the day that, while most of those at the ground clearly like to see good cricket, there is a percentage of people who are there for the sole purpose of abusing us whenever they see fit. It's something you can endure, so long as it doesn't get too personal. But too often today it did. Perhaps the worst of it comes during the long walk from the players' pavilion down to the playing surface, where we've copped a regular stream of abuse from the time the Test began. It's really starting to wear a bit thin, and I only hope this kind of thing doesn't go on for the remainder of the tour.

Just to cap the day off, back at the hotel, our keys wouldn't allow us access back into our room. Our angry efforts to loosen the locks and hinges proved futile, and I was designated to go and retrieve another set from the concierge. When I finally made it back, I was stunned to see Merv with a huge grin on his face, his body spreadeagled in a starfish-like pose on his bed. This did little to cheer me up, and neither did his response after I asked him how he had managed to get into the room.

'I went back to the lift and went up three floors,' he explained. 'We're staying on the 15th floor.'

I'm not sure how we got there in the first place, but we'd been trying to break into someone else's room on floor number 12.

PAGE 18

SPORT The Star

MONDAY MARCH 7 1994

Edited by Julian Kearns

Bradley leads SA golf sweep

South Africa's Wayne Bradley yesterday fired a six-under 67 to win the Ivory Coast Open golf tournament at Abidjan with a five-under total of 287. He was four shots ahead of compatriot James Kingston, while two other South Africans, Roger Wessels and Don Gammon, were joint third on one-over for the tournament.

BRIEFLY

Chappell guest speaker

Ian Chappell (above), former Australian cricket captain and current Channel Nine commentator, is the special guest speaker at a luncheon at the Wanderers club on Wednesday. The Qantas-Blue Chip Tours luncheon offers tables of 10 at an all-inclusive R95 a head. Book with Carolyn or Barbara on 884-08459.

Cullinan no to Boland

Transvaal batsman Daryll Cullinan and Northern Transvaal allrounder Steve Elworthy have both dismissed rumours that they will play their cricket for Boland next season.

No stopping AC Milan

AC Milan took a giant step towards their third successive league title with a 1-0 win over close rivals Juventus yesterday to stay six points clear at the top.

Snooker legend dies

South African snooker legend Jimmy van Rensburg (82) died in Johannesburg on Saturday night.

Lindenberg takes it

Peter Lindenberg stretched his lead in the SA powerboat championship when he won yesterday's 50-lap marathon on Germiston Lake from outsider Brian Lindsay.

Grondein's title

Colleen Grondein beat Sue Wilson 21-9 to win the Perm Southern Natal women's Masters bowls title in Durban yesterday.

Flying Jackson

Colin Jackson of Britain set a world indoor record of 7,30 sec in the 60 m hurdles at a track meeting in Germany yesterday.

SPORT ON TV

CRICKET: First test, SA v Australia (NNTV 10.25 am-12.35 pm; 1.05 pm-6 pm live); highlights (TV1 10.15 pm-10.45 pm)
WOMEN'S HOCKEY: SA v Australia, first two tests (NNTV 6 pm-6.30 pm)
POWERSPORT: Mr Olympia 1993 (NNTV 6.30 pm-7 pm)
SOCCER: Best of English (M-Net, 9 pm); Coventry v Aston Villa (M-Net 10 pm).

CRICKET: *Chastened Aussies left to reflect on sledging but it's . . .*

Heroes at your service

SHANE Warne and Merv Hughes each fined R1000 for verbal abuse in Wanderers controversy

BY PETER ROBINSON

Even before Merv Hughes and Shane Warne were hauled before the match referee last night, Hansie Cronje had, in the famous phrase, left the stadium.

The South African vice captain and his skipper Kepler Wessels shot out of the ground almost before stumps had been drawn, apparently to attend a Sunday evening church service.

It might be unwise, if not unfair, to draw too many conclusions from the way the South African pair and the Australians bowlers spent their evenings, but it was difficult not to escape the contrast.

Shortly after Wessels and Cronje had left the Wanderers, Hughes and Warne were in before head beak Donald Carr, trying to explain why they had, to use the official language, 'verbally abused' Gary Kirsten and Andrew Hudson respectively.

For their crimes they were each fined R1 000 and reprimanded, hardly the hanging, drawing and quartering that had been anticipated.

The fines amounted to roughly 10 percent of each player's match fee and certainly in the case of Hughes, who has twice before been called before an International Cricket Council match referee, appeared to amount to no more than a slap on the wrist.

In the Adelaide test, Peter Kirsten was eventually fined 60 per cent of his match fee for twice showing dissent when he was given out.

The maximum penalty which may be imposed in terms of the code of conduct is a three-match suspension and a fee amounting to 75 percent of the match fee. But since the code's introduction two years ago only one player, Pakistan's Aaqib Javed, has been suspended, for one match in New Zealand.

Last night's hearing tended to overshadow a splendid day for South Africa in general, as the home team reached 335/5 in their second innings, and Hansie Cronje in particular.

The Free Stater made his third test century in just over a year, 122 this time, to confirm his emergence as an international batsmen of genuine quality.

He wasn't around at the close of play last night to explain where all the runs were coming from, but coach Mike Procter described his innings as "fabulous".

Procter said the South African batsmen had been nervous and anxious on the first day when they had been bowled out for 251, but had settled themselves in the second innings to play their side into a commanding position.

As far as the sledging row was concerned Procter said there was an "unwritten code of conduct among our players.

"It depends on the timing and the state of the game and who's involved. We think we play it tough, but we cut it off at the right point."

Procter said that last night's disciplinary hearings were a matter between the players concerned, the umpires and the match referee.

Fine glance at a golden summer . . . batting hero Hansie Cronje takes more runs down to long leg off the Australian bowlers at the Wanderers. He made 122 as he compiled his third test century in twelve months. See Page 16. PICTURE: DUIF DU TOIT

SCOREBOARD

SOUTH AFRICA
First innings 251
AUSTRALIA
First innings 248
SOUTH AFRICA
Second innings

A Hudson b Warne	60
G Kirsten c Hughes b May	35
H Cronje c S Waugh b Hughes	122
K Wessels c Boon b Warne	50
P Kirsten not out	32
J Rhodes c Healy b S Waugh	14
F de Villiers not out	4
Extras	18
Total (for 5 wickets, 105 overs)	335

Fall of wickets: 1/76, 2/123, 3/258, 4/289, 5/324.
Bowling: McDermott 28-6-86-0; Hughes 25-5-86-1; May 23-7-67-1; S Waugh 10-3-28-1; M Waugh 6-2-14-0; Warne 19-5-31-2.

Sampras sticks to his task

Indian Wells (California) — World No 1 Pete Sampras yesterday won his third tennis title of the year when he beat Grand Slam Cup winner Petr Korda 4-6, 6-3, 3-6, 6-3, 6-2 in the final at the $1,7 million ATP Champions Cup.

Sampras, who lost to the Czech player in five sets in the final in Munich last December, trailed by two sets to one yesterday. But this time he surged back, serving down 23 aces against Korda. The match lasted just over three hours.

■ The Steffi Graf juggernaut rumbled onward yesterday as the world No 1 collected the Virginia Slims of Florida title with her 22nd consecutive straight sets victory of the year at Delray Beach.

Top-seed and defending champion Graf stopped second seed Arantxa Sanchez Vicario 6-3, 7-5 to pick up her fourth title of the year and 83rd career singles crown.

Sanchez, looking to avenge a 6-0, 6-2 humiliation in this year's Australian Open final, was on the verge of clinching the second set when she led 5-4, 15-40 on Graf's serve.

Graf collected $80 000 for her fifth Virginia Slims of Florida title.

Sanchez was already looking forward to a rematch with Graf on the next stop on the tour — the Lipton Championships, where the Spaniard beat Graf in the final last year.

"Next week is my week," Sanchez said. — Sapa-Reuter.

Barker to sweep clean

Changes in the composition and organisation of the national soccer side could be in store this year.

This follows confirmation that Clive Barker will be officially installed as the new national coach by the South African Football Association on Thursday.

Barker is expected to resign as coach of AmaZulu this week to take up the appointment created when Peruvian Augusto Palacios resigned in January.

One source said: "He intends involving all coaches throughout the country in the selection of players because he cannot be in all places at the same time."

SOCCER

Mixed fortunes for Bucs, Chiefs

BY PHIL NYAMANE

While Orlando Pirates are counting their luck after saving a Castle League point in their 1-1 draw with Cape Town Spurs at the weekend, Kaizer Chiefs were not as fortunate.

Chiefs, BP Top Eight finalists against the in-form Sundowns at the FNB Stadium on Saturday, were beaten 2-1 by unstylish Vaal Professionals at kwaMashu yesterday.

Chiefs accepted defeat in good grace. "We lost fair and square. Professionals deserved to win," assistant coach Trott Moloto is reported to have said.

The Cape side felt referee Robbie Williams and linesman Walter Mochubela cost them the extra point by ordering a retake of a penalty that had been saved by goalkeeper Andre Arendse.

The penalty was awarded when Spurs' Sebba Rodriquez handled the ball.

Arendse denied Ernest Makhanya's first attempt, but he was adjudged to have moved off his line. The kick was retaken, Edward Motale scoring from the spot.

At that stage Spurs were leading 1-0 through a goal from Reggie Jantjies.

"I have always said that South African football should get its act together. I did not think it was a penalty and Arendse did not move when the first kick was taken," said Spurs' coach Mich d'Avray.

Professionals, who lost and drew with Chiefs last season, netted twice in the first half through Victor Mazibele and Ruben Pitso.

Chiefs' second-half goal was scored by Tsepo Molatedi.

At Cape Town's Hartleyvale Stadium, Hellenic beat Chatsworth Rangers 2-1.

In Bloemfontein, Celtic drew 1-1 against Pretoria City while D'Albeton Callies and Real Rovers drew 3-3 at Chatsworth.

The match between Bush Bucks and Royal Tigers scheduled for Umtata's Independence Stadium yesterday was postponed after heavy rain ruled the ground unfit for play. The pitch was also damaged on Saturday following an ANC rally at the stadium.

ROAD RUNNING

SA championship course a disgrace, say marathon stars

BY MARSHALL HOWARD

East London risks losing out as a championship road race venue after athletes lashed out at the nature of the course for Saturday's Ohlssons SA marathon championships.

Runners and team managers were roundly critical of the circular route, which offered little relief over 42,2 km.

The course was sprinkled with a series of tough hills, sharp turns and stiff camber, only the final 5 km to the finish offering any respite.

"It's a disgrace that a national championships be held on such a tough course," team chiefs said.

"The runners don't expect to be pampered, but most train to run personal best times at a national event. This course was not acceptable."

Race convener Bob Norris said he was aware the route had come under fire, but countered: "I asked the great Matthews Temane what he thought and he said it was tough but fair."

With the news at the weekend that the SA 15 km championships — dropped last year because of financial restraints — are likely to return to the calendar in November, East London will again be in the hunt to host that race. The weekend's controversy, however, is sure to prompt organisers to find a quicker course.

See Page 16.

The back page of the Johannesburg Star *of March 7.*

DAY 30 *March 6*

A CAPACITY crowd, something of a rarity in Tests these days, welcomed the two teams onto the field for the third and probably game-deciding day of this match. Overcast skies hovered, but did nothing to dampen the day, or the spirits of the crowd because from the first over the South Africans held all the trumps. With a combination of skilful play and an element of luck they proceeded to put the match just about beyond our reach, and their score at stumps read 5-335.

It was one of those days when we didn't play as badly as the scoreboard suggests. But we couldn't quite get the bounce of the ball going our way, with catches not carrying to fieldsmen, a lot of play-and-misses from the South Africans, and some close lbw shouts going in the batsman's favour.

Our nemesis, Hansie Cronje, continued his golden run by scoring 122 and confirmed his status as a class player who will no doubt be recognised as one of the world's very best in the near future. Other batsmen to impress were opening bat Andrew Hudson (60), an aggressive type of player who likes to dominate if he can but has a reliable defence if needed, and Wessels (50), who we all know possesses a toughness that is essential at this level of competition.

Somehow, the press enclosure had prematurely discovered that during today's play two of our players, Merv and Warney, had been reported, and as a result our dressing room after play was swarming with cameras and pressmen all seeking to 'out-scoop' each other. Both incidents, in the opinion of Donald Carr (the match referee), were deemed serious enough to warrant a hearing, but strangely enough were not viewed that way by the umpires, who were willing to let the incidents in question stay on the field. This was disappointing, but what angered us the most was that the fact the two players had been reported was leaked to the media in the first place. The correct procedure is for the press room to learn of such reports after the hearings have taken place. But this did not happen, and consequently the two players in question were pictured by the media to be guilty, even before they had a chance to argue their case.

After waiting around for 90 minutes after the close of play, both players were found guilty of the charges levelled at them (verbal abuse) and were fined $A400 each. Later in the evening, Slats, Matty, Junior and I headed off for a quick feed at an Italian restaurant, but such is our notoriety over here we were constantly pestered for autographs, which somewhat spoilt a good meal.

DAY 31 *March 7*

DAY FOUR of the Test, a vital one for us, as we needed to claim the five remaining wickets cheaply to give ourselves any chance of a victory. A poor crowd was in attendance, mainly as a result of it being a Monday. But it was also another indication that Test cricket has taken a back seat to one-day cricket in the eyes of the fans, a situation that must be addressed shortly by the authorities if Test-match cricket is to survive. It is very rare these days for a Test to draw the big crowds that attended here on days two and three.

The first half of the day's play went smoothly, with four wickets coming our way for the addition of only 60 runs. However, a frustrating unbroken last-wicket partnership of 44 between Allan Donald and Craig Matthews took the wind out of our sails. A partnership of this nature may look innocuous on the scoresheet, but it can have quite impact on the mental approach of both teams in the period after it happens. Such was the case here, as it took the sting out of the momentum we had gained and it also lifted the spirits of the South Africans, who must have taken heart from seeing their two tailenders standing up when the odds were against them. Plus it gave the South Africans a lead of over 450 instead of nearer 400.

Only two teams have ever successfully chased over 400 in the fourth innings to win a Test match, so the odds of an Australian win must have been close to astronomical. Our best chance of attaining a famous win was to go out with an aggressive attitude, but, unfortunately, we couldn't have started any worse, with the first ball from Allan Donald crashing into Matt Hayden's thumb on his top batting hand, an injury that was later revealed as a double fracture and a minimum 10 days out of action. Matt battled on under difficulties, but was first to go, edging one back onto his stumps from Fanie de Villiers when he'd scored just five. This dismissal ended an unhappy debut match for him, but I'm sure there will be many better days and memories ahead during a long Test career.

A highlight of the day, and our entire tour, came at the tea interval, when we were introduced to the current South African President, F. W. de Klerk. He is a man who seems very humble and personable, and was keen to have a chat about the cricket.

Boon and Slater began to settle in during the final stanza of play, until Slater went in similar fashion to Hayden. Playing on is not a surprising mode of dismissal on this track, considering how the ball is beginning to keep low. Slat's demise was a huge blow to our chances, as we would have been well placed had we lost only one wicket at stumps instead of two. As it turned out, we require 331 runs tomorrow for victory – a huge task but one which we are keen to have a crack at so long as we don't lose any wickets early in the final day.

The key to a good day tomorrow for us is Boonie, as he can bat for long periods and stabilise our plans for an assault. I like the idea of our number three staying there for a long time, with the aggressive players batting around him.

During our time in South Africa we have all become very good friends with the security personnel who have escorted us everywhere. They are just about a part of the touring family we are all a part of. Rory Steyn, the head man of the outfit who loves to call the lads by their nicknames, invited Slats, Maysie, Heals and I out to his place for a home-cooked meal. Of course, we jumped at the opportunity, as there was the prospect of sighting a vegetable, which is something of a rarity in a touring cricketer's diet.

While having some batting practice during this afternoon's play, Jonesy managed to organise a helicopter flight from the medical service chopper that is situated near the practice nets. As someone who is always on the lookout for an exciting challenge, I boarded the helicopter with Dean, Warney and Pistol for a journey over Jo'burg that was more hair raising than an amusement park ride. The pilot was very keen to show off his manoeuvring skills over buildings and even in between them.

But perhaps the most haunting aspect of the trip was the sight of a township known as Alexandria. It is a squalid couple of miles, filled with makeshift huts of tin and bricks, and has rubbish scattered everywhere. Yet no more than 500 metres away there are suburbs full of mansions, all with beautifully manicured lawns, tennis courts and swimming pools. This was without doubt the most unsettling example we had seen in South Africa of the difference in living standards between the wealthy 'white' districts and the poor 'black' areas.

President F. W. de Klerk with Captain Allan Border.

DAY 32 *March 8*

NOT LONG after I woke this morning I was handed a couple of faxes that had been sent from Australia, wishing us all the best in our quest for a record run-chase. It's always great to know we have a lot of support back home, especially as the crowds here are so parochial.

As is always the case on a batting day, the team went straight to the nets to have a good knock-up before the start of play. However, after a promising start which saw the first 30 minutes safely negotiated, the following 90 minutes proved to be a disaster. Five wickets fell – the result of some intelligent South African bowling and batting below our usual high standard. By lunch, our chances of surviving rested with the two men at the wicket, Healy and Hughes, and with the weather, as the forecasters had suggested there was a 40 per cent chance of rain arriving during the afternoon.

My innings had been completed in the blink of an eyelid. The first delivery I faced (from Matthews) found the outside edge of my blade as I probed outside off-stump – a sickening feeling made even worse by the long trek back to the dressing room and the abuse I copped all the way up the steps to the players' enclosure.

When you're out first ball, in the seconds during and after the removal of your protective equipment back in the sheds, you feel as if the dismissal hasn't really happened. You're in something of a state of shock, and all you want is to be able to turn back the clock five minutes and alter the disastrous event that has just taken place. The next few minutes are spent watching a video replay over and over again in your mind, as you try to work out where you went wrong and whether or not it was your fault or perhaps the good work of the bowler. In this case, I believe I received a good ball first up, but I'm sure I could have been more positive – either by letting the ball pass through to the keeper or by pushing it through the covers with the intention of scoring runs. Instead, I was caught in two minds and this indecisiveness caused my downfall.

The confrontation between Merv and a spectator in the notorious players' tunnel at the Wanderers that caused such a storm in South Africa and Australia. The other batsman is Tim May.

Our predicament went from shaky to disastrous almost immediately after the resumption of play, as another four wickets fell in a display that had too

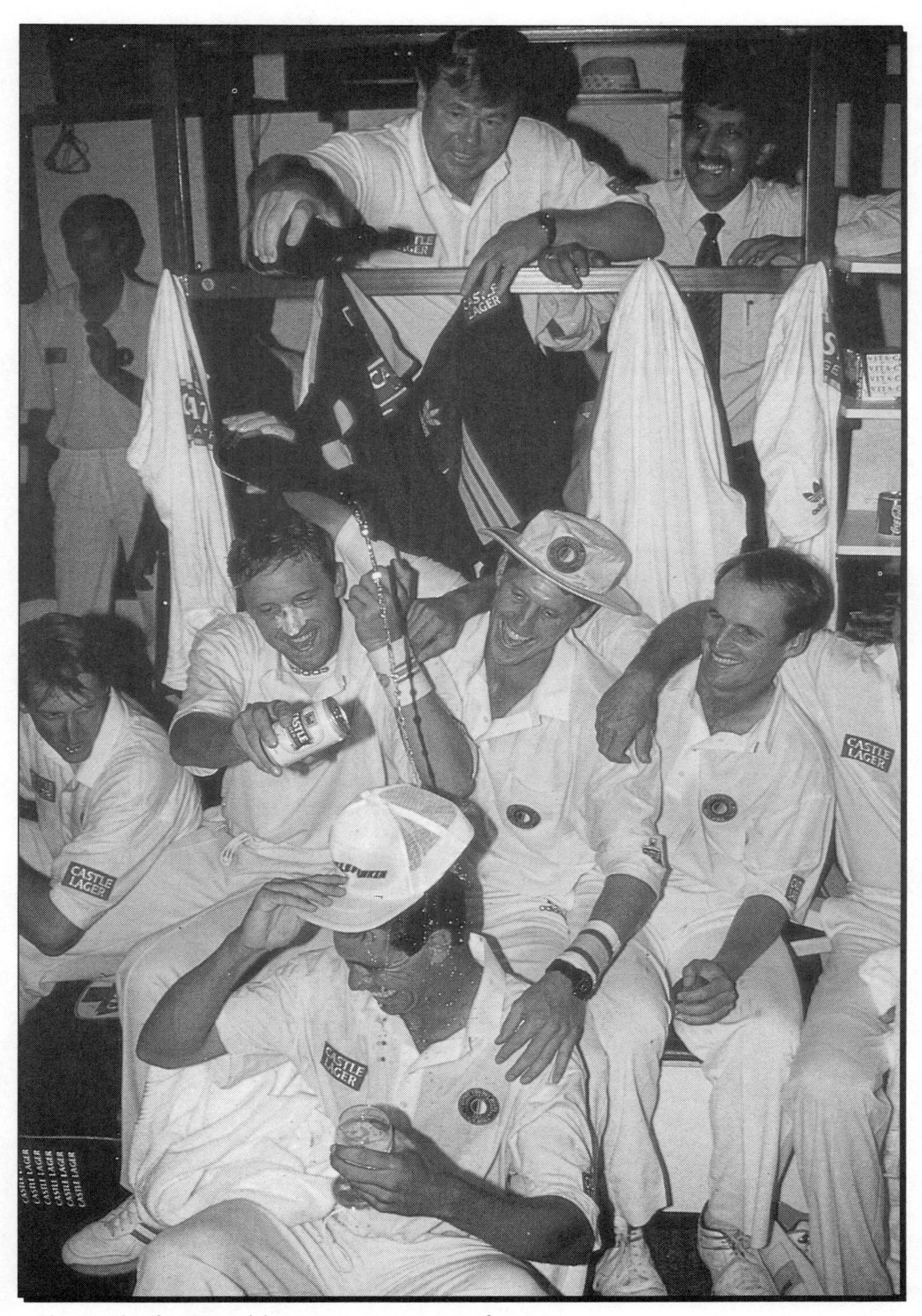

The South Africans celebrate going one-up in the series.

many similarities to the Sydney Test run-chase of two months before. No-one is really standing up to be counted in the tough times. Ironically, our best partnership was the last one, between Hughes and May, who gave their best in a defiant effort that looked as if it might even save the day when thunder and lighting began to menace overhead. The players even had to leave the field for a short time, during which our frustration and disgust with the South African 'fans' near the players' tunnel boiled over and Merv was involved in a clash with a spectator. Soon after, the players were back on the field and the rain wasn't sufficient to avoid the inevitable. The eventual margin between the two teams was 197 runs.

In trying to work out where we went wrong, I think our attitude after day one – when our commanding position led to us thinking it was only a matter of turning up to get the required results – let us down. A let-up in intensity was our downfall. As we know too well, once the South Africans get a sniff of a victory they are extremely hard to hold off. However, as long as we learn from our mistakes and can quickly recognise when our intensity is dropping, I'm sure we'll be able to get back in the winning circle.

Within 30 minutes of the presentations, the team boarded the bus for a journey to Sun City, which is two hours from the ground. The two choices confronting us as we set off were to re-hash the events of the day ... or have a get together down the back of the bus to try and revive spirits. The latter seemed a much more appealing option and we set about drowning our sorrows during the trip. Our morale is still high, and we see the loss as a setback rather than a disaster.

Tomorrow is a day off and will be followed by a charity golf day at a course just outside of Jo'burg, hosted by the Carousel Amusement Centre, when we will help raise funds for the development of cricket in underprivileged areas.

We were looking forward to seeing the world-famous resort city that was our destination ... and we weren't disappointed. Not even the effect of a few generous helpings of Southern Comfort and Coke could disguise the impact of my first sighting of the majestic Lost City complex – a group of hotels, casinos and golf courses situated in basically the middle of nowhere. It was a sight that took my breath away and one that can only be fully appreciated first hand. Tomorrow promises to be a fantastic experience. After getting settled in our rooms, and enjoying a complimentary meal courtesy of the hotel management, we spent what was left of the evening donating Rand to the hotel casino.

FROM SUN CITY TO TABLE MOUNTAIN

DAY 33 *March 9*

A 5AM WAKE-UP call shook me from a comatose state, and after a few curses and shakes of the head, it suddenly dawned on me that I had made myself available for a drive through a nearby game park that was to begin at 5.30am. This, I thought as I struggled to get out of bed, was an extremely foolish decision, especially considering the delicate state I was in. Nevertheless, I somehow managed to convince myself it was a worthwhile outing, but this was a verdict shared only by Glenn McGrath and our security mate Rory. The other half a dozen players who had indicated last night they wanted to come, now opted for the comfort of the sheets and serenity of a dark and peaceful room.

The game parks refer to the rhinos, elephants, cheetahs, lions and buffalos as the 'Big Five' and we were told that if you see one or two of these in a normal three-hour trip you've been lucky. We were lucky! Not long into our tour, we spotted three wild rhinos, happily sleeping underneath some trees. Then, no more than 30 seconds later, our driver became excited as he noticed some droppings and footprints along the road that belonged to elephants. Sure enough, there they were – just 50 metres further along the road.

To see an elephant demolish a tree just to satisfy its diet of 50 kilograms of food a day was awesome. However, something even more extraordinary was the sight of its partner charging at us, then stopping in its tracks not more than six metres away and letting out a monstrous noise to let us know very clearly that we were invading their territory. It was something I'll never forget. It truly was a magical morning, with animals such as giraffes, baboons, springboks, tessebys, wildebeests and zebras appearing around every bend in the road.

During our travels we were told by another sightseeing group that two lions were in the process of mating not far from our location at that time. The sighting of lions in this part of Africa is extremely rare, as there are currently only 19 lions in the 58-square-kilometre reserve. Just before we reached the right spot, another tourist group warned us to be careful as the animals were stressed and angry due to the amount of traffic that had been disturbing their peace. As a

Warney and Merv being interviewed by Australia's Channel 7's Brent Rees on the Sun City golf course. After the controversies of the first Test, the Victorian pair were very popular with the travelling media.

precaution our driver loaded his gun, and trouble did look like unfolding when the male began stalking our vehicle as we confronted it along the dirt track. However, after a few nervous moments, the two lions backed off and we were able to regain our colour and composure, and then sit back and marvel at their beauty.

This was how I had always imagined Africa to be like – it was a three-hour experience I will long remember. Then, after squeezing in some brekky, my next step was the golf course, where the quartet of May, S. Waugh, Hughes and Warne decided to play only nine holes so we would still have enough time to check out some other activities later on in the day. The team of May and Waugh started impressively, while Merv's first iron shot disappeared into some thickish woodlands. 'Did you use a tree iron there, big fella?' enquired Maysie. Then Warney hacked his tee shot into some dense growth and Maysie asked: 'Which scrub – I mean club – did you use?'

We all hoped the golf would improve, but, alas, it only deteriorated. Each hole developed into its own disaster. Our quest for good golf wasn't aided by a sickening collision between the two golf carts at the second hole, after Merv decided to test the brake pads out while the team of May and Waugh were taking in the spectacular views on offer. The result was a severe case of whiplash for each member of the foursome and a throbbing headache that failed to subside throughout the nine-hole debacle. By the time we stood on the fourth tee, our stocks of golf balls had dropped from 20 to four. To ensure the remaining holes were completed, a further 20 were purchased from a local who had obviously been spying on our shot-making abilities and collecting our wayward projectiles. He was kind enough to sell our balls back to us and make a tidy profit.

At the seventh, the golf carts nearly proved to be our undoing once again, as Warne and Hughes ran over a large rock, which sent them on a direct course towards a large gum tree. Soon after, May and Waugh lost all control on a steep section of the course. After a series of out-of-control sideways movements, the pair regained command only metres from a nasty ravine. As the golf standards reached new depths Merv suggested the introduction of what he called the 'Werribee 10-second rule', which turned out to be an interesting concept to say the least. The rule allows the player an opportunity to have a second shot at the same ball if he can retrieve the ball and place it in its original position before 10 seconds have elapsed since the original swing. Merv is obviously an avid disciple of the rule, and at the eighth introduced a loophole. His first shot was a shocker, and Merv was quick to give himself another bite at the cherry. His follow-up shot also left a lot to be desired – a ferocious looking swipe that sliced the ball into the scrub – after which Merv yelled out: 'It's safe!' This was a strange comment, considering it would have required postal stamps to get back onto the fairway, but we were quickly told the statement meant the ball was 'safely lost', and, according to the fine print of the 'Werribee 10-second rule', Merv had another shot.

The fixture was reaching an electrifying crescendo, but, alas, by the time the ninth tee was reached we'd run out of balls (with Waugh and May the main culprits), so the scorecard was ripped up and we headed straight for the safety of the clubhouse. Next stop was the water park, which is situated next to our hotel and features some frightening rides, one of which nearly ended my tour. One of the waterslides includes a section you go down in complete darkness – unfortunately for me, I came to a complete halt inside the tunnel. Realising the

Left: The group of Hughes, Warne, May and S. Waugh, whose golf at Sun City left a little to be desired.
Below: Heals and Junior have a quick look for an errant approach shot, before deciding the ball is clearly lost.

next rider was only a couple of seconds away I tried to push myself free, but a split-second before doing so I was hit at full speed from behind by a set of legs. For a split second I thought I was paralysed (a shocking feeling), but after I'd found two doctors who wanted to inject drugs into the affected area, Lindsay Tregar decided it was severe bruising that would last around 10 days. I was extremely lucky not to be seriously injured.

An emergency team meeting was hastily arranged in the manager's room, after we learned Merv and Warney have both been fined by our own board, in addition to the fine from the ICC's match referee. This has followed a lot of negative press the team has apparently received in Australia, with Warney's reaction after Andrew Hudson was dismissed in the second innings and the incident involving Merv and that fan in the players' tunnel being highly publicised. Apparently the boys have copped an additional $A4000 fine each. This was a shock to all of us as the two guys weren't given a chance to explain themselves. The point that causes us most concern is the lack of communication between the players and the Australian Cricket Board over the incidents, which led to the players discovering through the media that the fines had been imposed. We believe the players and the Board officials should have discussed the matter before the story of the fines appeared in the papers.

After the meeting, we attended a cocktail party at a 10,000 Rand-a-night penthouse, and the day was capped off by a dinner show at the Viva Sun City casino. Today has been an action-packed, enjoyable part of the tour – a vital boost to team morale after the setback of yesterday.

DAY 34 *March 10*

AFTER AN uncomfortable night's sleep, I woke to find my lower back was feeling much better than it had the previous evening, when I had been seriously concerned that I had a major problem. Our physio, who is happy with my progress, supervised an early-morning routine of stretching and swimming. Then I, with the rest of the team, boarded a special DC-3 plane that had been chartered for this morning's trip to the charity golf day just outside of Jo'burg. Our mode of transport caused concern among the poorer fliers in the team, who didn't like the archaic looking beast. We had a rather smooth flight, but experienced a turbulent approach that had some of the lads in a lather of sweat and thinking we had played our last game of cricket.

From the airport we were whisked straight to the course, where we were issued with shirts, hats, balls and shoes. Each member of the team was allocated to a different group, with partners who had paid either 1500 Rand or sponsored a hole. My group was made up of a good bunch of lads from a liquor company who obviously enjoyed their golf. However, as our round was beginning to blossom, their attitude changed from happy-go-lucky to tense and serious – which is not the way I like to play golf. The turning point in our round came at the eighth, where my three partners had all found the water hazard too great an obstacle. The competition rules were such that you had to use the team's best drive and all play a second from wherever that finished. Just as I was about to tee off, our team captain stopped me to suggest I should be playing with an iron for safety rather than trying to smash a wood as far as I could. I informed my concerned leader that my motto was 'never play safe, mate', which didn't seem to comfort him. Needless to say his facial expression changed for the worse when my Greg Norman imitation went horribly wrong and bounced a couple of times before sinking in the water hazard. From this moment our round was doomed and we eventually finished in the middle of the field.

The presentation evening was one that was enjoyed by all, with a cabaret-type show being put on at the casino. The only problem came afterwards, as the weekly allowance money was handed over to the croupiers on the gaming tables.

Contrasting emotions as we prepare to fly to a charity golf day. At the back of the plane, Merv is raring to go, whereas Matt Hayden, closer to the front in the sunglasses and Aussie cap, adopts a pose that more accurately reflected how most of us felt about the not-so-modern charter plane.

DAY 35 *March 11*

LUCKILY FOR us, we have moved on from Sun City. I say 'luckily' because trouble has flared up in the past 24 hours and it is difficult at present for people to move in and out of the surrounding regions. The elections are still six weeks away and, with quite a few of the parties still unsure as to whether or not they are going to take part in the vote, a major flare-up seems inevitable unless the friction that presently exists between certain groups is alleviated.

A two-hour plane flight to Cape Town, a city everyone raves about over here, was safely negotiated and we were greeted by another horde of school kids. The children were terrific, but some of their adult colleagues are really beginning to annoy us. As each day has passed on the tour it has become more and more apparent that the people over here are absolutely loving the fact that we are losing at the moment. The only way to resolve or address this situation is to begin winning – something we haven't achieved as yet, but something we fully intend to do..

More bad news awaited my roomie, Maysie, and myself, as we realised the size of our room (or more accurately, kennel) won't allow us to be separated enough for me to gain some shut-eye if his rather large nose begins to play up while he's horizontal. I'm not sure why we're staying at this hotel when there are numerous others of better quality around, although, to be fair, this one has got a relaxing courtyard with great views of table mountain.

A couple of weeks ago, the team had received an advanced invitation to a Cape Town health farm, and this afternoon Maysie, Slats, Cam B. and I took the option up. We were treated to a massage, then into the jacuzzi and, after a 10-minute rest, we ventured to the steamroom. We ended with another rest and then a swim. The order of events in the two-hour routine (which seemed a little strange) and the fact every employee was dressed in a white coat prompted Maysie to ask: 'Do you think they're conducting human experiments here?' It was a concept that didn't appear out of the question.

Back at the hotel, Maysie began to work himself into a frenzy over the thought of dining at an Indian restaurant called 'Talk of the Town'. He had made extensive enquiries as to the restaurant's quality, but when we arrived it was blatantly obvious Tim's sources weren't reliable. The decor rivalled a Chinese take-away and Maysie quickly made it clear he considered the menu inadequate. In his words: 'Can you believe they haven't got any mango chutney or nan bread!' Even more staggering, the restaurant was devoid of a Tandoori oven. I found it amusing to see Tim cowering in his seat, an obviously shattered man, as he perused his menu. However, the meals all turned out to be reasonable, although our 'experts', Tubs and Maysie, considered their curries to be nothing more than glorified stew.

DAY 36 *March 12*

WE HAD to rise early this morning, as our three-day game against Boland (who are newcomers to South Africa's equivalent of the Sheffield Shield, the Currie Cup), which commenced today, is being played 50 minutes from our hotel, in the wine-growing region of Stollenbosch. The backdrop to the ground is fantastic, as it is located among some beautiful mountain country, but we were a little taken aback by the playing field and wicket area, which weren't of great quality. Mind you, I've played on worse grounds around the world, particularly in the West Indies, Pakistan and India.

Although my back was still unbelievably stiff and sore, Lindsay assured me this was normal and that the stiffness would gradually clear up, so I was in the starting XI. The players to have the game off were the injured Hayden, plus May, McDermott and Border. Boland won the toss and sent us in, to the collective cheer of our bowlers who realised they could put their feet up for (hopefully) at least a day. And this they did, as we managed 7-254 in a day made forgettable by the negative approach of our opponents, whose tactics revolved around a ring field designed to stop us scoring rather than getting Australian batsmen out. I guess you couldn't really blame them, as their bowling was not up to first-class standard. As an added handicap, over an hour's playing time was lost, but Jones, Boon, Slater and M. Waugh all had a good workout, as did I, until run out for 32, a style of dismissal that has caused us a fair amount of anguish recently.

Without doubt the most interesting piece of trivia to come out of today was the reason why the wicket was uneven. We were told the groundsman was unable to roll the wicket yesterday because a Cape Cora snake has wrapped itself around the roller and the curator was unwilling to venture too close to the reptile. Consequently the roller was left untouched all day.

A quick getaway from the ground was required as the team had accepted an invitation for dinner at the Neederburg Winery. This was a keenly anticipated event, especially for the management who are rather partial to a drop or two. The enthusiasm of our hosts was commendable, especially as they knew we were in the middle of a game, and the team, being keen to make a good impression, didn't pass up the generous hospitality and sampled a few of the better vintages with great gusto. Of course, there were the few obligatory speeches that nobody listened to. But then one particular speaker rattled off the names of a few of our players who he regarded as being role models for the youngsters of South Africa – 'Merv Hughes, Shane Warne and Craig McMurray' – at which point the boys burst into uncontrollable laughter. We think he meant Craig McDermott!

The long trip home began with a singalong, to the title songs of television shows such as *Gilligan's Island, The Brady Bunch, Top Cat* and so on, until the numbers dwindled away to nothing as the cocktail of alcohol and tiredness took its toll.

WEEKEND Argus SUNDAY

sports

SECTION 2

CAPE TOWN, MARCH 12/13 1994

★ 23

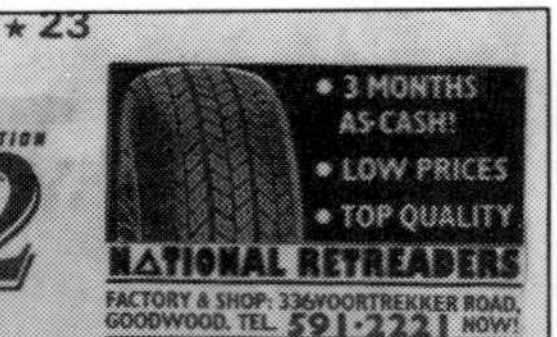

Transvaal whizkid takes title

GRANT WINTER

IN an explosive finish to a a hugely successful week, 18-year-old Transvaal whizkid, Bradford Vaughan, birdied six of the last seven holes he played yesterday to destroy Ryno Bougas of Western Province eight and seven in the final of the SA Amateur at Royal Cape.

WINNER: Bradford Vaughan

After going into lunch with a two-hole advantage, the tall, slim Emfuleni teenager turned the screws on his Somerset West opponent in the afternoon — one-putting the first seven greens to go five up in the match. That was a memorable enough start.

Then, at the 171m par-three eighth, Vaughan underclubbed, his ball coming to rest on the front of the green. This turned out to be his first two-putt of the afternoon but, incredibly, not before his "70-footer" for birdie actually hit the cup and bounced out. Here was the silky touch of a Mark McNulty.

Then, at the 385-metre par-four ninth, Vaughan hit a drive and an eight-iron to inside three metres and again trickled in the putt to reach the turn in just 32 strokes. That put him six up overall. He had needed just 10 putts in the nine-hole stretch as a new young star was born into South African golf.

Vaughan may be young and relatively inexperienced, but he was not prepared to back off even with such a comfortable lead intact. Further birdies followed at the 10th (a 322m par-four where he came close the green with his booming drive) and the par-five 11th where he was on the green for two.

"I can't believe what I'm seeing," said an exasperated Bougas.

Bougas, with respect, did not perform all that badly and in the afternoon was level par through the 11 holes that were completed. Ironically, it was the Cape golfer who took the early initiative on the day, with birdies at the second, fifth and seventh holes in the morning putting him three up. But, in an amazing run, Vaughan won 11 on the next 22 holes to turn the match around.

"Gee, I didn't realise that," said a non-plussed Vaughan after his victory. "Mind you, I tried to think positively out there."

Even though he was not entirely happy with his short game a few days back he did manage joint second place on 282 in the SA strokeplay championship which ended on Wednesday. Neil Homann won the event.

Vaughan is a member at Emfuleni but plays league for Krugersdorp Golf Club and as such is in the Western Transvaal side. At last year's interprovincial he went through the week unbeaten to help his team gain promotion to the A Section.

It is such a pity that all is not entirely well in the administration of amateur golf. There is certainly no shortage of talent. It would have been fitting if at least Vaughan and Homann could have received national colours at last night's prizegiving. They deserve to be playing internation golf but, sadly, it is still not definite whether there will be tours this year.

Homann aims for the top, see page 24
Losing finalist, picture on page 25

AUSSIE OPENS UP: Australian opening batsman Michael Slater hits out against Boland yesterday. Slater made 40.

Picture: OBED ZILWA, Weekend Argus

Cape rain fails to foil Aussies

Dean Jones slams the Boland bowlers

PETER ROBINSON in Stellenbosch

AUSTRALIA dodged around the changeable Cape weather and made the best of a stodgy Coetzenburg pitch to give most of their top order some batting practice on the opening day of their three-day match against Boland yesterday.

Despite two interruptions for rain which lasted 114 minutes, the tourists were able to use up 77 of the day's quota of 104 overs as they made 254/7 declared. There were no innings of major significance — an adventurous 83 from Dean Jones being the day's top score — but with the exception of Mark Taylor, who scored only 10, the Australian batsmen all had time at the crease.

Sent in by Boland, Australia quickly lost Taylor, caught at midwicket as he ventured a pull off Marais Erasmus, but thereafter settled into the day.

They were mostly denied a view of the breathtaking backdrop to this university ground sited in the heart of South Africa's rugby establishment, but after viewing a slow pitch with some suspicion, batted brightly through most of the day.

Apart from Jones, whose runs came in 101-minute stay at the crease, the most entertaining interludes were separately provided by the Waugh twins, Mark and Steve.

Mark took an age to settle in, finally moving to double figures after facing 38 balls. He did so, however, with a six off Erasmus and promptly scored 29 more off the next 17 balls he faced.

He hit Erasmus for three successive fours, took three fours in four balls off offspinner Brian Drew, but was then stumped for 43 as he launched into a heave in the direction of midwicket off Claude Henderson.

Steve, who came to the crease at his brother's dismissal, rattled along to 32 off 39 balls before he was sent back by Dean Jones and run out at the bowler's end by a direct hit from Erasmus.

Earlier, Michael Slater had helped put on 73 for the second wicket, the day's highest partnership, with David Boon.

While Slater looked characteristically busy, he never quite found his touch, batting for 108 minutes for his 40 before lifting a drive to extra cover.

Boon, though, played the anchor role at the top of the innings, making 52 before Drew trapped him leg before with his first delivery of the innings, one that kept low, and later in the afternoon it was left to Jones to hold the bottom half of the batting together.

It was a bitty day's cricket, one which never quite caught alight and the Australians may feel that they should have taken greater advantage against relatively ordinary opposition.

Allan Border, Craig McDermott, Tim May and Matthew Hayden, who has a broken thumb, sat out this match.

Taylor is acting as captain for this match and went some way towards restoring Australia's tarnished image by allowing the home team to replace middle order batsman Wayne Truter with Robbie Dalrymple after the match had begun.

Truter aggravated a hand injury while fielding, but Taylor agreed to allow Dalrymple to come in for him as a full player, able to bat during Boland's innings.

The declaration came just on 18h00 at the fall of Jones' wicket and more drizzle and bad light prevented Boland beginning their first innings.

Play will start 30 minutes early at 10h30 today and tomorrow to make up lost time.

STELLENBOSCH SCOREBOARD

AUSTRALIA first innings

M Slater c Henderson b Erasmus	40
M Taylor c Erasmus b Smith	10
D Boon lbw Drew	52
M Waugh st Erasmus b Henderson	3
D Jones b Drew	63
S Waugh run out	32
I Healy c Henderson b Drew	1
P Reiffel not out	8
Extras	5
TOTAL (for seven decl)	254
	77 overs

Falls: 1/15, 2/88, 3/135, 4/156, 5/221, 6/229, 7/254

Bowling: Smith 12-2-32-1; Roos 13-3-40-0; Henderson 15-2-49-1; Erasmus 21-4-84-1; Drew 16-2-68-3

A TALE OF TWO TEST HEROES

KAPIL DEV on page 25
HANSIE CRONJE on page 30

Hooper returns

BRIDGETOWN (Barbados). — Middle-order batsman Carl Hooper was yesterday named in place of Roger Harper in West Indies' 13-man squad for the second cricket test against England starting in Bourda, Guyana on Thursday.

Hooper missed the first test and the one-day series because of a back injury but he is leading a West Indies President's XI in their current four-day match against England at Bourda.

The squad is: Desmond Haynes, Phil Simmons, Richie Richardson (captain), Brian Lara, Keith Arthurton, Jimmy Adams, Carl Hooper, Junior Murray, Anderson Cummins, Winston Benjamin, Kenneth Benjamin, Curtly Ambrose, Courtney Walsh. — Sapa-Reuter

McLean set to clinch Giro in today's Tour

ANDREW McLEAN is a stone's throw away from winning his third consecutive Pick 'n Pay Giro del Cape, writes Bryan Grieve.

Going into today's final leg — The Argus/Pick 'n Pay Tour — the defending champion has a 40-second advantage over Russian Igor Protskikh who, in turn, is 44 seconds ahead of third-placed Willie Engelbrecht.

McLean moved farther ahead of his rivals in the 53km hill climb third stage yesterday when he was second to Briton Lee Davis, who clocked 13min 14sec. McLean was only four seconds in arrears.

A surprise was the time of Engelbrecht, who does not enjoy racing in wet, misty weather. He took 14min 40sec to finish in 62nd position.

ALL the results of tomorrow's Argus/Pick 'n Pay Cycle Tour will appear in a special souvenir section in next Sunday's Weekend Argus Sunday.

Don't miss it — The Weekend Argus Sunday of March 20.

Picture, see page 25
Lange wins, see page 27

TV SPORT

M-NET: TENNIS: ATP highlights (22h00). BOWLS: Midland World Indoor Championship, England recent, highlights (23h30).
CCV: SOCCER: NSL league, Moroka Swallows v Wits, Dobsonville, live (14h30-16h50). BOXING: SA Junior middleweight title Johannes Mabaso v Mzukisi Marambi, Eldorado, live (16h55-17h55).

Hansie joins world's batting elite

LONDON. — Hansie Cronjé, man of the match in South Africa's first test victory over Australia, has jumped into the world's top five batsmen.

The 24-year-old SA vice-captain leaps 11 places by virtue of his second-innings century at Johannesburg earlier this week.

England's Graham Gooch still heads the list, despite not taking part in his country's Caribbean tour, by one point from West Indies veteran Des Haynes.

Pakistan paceman Waqar Younis is still the world's top bowler from Indian spinner Anil Kumble.

LEADING RATINGS

BATSMEN: 1 Graham Gooch 811 points, 2 Des Haynes (W Indies) 810, 3 Sachin Tendulkar (India) 785, 4 Richie Richardson (W Indies) 784, 5 Hansie Cronje (S Africa) 744, 6 Brian Lara (W Indies) 730, 7 David Boon (Australia) 728, 8 Steve Waugh (Australia) 675, 9 Vinod Kambli (India) 673, 10 Mohammad Azharuddin (India) 668.

BOWLERS: 1 Waqar Younis (Pakistan) 907, 2 Anil Kumble (India) 890, 3 Shane Warne (Australia) 867, 4 Curtly Ambrose (W Indies) 861, 5 Allan Donald (S Africa) 788, 6 Wasim Akram (Pakistan) 755, 7 Winston Benjamin (W Indies) 690, 8 Craig McDermott and Merv Hughes (Australia) 678, 10 Angus Fraser (England) 667. — Sapa-AFP

Bellville win WP cricket title for first time

BELLVILLE clinched this season's Western Province Premier League cricket title when they beat Avendale by five wickets at PP Smit Stadium yesterday.

The northern club finished the season strongly with four consecutive victories while Green Point, log leaders for most of the summer, couldn't force the win they needed against Western Province CC at Newlands yesterday, a result which would have sealed them the trophy. It was the first time in their history that Bellville have won the title.

The first semi-final of the Protea one-day competition between Green Point and Fish Hoek takes place today at Stephan Oval while the second semi — against Constantia and Montrose — will be played at Burt Oval next Saturday.

Scores and report on page 28

The front page of the Cape Town Weekend Argus *sports section describes the first-day action at Stellenbosch.*

DAY 37 *March 13*

DURING THE warm-ups this morning those two Australian classics *True Blue* by John Williamson and *Khe Sanh* by Cold Chisel were broadcast over the public address system at the ground. A local radio station, 5FM, who is sponsoring our game against Boland, played my CDs to the masses and had the Aussie squad singing while they worked. It's interesting how a bunch of guys who begged me unmercifully to bury the *True Blue* CD when I first introduced them to the song are now singing the words at every opportunity. Well ... almost every opportunity.

By tea time, we had bowled the opposition out for 155, a score that frankly flattered their ability. We are finding it difficult to understand why a game such as this was scheduled at such a vital stage of the tour, with the second Test just days away. There are many provincial sides we don't get the opportunity to play and they would have provided a much better preparation. The man most responsible for bowling the opposition out today was Glenn McGrath, who captured 4-38 in a workmanlike spell that wouldn't have done his chances of a Test recall any harm at all.

The quote of the day came from the opposition's original 12th man, who had been allowed by Mark Taylor to play in the game after one of their other players became ill after the start of play. Paul Reiffel had bowled unsuccessfully to him for an hour, but during that time Pistol had beaten this poor bloke's bat time and again. Unfortunately, the guy lacked the talent to hit the ball where he wanted – some of us thought he lacked the talent to hit the ball at all. 'You know pal,' said a weary Pistol, 'you should have stayed 12th man.'

To which the indignant batsman came back with: 'Well, who did you expect to be 12th man ... Don Bradman!'

By stumps, we had moved quickly to reach 2-150. Tubs had his first decent hit for a while in compiling 74, which was a good workout for him, and I'm unbeaten on 49. And that was it for the day. By the time the bus pulled into the hotel most of the occupants were well and truly asleep and, inevitably, a quiet night was had by all.

On the attack during the final session of the second day at Stellenbosch.

DAY 38 *March 14*

DAY THREE of the most boring first-class fixture ever staged began with *True Blue* filtering around the oval once more. The boys, patriots all, are now admitting they've begun to take a liking to the lyrics, but unfortunately their singing was curtailed when someone told us the day's play was going to start at 10am. A decision had been made to start today's play half an hour early, but it was a bit of a shame no-one had told the captains. Apparently the umpires wanted to make up for some time that had been lost on day one, but, after some hurried negotiations, everyone agreed 10.30 was as good a starting time as any.

My innings came to a sudden and unexpected end (out lbw) with my total on 71, just when I thought I was in complete control and a century was on offer. I was a little disappointed not to get the three figures but pleased with my footwork and timing. Jonesy reached 20 courtesy of two of the biggest sixes of all time, but his hitting proved to be his undoing, as he spooned a catch to cover point trying to reach the summit of the adjoining mountain ranges. His dismissal was the start of a mini collapse, in which four wickets fell for 20, before Tubs called the 'jam' off, setting Boland 328 to win in about four hours.

During a break in play Maysie, Merv and Warney found a quiet corner where they could sit back and regain their strength.

The boys whipped themselves into a frenzy in the change rooms as we prepared for our quest for victory. Unfortunately, that's not exactly true. In fact, we had Tubs bailed up in the corner of the room and were busily and painfully inflicting revenge for his unpopular (with the team) declaration. In the end, Boland's quest for survival was made a little easier by the slow wicket and some average cricket on our behalf. But we were able to practise our throwing and ducking techniques, after a benevolent spectator handed over two handfuls of acorns (from trees overhanging the boundary) to Merv, who proceeded to sharpen his accuracy on the rest of the team. Within 10 minutes, each player was armed with a pocketful of acorns, and all hell broke loose. Heals copped the biggest barrage, as he was a sitting target and couldn't fight back. And his nose is an easy target for a sniper. During the battle, an umpire was stuck a painless blow and the cricket held up on at least one occasion (so the wicket could be cleared of debris), but, more importantly, we had a few laughs.

Boland managed to dodge most of the missiles, and crawled to 5-132 by the close of play. When the match finally ended, the lads all breathed a sign of relief and immediately headed for the change rooms to pack our bags and channel our thoughts towards the upcoming Test match, which begins at the Newlands Ground in Cape Town in two day's time.

On a sobering note, I'm beginning to get the feeling I've run over a black cat or stepped under a ladder, as my elbow, which I grazed yesterday, has suddenly shown signs of infection. Lindsay took one look at it and put me straight on some antibiotics. He reckons I have an inflamed bursitis and if it's not treated correctly I may miss the Test. I thought initially that our physio had over-reacted and prepared myself for a good night's sleep, but at 11.30pm I called for a doctor, as my elbow had doubled in size and was causing me a lot of discomfort. And the nauseating feeling in my stomach didn't help. After consultation with the doc, a stronger dose of antibiotics was prescribed along with a five-day embargo on alcohol – a tough ask on a tour such as this. As the doctor left, I asked him if he had any solution to Maysie's snoring talents, but he couldn't help me. As my off-spinning colleague drifted off to sleep I could do no more than grimace at the pain from my bung elbow, and listen to another of his symphonies.

DAY 39 *March 15*

I FINALLY did get to sleep, but when I woke this morning I found my arm swollen and shining red due to the infection. The only bonus to come out of this mishap was that the doctor demanded I sit out training this morning. Even though I was unable to go through my paces at training I was there to encourage the lads, although I learned that quite a few complained to Lindsay about my 'inadequate' excuse. They seemed far from happy as I sat there on the sidelines with a smile like a split watermelon.

The boys all seem in good spirits, although one gets the feeling that playing and preparing for cricket in 19 months out of the last 20 has taken its toll physically and mentally. I think at least a few of the team are getting pretty frustrated at continually being away from home. I just hope we can muster the inner strength needed for success in the remaining two Tests. I don't think the South Africans are feeling the strain as much as we are, as they are still in their 'honeymoon' period in international cricket – every tour and Test series for

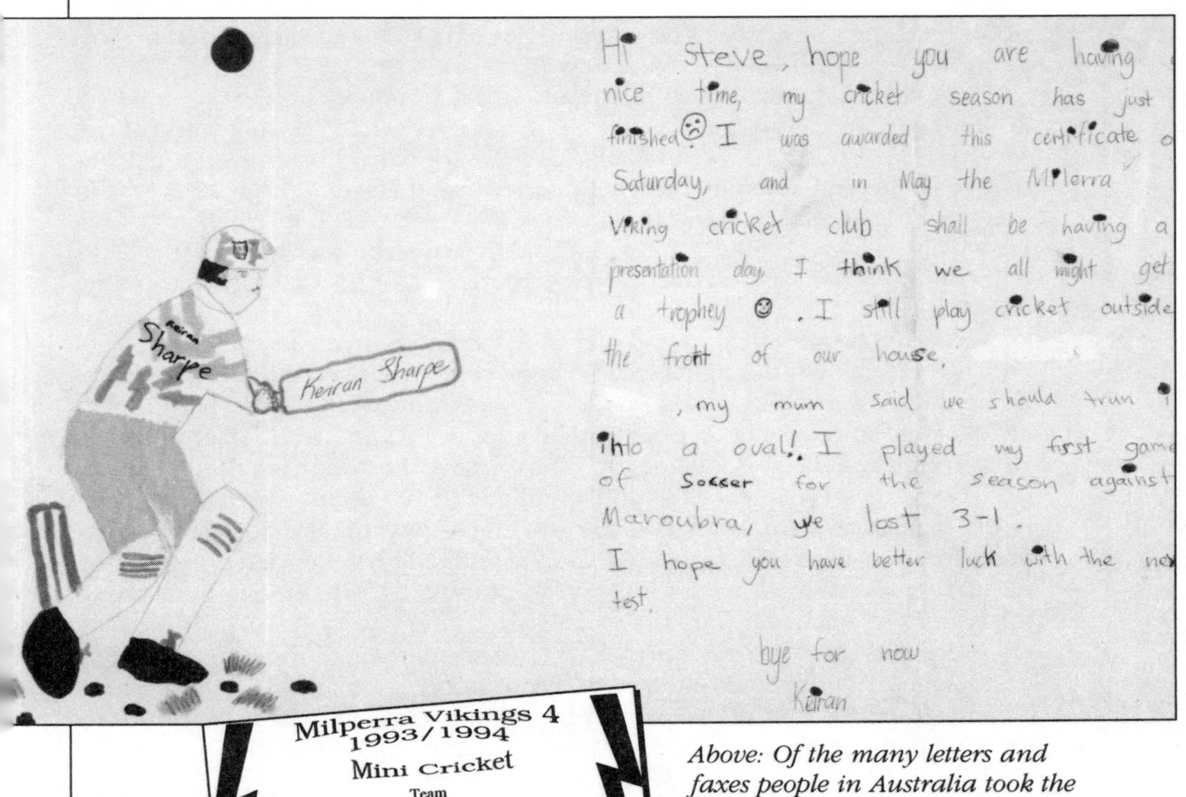

Keiran Sharpe

Keiran Sharpe

Hi Steve, hope you are having
nice time, my cricket season has just
finished ☹ I was awarded this certificate o
Saturday, and in May the Milperra
Viking cricket club shall be having a
presentation day I think we all might get
a trophey ☺. I still play cricket outside
the front of our house,
, my mum said we should turn
into a oval!. I played my first gam
of Soccer for the season against
Maroubra, we lost 3-1.
I hope you have better luck with the ne
test.

bye for now
Keiran

Milperra Vikings 4
1993/1994
Mini Cricket

Team
Stuart Lester, Keiran Sharpe,
Tim Cox, David Raft, Andrew Cook,
Sarah Bariss, Daniel Bariss,
Drew Munro, Bryce Bentley
& Luke Enevoldsen.

Keiran had a run up to rival Craig McDermott with bowling figures to match, taking a total of 8 wickets, with his best figures being 3 for 2. He also backed up his bowling with a total of 125 runs in the season.

Above: Of the many letters and faxes people in Australia took the time to send to the team, one of my favourites came from my next-door neighbour in Sydney, Keiran Sharpe, which included a copy of a certificate (left) he received at the end of his 1993-94 season.

them is a new adventure and each opposing team a whole new experience. It will be interesting to see how they are travelling in 12 months time, when a few injuries occur and mental and physical tiredness start to creep into their game.

In saying the lads are a little homesick, I know we all have immense pride in wearing the baggy green cap and will give it our best shot. And I believe we are a better side – it's just a matter of showing it consistently. Once training had been completed, a short bus trip was required in order to have the famous and fantastic Table Top Mountain as our backdrop for our team photo. The mountain is a glorious sight, a description many people wouldn't associate with us in our pin-striped suits.

We found time for a quick bite to eat back at the pub before our expedition to the top of TableTop Mountain by cable car. This excursion turned into one of the highlights of the tour. The ascent to the top was quite exhilarating, especially as the cabin has no glass in the windows and the climb is almost vertical – a fact that didn't escape Tubs' notice and he began to sweat profusely and curse the rest of us for talking him into coming along. However, moments like these are to be savoured and consequently (and to Tubby's immense displeasure), the taunts came his way thick and fast, with comments such as 'no cable car has ever crashed, one must be due soon' and, 'there's no way we'd survive if the cable snapped and we fell from this height'. Tubs was a relieved man upon reaching the safety of terra firma, but didn't look to flash when he was reminded we still had to get back down.

The outlook from the top of the mountain is outrageous, with views all around the Cape. With the weather being close to perfect, it truly was a scene straight from a postcard. I could have sat there for days checking out the beautiful coastline and adjoining mountain ranges. Matt Hayden thought he was in heaven as he spread himself out on a rock ledge with a 600-metre drop below. He was just trying to take it all in, and didn't realise he was giving Tubs heart palpitations – our vice-captain clearly had visions of his team-mate toppling over the edge.

Matty is a country boy who is very much a nature lover, and he likes to get away and check out the sights whenever he can. This is something I also enjoy doing if the opportunity arises, while there are a few of the lads who appreciate the comforts of the hotel pool and facilities more so than a look around. We were so impressed by the sights on offer that we elected to stay until sunset. And we weren't let down, as a calm engulfed the mountain range. The change in the landscape's appearance as the sun edged towards the horizon was extraordinary, as the sun disappeared and the temperature dropped dramatically. All up, we spent about four hours on top of the mountain enjoying a view of the world we will never forget.

Afterwards, we enjoyed dinner at the world-renowned Cape Town 'Waterfront', where Matt and I overdosed on the seafood extravaganza. I think it was a meal meant for four people, but we tried our best and then waddled off to the taxi rank feeling like we'd swallowed half a dozen bricks each.

DAY 40 *March 16*

WHEN I picked up this morning's paper I discovered I was in serious doubt for tomorrow's second Test because of a spider bite. Apparently it's some errant little arachnid that's caused the infection in my elbow. This, of course, is news to me, and only goes to show that what you read in the papers isn't always what's true but what the reporter thinks will make interesting reading.

The media has not been very kind to the Australian team over the past week. The criticism of the team, especially Merv and Warney, over what went on in the first Test has hardly let up, and we have received continual reminders, by way of feedback from home, that a number of Australian writers and commentators have said we are a team of loud mouths and prima donnas. The severity of the censure has hurt the team badly, and made us all the more determined to do well in the coming Test and put the record straight. That determination was evident at today's training session, where a greater intensity was displayed and a feeling of urgency was evident among the squad.

I feel comfortable with my game and mentally strong, the latter being the most sought after factor at this level of sport. But, after training I had another check-up from the doctor concerning my elbow and he rang the alarm bells by

The Australians prepare to take off on a sometimes scary but always spectacular helicopter flight over Cape Town. The Aussies are: (back row) Glenn McGrath (in sunglasses), Paul Reiffel, Cam Battersby, Tim May (wearing cap), Allan Border; (at front) Dean Jones (second from left), Mark Waugh, Ian Healy, Matt Hayden, myself, Michael Slater, Bob Simpson.

saying there was no way I could play with the infection as it was because I would feel sick and run a high temperature. I immediately told the doc there was no way a high temperature was going to stop me playing in a Test match, so he went to Plan B and sent me to an orthopaedic surgeon for an intravenous injection of a stronger antibiotic. However, the specialist declined in favour of a continuation of the current prescription. Perhaps the medical people think I'm in some doubt for the Test, but I know I'm going to be okay.

When I returned after seeing the specialist, I allowed the hotel hairdresser to attempt a quick haircut , but he didn't give good value for the 30 Rand I was charged. The rest of the afternoon was spent flying around the Cape in Puma Helicopters, courtesy of the local Maritime Services, and the views we had the chance to see were another of the tour's highlights. It was like being in one of those simulated rides at an amusement park and was made all the more thrilling when the chopper's doors were opened, leaving us sitting directly over the edge. One of the most amazing things we learned came when we saw precisely where the Atlantic and Indian Oceans meet – apparently the water in the Atlantic is at least 10 degrees Celsius cooler than the Indian. Then, after an hour in the air taking in this magnificent city and coastline, it was back to the base where a social function in the officers' mess was laid on.

As per usual, a team meeting was conducted the night before the Test, and much emphasis was placed on using the bad press of the last week to our advantage. We need to stick together so we can prove all the doubters wrong. The only change to the XII (apart from the recovered Taylor for the injured Hayden) is McGrath is in for Reiffel – a tough call for the latter but well deserved for the former, who has bowled well of late. After the meeting, instead of having the team dinner at a restaurant, we went only as far as the barbecue area in the hotel, with lobster, fish, and a variety of meats satisfying the boys' hunger. The air among the team is nervous, yet we remain confident. And we are happy that the ACB has finally agreed to a request for single rooms here in Cape Town. Unfortunately, the twins in which we having been sleeping have been far too cluttered for two people to spend 10 days together. So everyone has now got a single, except Maysie and I, as we both prefer some form of company. But our set-up is fine, as the beds are well separated so as to block out the harmful noise disturbances that can permeate from his nostrils.

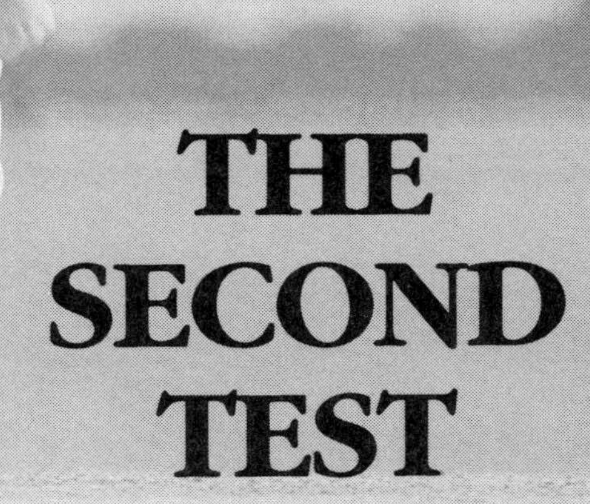

THE SECOND TEST

DAY 41 *March 17*

THANKFULLY THE antibiotics had begun to work on my elbow, with a noticeable decrease in the swelling, but my lower back and buttock are still extremely stiff and sore from my Sun City accident. But there was no question of me even having to undergo a fitness Test.

Newlands is only a short distance from our hotel, and I couldn't help but notice the good spirits of the team as we made the brief journey to this extremely important Test match. Again the importance of the game has been stressed, not only because of the state of the series but also because the way we play during the next five days will show up the character of the team. In a tough decision the selectors opted for three pacemen rather than two spinners, which meant McGrath played instead of May. That decision must have been a toss up, as the wicket hasn't got a lot of grass on it and won't be all that helpful for the quicker bowlers.

We saw the toss as crucial, and the home team won it. Wessels chose to bat, no doubt hoping for a big score that would kill off our chances of victory, and the way we began wouldn't have upset him. Our opening combination of McDermott and Hughes made a disastrous start, and by the first drinks break the scoreboard read 0-66. This was probably the first time I've ever seen both of these guys bowl poorly at the same time – neither were able to gain any rhythm and bowled without fire or consistency. Fortunately, we had a much better second hour with myself and Glenn McGrath stemming the flow of runs and seeing two wickets fall – Gary Kirsten run out and Cronje bowled by McGrath.

A poor lunch was had by all, with a curry the only dish on offer – not exactly what you want with another four hours in the field a possibility. A pasta dish is the preferred option. It appeared the curry had done us few favours,

South African opener Gary Kirsten hooks Glenn McGrath on the opening day of the second Test at Newlands.

The end of Gary Kirsten's first innings ... run out by a quick and athletic pick-up and throw by Michael Slater.

and South Africa were in control at 3-189 when a potentially major turning point in the game occurred. It was a dismissal that brought back memories of the crucial run out of AB in our first innings of the first Test, when Jonty Rhodes had dived full length to stop a ball. Here it was S. Waugh who did pretty much the same thing, diving to stop the shot and then throwing down the stumps from a kneeling position to catch Andrew Hudson centimetres short of his ground. Hudson had just completed an excellent century. A dismissal of this nature tends to lift the fielding side as it is really a bonus wicket. And it also has the effect of annoying the opposition, who see it as a tragic waste – especially if the player dismissed has been 102 not out.

From that moment on we clawed our way back into the game, thanks to some excellent bowling from Norman and Warney and some very good ground fielding. At stumps, the South Africans were 5-237, after a day when honours were evenly shared. Tomorrow morning looms as a crucial section of play, because a total of around 350 would be an excellent result for us, while they no doubt would be hoping for something closer to 450.

After a long day in the field it's a nice change to be able to go back to the dressing sheds and relax in a room that is larger than a reasonably sized bedroom. The rooms here at Newlands are the biggest I've seen, which suits me perfectly as some of my neighbours over the years have been known to complain about my ability to spread my gear over a wide area. But who needs to worry when there's no-one within two metres of my kit bag? I think I could have stayed there forever, but instead decided on a quick feed at the Hard Rock Cafe, followed by a tussle with a pinball machine, before opting for the comfort of the bedsheets.

DAY 42 *March 18*

AFTER LINDSAY had taken us through a full warm-up routine, the vital morning session developed into a tough grafting one, with South African wickets not easy to come by. But, at the same time, they weren't scoring many runs, which was as much as a result of their strangely negative attitude as the quality of our bowling. But perhaps we forced their caution – especially Warney, who was brilliant.

As we walked back on the field after lunch, an announcement was made that the winner of a competition for the 'banner of the day' had gone to one which read, 'The Good, The Bad and The Merv Hughes'. The winning owner or owners earned five cartons of the local brew, Castle Lager, and a loud cheer from the 15,000-strong crowd. Meanwhile, in the middle, the persistence of our efforts in the field was rewarded when the last South African batsman was dismissed with the total on 361. The Australian stars were Warne (three wickets) and McGrath (three), both of whom bowled particularly well considering the large amounts of overs (73.1 between them) they had to deliver.

The South Africans have left the door open for us, as a total of around 500 will have them panicking in their second innings. But first we had to knuckle down and play hard, disciplined cricket, which was something we didn't provide a lot of in the first Test.

Taylor and Slater once again got us off to a solid start, until, with the score on 40, Slats drove too hard at a wide ball and departed, caught in the gully, just when he looked to be getting on top of the bowling. I'm sure a big Michael Slater innings isn't far away, if only he can curb his natural aggressive instincts just a little. However, there were no further dramas before stumps, as Taylor and Boon cruised to 1-112. Tubby looks in ominous touch (from the South Africans' viewpoint), reminiscent of his Ashes '89 form when he scored 839 runs in six Tests.

At the end of the day's play, we were joined in the change rooms by two of our greatest supporters, John Cornell (one of Australia's most successful businessmen, but perhaps best known as Strop from the old Paul Hogan TV shows) and Austin Robertson (AB's manager), who have travelled over here to catch the action. I felt much wearier than I did at stumps yesterday even though I didn't do a thing today other than field through the last part of the South African innings. I'm sure it's much more draining actually watching others guys bat than batting yourself.

DAY 43 *March 19*

AS TODAY was a batting day, we headed straight for the two practice nets this morning, to prepare for what we intended to be a match-winning first-innings total. However, when we arrived we were surprised to find the South Africans wanted one of the nets. This was, no doubt, some form of tactical ploy and one that we will try ourselves when the situation is reversed.

The morning's session was moving along nicely until Tubby was given out caught behind – a decision he wasn't all that pleased about – for a well-made 70. He was soon followed by Junior, who chased a wide delivery and was well caught in the gully, an out that continued his disappointing run in recent Tests. It's hard to work out the reason for his low returns, especially as he is scoring heavily in the fixtures between the main matches. However, I'm sure a big score is just around the corner if he stays positive.

Boon and Border saw us through to the serving of the 'hospital' food at lunch. AB was extremely determined to post a big score. Our captain has been a little on edge lately, probably as a result of the press hounding him for his retirement date, and also the fact we butchered the first Test. He's a man who takes defeat very heavily, which is one of the reasons he is such a great player. Allan Border is so tough and determined. Which he needed to be through the middle session, as the locals' negative field placings and bowling turned the match into a grinding affair. Our batsmen's response was to not give in to such tactics by throwing their hands away, and the two-hour session yielded only 50 runs without the loss of a wicket. It might have been dull, but the efforts of AB and Boonie built a platform for a later assault.

Not long after tea, Boon fell when only a tantalising four runs short of another Test century, which brought me to the crease with the score at 4-244, still 117 runs behind. My start was ideal – the first ball found the middle of the bat and went for four – and from there, while AB gradually wore their bowlers down, I took advantage of my confidence and attacked the bowling. We complemented each other well and added 66 before AB edged an attempted hook shot to the keeper

I was then joined by Heals, who is one of the two blokes in the Aussie team I've had the most success batting with (AB is the other). Heals is a busy cricketer who usually makes something happen and is always willing to try all the shots. He'll attempt to cut a yorker, or hook a bumper off his nose no matter what the situation, and has the ability to swing the match in his team's favour if he gets away with his shots. And this was the case this afternoon especially during the final six overs of the day, which were bowled in 'overtime' after the South Africans were unable to get through their 90 allotted overs by the scheduled finishing time. Sensing their bowlers were jaded, we took 30 more runs from them, and now need just 27 more before we can begin establishing a first-innings lead.

We see ourselves as being in the box seat, and intend tomorrow to put the match beyond our opponent's reach. I finished the day 50 not out and in the kind of form I must make the most of. I dined tonight in my room with my unbeaten batting partner and, while sampling the hotel's pasta and milkshakes, discussed the possible outcomes of the game. We've decided we're going to win.

David Boon lofts Gary Kirsten for four during his first innings of 96 at Newlands.

DAY 44 *March 20*

THE DAY after the media reported I had been bitten by a spider and was consequently in doubt for the Test, a fan sent me 18 red roses. By this morning, despite my best efforts, they were beginning to wilt, and I just hoped that wasn't an omen for today's play. I was also intrigued by an interesting quote from Fanie de Villiers that appeared in this morning's paper. He suggested we should declare now so Kepler could set us a target tomorrow afternoon! He must have been joking – from our side of the fence we see ourselves building a big first-innings lead and the game ending in an Australian victory – and I'm sure if the two sides' positions at the start of play today had been reversed the South Africans wouldn't have even thought of adopting such a benevolent strategy. Sometimes a statement such as de Villiers' can be very beneficial to a side, as it spurs them on to greater deeds. I know in this case it made us just that little bit more determined.

When play began, Heals and I continued to build a useful partnership, with our keeper playing the more dominant role in a partnership that eventually yielded 118 runs – beating an Australian record for the sixth wicket which has stood since 1910-11. The stand was ended by the fourth ball of the last over before the lunch break, which Heals hit to mid-wicket, and then, as if to underline the impact of that dismissal, Merv was trapped lbw by the following ball.

The lunch-time spaghetti bolognaise didn't provide me with the necessary impetus to bring up my century because, when I was 86 and the total 7-430, I became Craig Matthews' fourth wicket after a ball skidded through low and crept under my bat. The hundred was a milestone I was keen to achieve, especially this time as I felt I batted as well as I ever have. Unfortunately, the remainder of our batting offered only token resistance and our first-innings lead was restricted to 74.

The best for the South Africans were the ever reliable Matthews, who exploited the conditions well for a five-wicket haul, and de Villiers, who, despite not feeling well, gave his usual 110 per cent in a 44.4-over spell. I could never imagine Fanie giving anything less than his very best, just as I could never have believed something else that *did* occur today. Jonty Rhodes misfielded – which must be a very rare experience for this freak of a fieldsman. Without doubt Rhodes' greatest ability is being able to make great angles while coming in to field the ball. His judgement is uncanny, and because of this he is able to get to balls that would evade any other fieldsman and catch batsmen off guard if they don't anticipate his early arrival onto the moving ball. Hence, his ability to create run out chances and save runs.

Before we returned to the field for the South Africans' second innings, we gathered around and reinforced to each other the fact the game was there to be won if we really wanted it badly enough. However, for most of the afternoon we couldn't get the breakthroughs we needed, and into the last hour the locals had reached 1-69 and the point where many at the ground thought the match was destined to become another boring draw. But we still believed a result was possible, and when I had Cronje caught and bowled with probably my best catch in Test cricket, we gave ourselves a chance of forcing a collapse. We always feel Cronje is the man we need to get out to make things happen.

The impact of Cronje's dismissal was emphasised 25 runs later when, unbe-

The Australians celebrate the final wicket of the fourth day – nightwatchman de Villiers, lbw Warne, 0.

lievably, another run out occurred, with the third umpire ruling Wessels had his bat on the line after Border had done some brilliant work at mid-wicket. That took the run out total to five in two Tests, a staggering number, and especially significant when considering the batsmen involved (Mark Waugh, Border, Gary Kirsten, Hudson and now Wessels) and the way each of the run outs have altered the nature of the contest. To help us along, Wessels gave his surviving partner, Hudson, a serve on the way past which seemed to affect the opener's composure. It came as no surprise when Hudson, with his concentration shot, went three runs later, lbw to an S. Waugh slower ball, to complete a trifecta of wickets that completely changed the course of the match. We could sense victory and, aided by some excellent bowling and field placements, went in for the kill. Warney struck twice in the dying moments, giving him three wickets, to shatter a South African line-up whose batsmen late in the day had looked like they were going to the gallows. The end result was a scoreline of 6-100, leaving the home team with a fragile lead of just 26 runs. For a change, today's winning banner had been quite appropriate – 'It Ain't Over Till The Fat Man Spins'.

Believing in yourself is a major factor at this level and was something we all did today. We somehow knew it was going to go our way, as if a sixth sense was taking over. Now we must forge on for victory tomorrow. There was further good news waiting for the Bluebag contingent (Taylor, Slater, M. Waugh, S. Waugh and McGrath) when we reached the change rooms – a further six Sheffield Shield points had been won via an outright win over Queensland. This means a final against Tassie, but perhaps even more enjoyable, the knowledge that the Maroons are now the owners of the wooden spoon. This might be undeserved, but it's still a fact we won't let Messrs Border, Healy, Hayden and McDermott miss out on too often.

Philadelphia was the replacement movie for Slats, Matty, Heals, Norman and myself, after our first choice at the cinema, *Schindler's List*, was fully booked, and it turned out to be an adequate fill-in as we made our way through a mountain of junk food in the neck-paralysing front-row seats.

DAY 45 *March 21*

I TOSSED and turned all night, finally giving in at 7am when I took an early shower. But before I stepped under the water, I checked the weather and was much relieved to find not a cloud in the sky. Rain appeared to be the major obstacle in our quest for victory. At the ground, we did no more than a light routine of stretching and catching before play began, and when we did take our places in the field we had immediate success, as I trapped McMillan in front in the third over of the morning. AB had considered the way the wicket was playing and decided that I, rather than our frontline quicks, was most suited to aid Warney. The ball wasn't bouncing a lot, a factor that always helps me as I'm more of a 'skidder' style of bowler rather than a 'bang it in' type such as Merv, who appreciates wickets with more bounce and lift in them.

Just when we thought the game was in the bag and it was only a matter of time before we could start celebrating, the South African pair of Rhodes and Richardson dug deep and kept us wicketless for the remainder of the morning session. Having played quite a bit against these guys recently, it is obvious they are an under-rated bunch of cricketers whose greatest asset, without question, is their 'never say die' attitude. Such was the solidity of this eighth-wicket stand, the Australian end of the lunch room was fairly quiet. We were at a point where we realistically had only a session in which to take the remaining three wickets so we would have enough time left to score the required runs.

After the break, AB once again put his faith in Warney and me, although I felt my body was beginning to tire. But I knew I had a great opportunity to help us win the Test, so I put my weariness to one side. The South African's stubborn resistance continued for a further 25 minutes, when AB decided on a change bringing McGrath on for Warne, and it did the trick. In his second over, McGrath enticed Richardson into chasing a wide delivery and the subsequent faint edge ended, much to the delight of all the Australians, in the safe hands of Healy. The scoreboard now read 8-164, a lead for the home team of 90.

AB must have thought I had no more to offer, because he informed me Merv would be coming on at my end. But I insisted on one more over, as I had a good feeling about it. Not only did he give me another chance, but acting on his own instincts, AB moved himself into a catching position at mid-wicket. I knew nothing of the move, and couldn't believe it when he pulled off a great catch next ball to put paid to Rhodes' determined innings. There is often a fine line between luck and skill, although this was a great piece of captaincy by a man who has never been afraid to do something unusual in order to pick up the wicket.

At this moment in time I was faced with a major dilemma. Should I try to take my fifth wicket of the innings and pay the price for doing so – Merv promised he would hug and kiss me if I accomplished the feat – or be happy with four. Two balls later, I shattered Donald's stumps to complete my best ever bowling analysis in Tests, 5-28 off 22.3 overs, statistics I would never have thought possible. Jonesy turned up with a nice surprise 10 minutes later when he handed me the match ball – a nice touch, especially as he had to run down to the umpires' room to retrieve it. It's acts like this that bond a team that little bit closer.

With 91 runs to win and the lessons learned during the Sydney Test debacle

Times Sport

20 • TUESDAY, MARCH 22 1994

● CRICKET

Aussies square it

By GUY HAWTHORNE

ANOTHER mini-collapse, which epitomised SA's batting fortunes during the second cricket Test at Newlands, ended their faint hopes of a draw as Australia cantered to a comfortable nine-wicket win to level the series 1-1 yesterday.

SA batted poorly on Sunday to give Australia the edge. But although they had one foot on the podium, Allan Border's side still had to take that final step.

The loss by SA of their last three wickets yesterday in just five balls, and without the addition of a run, earned Australia the richly-deserved laurels.

Bowled out for just 164 shortly after lunch, SA left Australia requiring 91 for victory. That they achieved just before 4pm for the loss of vice-captain Mark Taylor.

SA resumed Monday on 100/6, an effective lead of just 26, and when Brian McMillan was trapped lbw by Steve Waugh in the sixth over of the morning, the match looked like being all over before lunchtime.

Wicketkeeper Dave Richardson and Jonty Rhodes gave the 6 346 spectators a glimmer of hope with a gutsy 61-run eighth wicket partnership that, although painfully slow, improved SA's chances of salvaging a draw they hardly deserved.

Rhodes, who had resumed on one, faced 79 deliveries before he reached double figures and the first time the ball was hit to the boundary — four byes had earlier come off Shane Warne — was in the 24th over of the morning when Richardson smashed a drive through the covers off Craig McDermott.

By lunch, with SA on 153/7, Australia were looking anxious. Eight overs later, however, their trepidation turned to delight.

Glenn McGrath and medium-paced seamer Steve Waugh had, somewhat surprisingly, had been asked by Border to share the new ball at the expense of regular opening pair McDermott and Merv Hughes.

The impressive McGrath, who bowled tidily throughout the Test, made the vital breakthrough when Richardson, on 31 and in good nick, needlessly threw his bat at a wide delivery and edged a simple catch to wicketkeeper Ian Healy.

SA were suddenly 164/8 and Australia, sensing victory, went for the jugular.

In the very next over, from Waugh, Rhodes, on 27, clipped the ball away to the on side where Border, who had moved in from regulation midwicket to short midwicket, snapped up the chance.

Two balls later, without further addition to the score, Allan Donald played down the wrong line and his stumps were shattered by Waugh, whose second innings return of 22.3-9-28-5 and his fine 86 in Australia's first innings earned him the man-of-the-match award.

After the loss of Taylor for 14, Michael Slater (43no), who passed the 2 000 run mark in Test cricket, and David Boon (32no) knocked off the required runs with a minimum of fuss.

THE WINNER! . . . Australian opener Michael Slater hits the winning runs to make the series all square at 1-1 at Newlands yesterday. Dave Richardson is the SA wicketkeeper. Picture: ANNE LAING

OUT! . . . The stumps are shattered as South Africa's Allan Donald is clean bowled by Australia's Steve Waugh at Newlands yesterday. Picture: ANNE LAING

SECOND TEST SCORECARD

Result: Australia won by nine wickets.

Australia's Steve Waugh, the 'Man of the Match' of the second Test. Picture: ANNE LAING

SA squad is left unchanged

THE convener of the national selectors, Peter Pollock, yesterday announced that the same 13-man squad for the Newlands Test will do duty for South Africa in the third and deciding test against the touring Australians, starting in Durban on Friday.

The SA squad is: Kepler Wessels (capt), Hansie Cronje (vice-capt), Andrew Hudson, Gary Kirsten, Peter Kirsten, Jonty Rhodes, Brian McMillan, Dave Richardson, Craig Matthews, Fanie de Villiers, Allan Donald, Eric Simons, Tim Shaw.

● RUGBY

Chiat comes in for injured Stransky

By IAN GAULT

VILLAGER flyhalf Anton Chait was yesterday called into the Norwich Western Province team for tonight's Ford M-Net night series clash against Transvaal at Ellis Park.

Chait, who played four games for WP in 1989 and two last year, takes over from the injured Joel Stransky and will also assume the goal kicking duties. The Villager player had a solid game for his club on Saturday, landing two dropped goals, a penalty and a conversion in their 26-11 win over UCT.

WP coach Alan Zondagh said yesterday that the late change was a disruptive influence but the sort of thing that can happen at any stage of a season. It was better that Stransky sit this one out and give himself 10 days to be fully restored to fitness. It automatically means that Stransky will miss Friday's final, should WP beat Transvaal tonight.

"Joel is not happy to play with an injury like this and though his hamstring injury is better than it was, it is not good enough to withstand the pressures of a game like this," said Zondagh.

While tonight's game is being billed as the "real" final, rather that that which is due to be on Friday between tonight's winners, it's worth remembering that WP beat Transvaal 42-32 the last time the two sides met. That was at Newlands in September last year, admittedly when Transvaal were already assured of a place in the Bankfin Currie Cup final.

Teams

● ATHLETICS

'Hungry' SA team set off for Hungary

. . . ual South African cross . . . es out to Hungary today . . . etermination and pur- . . . test their ability . . . untry athletes in . . . Snickers IAAF . . . ips in Buda- . . . ined to im- . . . g inaugural . . . that cross . . . stepped in to rescue the South African team means that the full compliment of 27 (nine senior men and six of each of the senior and junior women and junior men) will board the flight via Frankfurt to Budapest.

Last year South Africa were tipped as possible gold medallists in the women's championship but below-par performances by Gwen Griffiths and, to a lesser extent, Colleen de Reuck, saw them edged . . . margin.

This year South Africa's chances do not appear as favourable. True, Elana Meyer and Zola Pieterse are there and will both be determined to at least match their performances last year (Pieterse placed fourth and Meyer sixth).

But the unavailability of De Reuck (who has been in great form) and the omission of Griffiths, whose illness on the day of the trial proved no mitigating factor for the selectors, places a question mark over . . .

● SOCCER

Full house for Hellenic?

By HERMAN GIBBS

THE last time Hellenic played Kaizer Chiefs in the NSL First Division log-leaders three seasons ago, Athlone Stadium was packed to capacity.

On Saturday, Hellenic, the current league log-leaders, meet the Amakhosi at the Rand Stadium and the afternoon contest again has the potential to attract a capacity crowd.

A fortnight ago, almost 75 000 spectators watched Chiefs lift the BP Top 8 trophy with a 3-2 victory over defending league champions Sundowns. Chiefs were unable to repeat that performance over the weekend and eventually relied on an own goal to see them home against Bloemfontein Celtic.

Chiefs, under Frenchman Philippe Troussier, the former Ivory Coast national coach, suffered a shock setback in their opening league fixture against Vaal Professionals and have since dropped another point after three league outings.

Budgie Byrne is back at . . . after a three-week UK sojourn. This is just the sort of contest he'll savour to announce that he's back in the 'office.'

Lanky Zambian striker, Wedson Nyirenda, has emerged as a key player in the Amakhosi line-up and his two headed goals in Chiefs' Top 8 triumph were arts of sheer class.

Byrne is not one to send his charges onto the pitch without doing his homework and Nyirenda can bet on being a closely marked man at the Rand Stadium on Saturday.

Cape coaches usually don't have a problem working out a strategy for encounters against Chiefs. The good old fashioned approach of first-time tackling has often reduced the mighty Amakhosi to the ordinary.

● Cape Town Spurs, following their 1-0 away victory over Vaal Pros last Sunday, return to local action against Wits University at Athlone Stadium on Friday night.

Albertyn in great form

English soccer

The back page of the Cape Times *of March 22 recalls the final day at Newlands.*

not forgotten, we set out in search of the target aggressively and completed it for the loss of only Tubs, to give us a stunning nine-wicket victory. This is a win that I'm sure will provide us with the necessary impetus to win the next Test in Durban and so wrap up the series.

Having won the Man of the Match award, I had to face the press with AB immediately after the Test was won. When the questions had all been asked, we returned to the dressing room where the team congregated around Boonie, who had perched himself up on top of two coffins in readiness for the team's victory song, which he always leads us in. It was sung with a passion I haven't experienced before, so much so I had goose bumps all over my body. At that moment, I was very proud to be an Aussie.

From this point, the celebrations became more raucous, with the lyrics of *Khe Sanh* getting a hammering from the lads, especially Slats, who fancies himself as a man with abundant musical talent. He's a sorely mistaken lad indeed. Two hours later the team was still gathered in a small section of the room, singing victory songs and loving every minute of it – a complete reversal of the Wanderers rooms two weeks earlier. A party had been organised back at the hotel in preparation for our victory, but in fact turned out to be a pretty tame affair as the lads were exhausted from the dressing-room celebrations and the mental tiredness that resulted from watching and playing today.

However, at least one humorous incident occurred after we arrived back from the ground. Because the ugly process of packing bags had to be completed tonight (they go to the airport before we do and therefore have to be in reception early tomorrow morning), the boys set out to gather all their belongings together, and get them down to the front desk. Boonie, who may have been influenced by a drop or two of alcohol, was feeling pretty pleased with himself after accomplishing this impressive task, and chose not to annoy the porter's desk. Instead, he began carrying his three bags down the hallway and was just about to enter the reception area when he was confronted by a member of the hotel staff, who informed him: 'You can't take them any further, Mr Boon.'

To which the tough little Tasmanian replied: 'It's all right, mate, I just have to go around the corner with them.'

But the hotel employee wouldn't budge. 'Please, Mr Boon,' he said, 'you cannot take your bags into the reception area.'

By this stage, Boonie was getting a little hot under the collar. After all, he was just trying to do the bloke a favour. 'Why,' he asked, 'can't I take them any further?'

'Because Mr Boon,' our intrepid hero was told, 'you only have your boxer shorts on.'

At this moment, Boonie realised he had met his match and scurried back to the safety of his room, glowing the same colour as the Cabernet Sauvignon he had been consuming a little earlier.

THE THIRD TEST

DAY 46 *March 22*

I WOKE up this morning not feeling all that sprightly – hardly a real surprise after the events of the previous evening. The only consolation was that I wasn't the only one slightly off colour. We were scheduled to depart for the airport at 8.30am, for a two and a half hour flight to Durban, which was a concept that didn't thrill me all that much. I searched for a saviour, and discovered the airport's 'Juicy Lucy's', where a toasted sandwich and bacon-and-egg burger did the trick.

The last thing our fragile states needed on our arrival in Durban was a welcoming committee, but one had been organised, complete with a traditional rickshaw ride to our hotel for each member of the party. My new roomie is Glenn McGrath, who has successfully achieved what everyone had considered impossible – he is now recognised as a greater menace than Merv. The lad is a natural. I tried in vain to catch a few hours of shut eye, but Norman had other ideas and proceeded to toss a variety of implements in my direction in a bid to keep me from achieving my goal. All I could do was accept my lot in life, until finally my patience won the day as my beloved new roomie eventually succumbed to his own tiredness and drifted off to sleep.

For a city the size of Durban, which has a population of two and a half million people, there appears to be a distinct lack of quality restaurants. As social director, I sent my scouts out in search of a decent feed, but did not receive a single positive report from any team member. An assault on what was supposed to be a top-notch Chinese restaurant turned out to be yet another disaster, with the product turning out to be only marginally better than a quick take-away. We did learn, to be fair, that many of the establishment's employees were on strike. It seemed pretty clear the chef was one of them.

Earlier in the day, Warney and Heals had gone shopping in town and purchased a roulette wheel and blackjack kit, which they tested out on the boys tonight. The only big winner was Jonesy, who walked away 1000 Rand richer after a run of superb hands at the blackjack table. There was a point during Jonesy's golden run when the owners of the portable casino, who doubled as bankers, were sweating profusely and trying to work out whether selling their cricket kits would bring enough for them to be able to pay off their gambling debts.

Later in the night, just before Norman decided I could get some sleep, I rang home to catch up on all the news and learned that Lynette had rescued a bird that had been run over. After a couple of veterinary bills, the 'poor little fellow' had recovered sufficiently and is soon to be returned to the bush, no doubt to make room for the next stranded animal Lynette stumbles upon.

DAY 47 *March 23*

A SEVEN o'clock wake-up call would normally be an unthinkable act on a day off, but this morning it was a must, as it was the only time we could arrange a game at the highly rated Durban Country Club golf course.

When we reached the course we had to organise teams, arrange clubs and pick out a caddy, someone every golfer must hire as it provides employment for quite a few people. My man was a gentleman by the name of Harry Mathamuthulu, who has been a caddy at this course for over 50 years. I thought I was on to something – with that sort of experience I figured I'd be able to read the greens and avoid the pitfalls of a difficult layout. So with great enthusiasm I teed up on the first with my partner Heals, to take on the formidable duo of Junior and McGrath. Eighteen holes later, despite the best efforts of my caddy, we'd been soundly thrashed, but we'd all had an entertaining time on a course that exceeded our expectations.

In the afternoon, the team's mobile casino was back into action, with the bankers keen to recoup some of the lost loot of last night. They found the travelling press contingent just the men to achieve their objective. Then, as the last of the press boys' banknotes was handed over, it was decided a Nerds v Julios clash was long overdue, and a re-match of the titanic 1993 ten-pin bowling clash at Manchester was scheduled for tonight. The Nerds retain bitter memories of their shock loss on that occasion, and for this contest Tubby took over the captaincy from Maysie, to lead a new-look outfit consisting of S. Waugh, Reiffel, McGrath and Lindsay Tregar. But sadly, we weren't up to the task and went down by the embarrassing margin of 150 pins to the combination of Warne, M. Waugh, Jones and Slater. What was disappointing was the behaviour of the victors, who carried on like good sorts when the result became obvious.

With David Boon (left) an observer, Messrs Warne (centre) and Healy seek bets at their makeshift blackjack table.

After such a heavy mauling, I was keen to make amends and headed for the putt putt course. Unfortunately, our aim was no better here, but a few laughs were had as Warney, after a succession of poor putts, attempted to reshape his putter on the framework surrounding the holes. Next stop in our action-packed night was the pinball machines where I finally achieved a victory, over a very physical Glenn McGrath, who tends to become emotional about his poor performances and likes to take out his frustrations on the machine.

A different type of night such as tonight's activities may seem childish (and probably is) but it helps relax the players, promotes team spirit, and ensures that a few laughs are had between the guys.

DAY 48 *March 24*

WE WERE back to the serious stuff this morning with a net session designed to get us into the right frame of mind for the third Test match, which begins tomorrow at the Kingsmead ground in Durban. The team is fairly settled with the exception of Merv, who looks a doubtful starter on his recent form, although I hope it's not forgotten that he can always be relied upon, especially when the going is tough.

I'm confident of doing well, a feeling that goes right back to the 47 not out I managed in the second innings of the third Test, at Trent Bridge during the '93 Ashes series in England, when I batted through the final session with Brendon Julian to save the match. I really believe that knock turned my career around. At that point of my career I had something I needed to prove to myself – in that innings I achieved what I was looking for – and suddenly I felt a type of inner strength or belief that might have been missing. Ever since, that inner strength has given me the confidence to do well every time I walk onto a cricket field.

Unfortunately, my body has not responded well to the added responsibilities of having to bowl a lot of overs recently. My old ailment – shin splints – has flared up again, while the back problems that resulted from the kick in the back at the Sun City waterslide refuses to go away. With a need to stretch out and loosen up, the swimming pool was the most obvious place to try and remedy the situation, and I followed that with a sports massage that improved the situation dramatically.

The afternoon was spent walking along the beach-side promenade opposite the hotel, where we had the pleasure of watching Matt Hayden perform, in his own words, 'a couple of radical manoeuvres' on the waves. Matt was in the water with his new found surfing mate – former number five in the world Pierre Tostee. As Durban has a large number of Indians among its population, it is impossible to walk anywhere without being recognised. This can sometimes be a hassle but generally is okay, as long as the people are polite – which they are here.

At one point, Merv was confronted by a local, who commented: 'Gee, Merv, it's great to see you in Durban. It's just a pity we didn't get a chance to see you play when you were at your peak!'

An ego-damaging line if ever there was one!

Tonight, the team meeting was one of the briefest on record. The main theme coming through was that we had to continue to play the aggressive but patient cricket we had performed so profitably in the second Test. We all realise we have a genuine chance to pull off something special – to win a series away from home against world-class opposition. Another barbecue-style dinner was held, as we enjoyed the ocean views from the Beverley Hills Hotel. All the guys are in good spirits – even Merv, who had earlier been informed he had been excluded from the XII for this game and replaced by his good mate Paul Reiffel.

Before retiring for the night, I received a call from Jo'burg from a great friend of the team, John Coutis, who's just arrived in South Africa. Johno, as we know him, is a guy who has no legs, but he still manages to live a fuller life than many able-bodied people. We first crossed paths two years ago and have become very good mates.

The fact Johno's here in South Africa is a story in itself. He was at the recent one-day finals in Sydney and happily celebrated our victory with a few ales. Also there that night was John Cornell, who was so impressed with Johno's zest and attitude to life that he insisted on paying for him to join up with the touring party in South Africa. Johno's always an inspiration to the people around him – it will be great to catch up with him when he arrives in Durban tomorrow.

It's not always easy to concentrate on this diary with the Atlantic Ocean and the beach at Durban so close to the team hotel.

DAY 49 *March 25*

OUR 12TH MAN was announced after the warm-ups, with the tough decision as to who played favouring Paul Reiffel over Tim May. The wicket has a good covering of grass which should aid our seam bowlers, especially Pistol, as he hits the seam with every ball he delivers.

There may have been a special significance in the toss that preceded the start of play. In what we believe will probably be his last Test match (although he hasn't officially told anyone) AB called unsuccessfully. That made it three tosses to South Africa in a row and, not surprisingly, we were given first use of the wicket to bat on. The morning sky was very overcast, and that, plus the grass on the pitch, obviously influenced Wessels' decision to send us in.

The South Africans achieved the early breakthrough they craved when Taylor was leg before to Allan Donald for one. This was a critical setback for us, as Tubs is rarely dismissed in the opening overs and is the player the rest of us tend to bat around. His solid and steady accumulation of runs is usually the perfect complement to our slightly more aggressive approach. Midway through the session came another blow, when Slats was out trying to demolish an advertising board on the point boundary. Unfortunately, he picked the wrong person to hit to – Jonty Rhodes, who paroles this region like a predator. But we managed to reach the safety of the lunch interval without further loss, and hoped the 40-minute break would allow the remaining moisture to evaporate from the pitch.

In fact, the only other pre-lunch damage inflicted was to Boonie's reproductive organs, where an Allan Donald thunderbolt caused a deal of pain. The only relief our physio could offer was by way of an ice pack ... very carefully applied. This type of injury always gets a few laughs at the time, but can be very serious, and this blow was severe enough for Boonie to require medical attention after the close of play.

After lunch, our comfortable position crumbled as Boon, Border and M. Waugh fell within the hour, leaving the score at a sorry 5-123 and both Heals and myself at the wicket without a run to our names. This was something of a crisis, but in typical Healy fashion, his aggressive attitude took over and the score grew rapidly. Heals' approach always gives the bowler the feeling a wicket could fall at any time, but our keeper is a much better player than that impression implies. Our partnership blossomed and was worth 92 when, just when we thought all the hard work had been done, Heals unluckily played a shortish length ball onto his body and then back onto the stumps. The remaining 20 minutes were negotiated safely by Pistol and myself, in conditions that should have seen us go off for bad light. However, I shouldn't complain as I reached my 50 off the final ball – a performance I was pleased with, especially as it was so important for the team.

Today's crowd was extremely disappointing considering the build-up to the Test, but totally understandable when matters not directly related to cricket were explained. The Zulus held a march through town this afternoon and trouble was expected, so most of the locals took the safer option and stayed indoors. Our schedule (and our concentration on the cricket) has been such that it is easy to believe that there is little trouble around. We've hardly seen any direct evidence of a disturbance, and if something has occurred, we have been diverted away from it. But we were brought down to earth today when instructed, for our own safety's sake, not to venture more than 200 metres from the hotel.

With this advice firmly in mind, Maysie, Johno and I headed off for dinner at a nearby Chinese restaurant. The restaurant was just down the road, but it was too far away for Johno to manage without his skateboard, which he left in the room. So Maysie and I each grabbed an arm and carried him down the promenade. You couldn't help but notice the disbelieving eyes on passers-by, but we set them straight by explaining that Johno was no more than proof the local surf was unsafe. Look what the sharks had done to him!

South Africa's fastest bowler, Allan Donald.

Day 50 *March 26*

AFTER A quick warm-up routine this morning, it was straight to the nets, where I had a reasonably lengthy hit up – something I like to do if I'm straight in at the commencement of play. The first session loomed as a crucial one for Australia, as a score of around 350 would put us in the box seat, while anything less than 300 would not be satisfactory. But, from our overnight score of 6-241, a steady flow of wickets found our eventual total 31 runs shy of 300, which was, of course, extremely disappointing. My contribution ended at 64, well short of what I wanted but my long term plans had been ruined by the falling of wickets around me

Although I believed we needed around 350, our total was still competitive if our bowlers started well, but unfortunately that didn't happen and the much under-rated opening pair of Hudson and Gary Kirsten took to the inconsistent bowling. Things weren't looking good until, with the penultimate ball before tea, a Reiffel off-cutter trapped Hudson lbw to give us some hope, although the 1-100 scoreline was not we'd been hoping for.

Even with Hudson's demise, we were still far from happy as we made our way to the pavilion for the tea break. However, a banner caught our eye that lifted our spirits a little. It read: 'A bad day at cricket is better than a good day at work.'

After a poor opening spell (which was at least in part due to a knee injury) Billy came bouncing back after tea with a tremendous, sustained burst of high-quality pace bowling. He completely out-pointed Cronje and dismissed Wessels, to prove he is among the pace-bowling elite when in peak form. The rest of our frontline bowlers also fought back magnificently and the net result was a meagre 43 runs from 32 overs and at a cost of two wickets, in the final session. And we felt we bowled without luck! Cronje remains not out and something of a danger man, but the home team lost a lot of the initiative this afternoon. These two hours were crucial for us, as the bowling and fielding not only stemmed the run flow but also showed we were willing to give it everything we possibly had to ensure a victory or draw was going to come our way. In recent years, our away form (with the exception of the '89 and '93 Ashes series in England) hasn't been good, but we are all very keen to correct this imbalance and set the record straight with a few Aussie journalists who only seem to recognise our defeats and dismiss our victories.

Tonight was a very quiet affair, as the team gathered its physical and mental resources for a vital day tomorrow. However, before we retired for the night, the Blues contingent in the tour party gathered to send the team our best wishes via a fax, before the start of the Sheffield Shield final against Tasmania in Sydney.

Shane Warne appeals for lbw against Andrew Hudson, who followed up his century at Cape Town with a half century in his only innings at Durban.

DAY 51 *March 27*

THE DAY started on a bright note, with news from back home that my Sydney club Bankstown/Canterbury looks like wrapping up the first-grade final against Parramatta. This is a triumph that means as much to me as any other victory by a team I'm directly involved in.

More good news followed, for when I stepped outside I was greeted by an overcast sky, which should help the quicker bowlers in their quest for swing. When play began, Cronje, obviously stung by media criticism of the home team's slow batting, adopted a much more positive approach but, ironically, this aggression led to his downfall. With his score on 26, he attempted to hit Warney over the infield but instead spooned a catch to me at backward point to give us the perfect start to the day. Then, only a couple of overs later, an incident took place that may eventually turn out to be the turning point in the game.

The score was 4-157 and Jonty Rhodes had scored just 2, when he fended at a Warne delivery and appeared to edge a catch, via his pad, to Boonie close in on the off side. The only problem was that Boonie not only had the ball in his hand, but also a few blades of grass, and this led to the fieldsman not being 100 per cent sure whether or not it was a fair catch. That indecision prompted the umpires to give a verdict in favour of the batsman, although Ian Healy is positive the catch was fair.

With this controversial moment behind them, Rhodes and Peter Kirsten began to slowly turn the match back in the home team's favour, until I trapped Kirsten lbw with the score on 256. Then, in the last over before tea, another strange event took place. The last ball before the interval was a no ball from Warne to Rhodes, which the South African smashed to the boundary while Warney cried in anguish at having to bowl another ball and at the same time take up some more of our precious 20 minute tea break. However lady luck smiled upon us, because the next ball, a flipper, beat a casual looking defensive prod and trapped Rhodes lbw for 78. This was a breakthrough we sorely needed, and it left South Africa only five runs ahead with four wickets still in hand.

But, alas, this proved to be our last success of the day. After coming into this series with a string of low scores to his name, Brian McMillan has proved to be something of a stumbling block for us, and in the final session he once again proved his mettle by managing to bat through, with the under-rated keeper/batsman David Richardson, until bad light intervened before the scheduled end of play. The score at stumps was 6-322, which meant just 179 runs had been scored in the day.

In summing up the day, I thought we bowled particularly well without having anything run our way. McDermott bowled magnificently – the best I've seen from him for many years – without reaping rewards for his hard work. I bowled a lot more overs than I've been used to in previous series (17 overs for the return of 1-34), and right at the moment I feel like I've been run over by a Mack truck.

This is not exactly how I would like to feel with four more one-dayers still to come after this Test match, and then a quick trip to Sharjah. The squad for that Sharjah tournament was announced today, and there were a few surprises.

Out of the present team are Hayden and Hughes (dropped), Border (unavailable), and McDermott and Healy (injured), with the incoming players being Michael Bevan from NSW, Western Australia's Justin Langer and Victoria's Damien Fleming. We're all pretty stunned that there is no specialist keeper in the squad. Damien has also been chosen to link up with us before the next one-dayer to be played in East London, because Billy is flying home immediately after the finish of this Test to have an operation on his knee. With AB unavailable, the new captain is Mark Taylor, and I have the honour of being vice-captain.

Without doubt, Matthew Hayden is extremely unlucky to have been dropped. His statistics over the past three years have been outstanding, particularly this season in the Sheffield Shield where he totalled a phenomenal 1136 runs (including seven centuries and a 96 not out) in just six games. Hopefully, he'll get a chance in the last four one-dayers to prove a point, as the rest of the team are fully behind him and hope he does well.

This evening's meal, at a nearby Italian Restaurant, was courtesy of John Cornell and Austin Robertson, and the former kept us amused with stories of his days as the character Strop on *The Paul Hogan Show.*

DAY 52 *March 28*

WE HAD an early start today, as we were obliged to make up the 30 minutes of play lost the previous evening. Turning a day's play into six and a half hours may seem only a small change, but I can assure you it's very noticeable when you're in the field all day. Ironically, heavy overnight rain and menacing clouds hovering above suggested the start might be delayed, but the sun burst through the clouds shortly before the amended starting time and play began as planned.

The morning session loomed as a crucial period in the game, as we needed to wrap the innings up quickly – the last thing we wanted was a 200-run deficit, and the prospect of having to save the game on the last day. South Africa needed to come out playing some shots so they could quickly build a substantial lead and give their bowlers time to achieve a victory, but this seemed unlikely given that their attitude throughout this game has clearly been to avoid defeat at all costs. It seemed that if a victory came that would be a bonus. It's been hard to fathom why, after bowling us out cheaply, they have crawled along at two runs per over with no sense of urgency in their play. I know if the state of the game was in our favour, and the series was there to be won, we'd be pushing hard for a victory. There's no way we'd be satisfied with a draw.

The first session was as exciting as watching paint dry. The South Africans refused to take any chances and, with the possibility of an Australian victory gone, this played into our hands. By lunch, the partnership remained unbroken, with over 100 runs to McMillan and Richardson's credit, and we weren't sure where to turn for the breakthrough. But after the mushroom pasta had been devoured, Warney and I managed to quickly polish off the last four wickets, leaving South Africa with a lead of 153 runs. Warney had the best figures – 4-92 off 55 overs – while I chipped in with 3-40 from 27.2.

I have been surprised by how effective my bowling has been over here. It certainly has been helped by the South Africans' negative approach – as I bowl 'stump to stump' I can wait for their patience to run out and pick up wickets either bowled or lbw. And the fact that the wickets have played low hasn't hurt at all. Bowling is a part of my game that I enjoy, as it keeps me involved, but it has been somewhat tormenting over the past couple of years because of the problems I've had with injury. Hopefully, that's all in the past, and I can bowl as I want to from now on.

With four and a bit sessions left in the match, and only a draw to play for, the hard grind of saving the Test match now began. This challenge will show whether or not we are a good side. It's easy to play well from the front, but much harder to come from behind.

After a reasonable start, Tubby fell victim to a dubious lbw decision to complete an unusually low scoring match for him. Not long after, he was joined by Boonie, who was out for the same score as his vice-captain (12). At the close of play, we were 2-89, with Slats on 54 and nightwatchman Warney on 8. With one day remaining we are well aware one bad session tomorrow could cost us the game and the series.

After each day's play of this Test the non-playing personnel of May, Jones and Hughes have released all their pent-up energy by kicking around an AFL ball on the field. The routine includes the inevitable assortment of fancy kicks, death-defying marks and a series of dummies that inevitably embarrasses the imaginary opposition. The show these three lairs put on has provided much amusement for their team-mates.

After it finally ended tonight, and we made our way back to the team hotel, the casino run by Heals and Warney began business for the evening. For tonight the owners offered free beer as a lure to get as many players involved as possible. Apparently profits have been down, and they saw this incentive as a means of getting some mug players involved in proceedings.

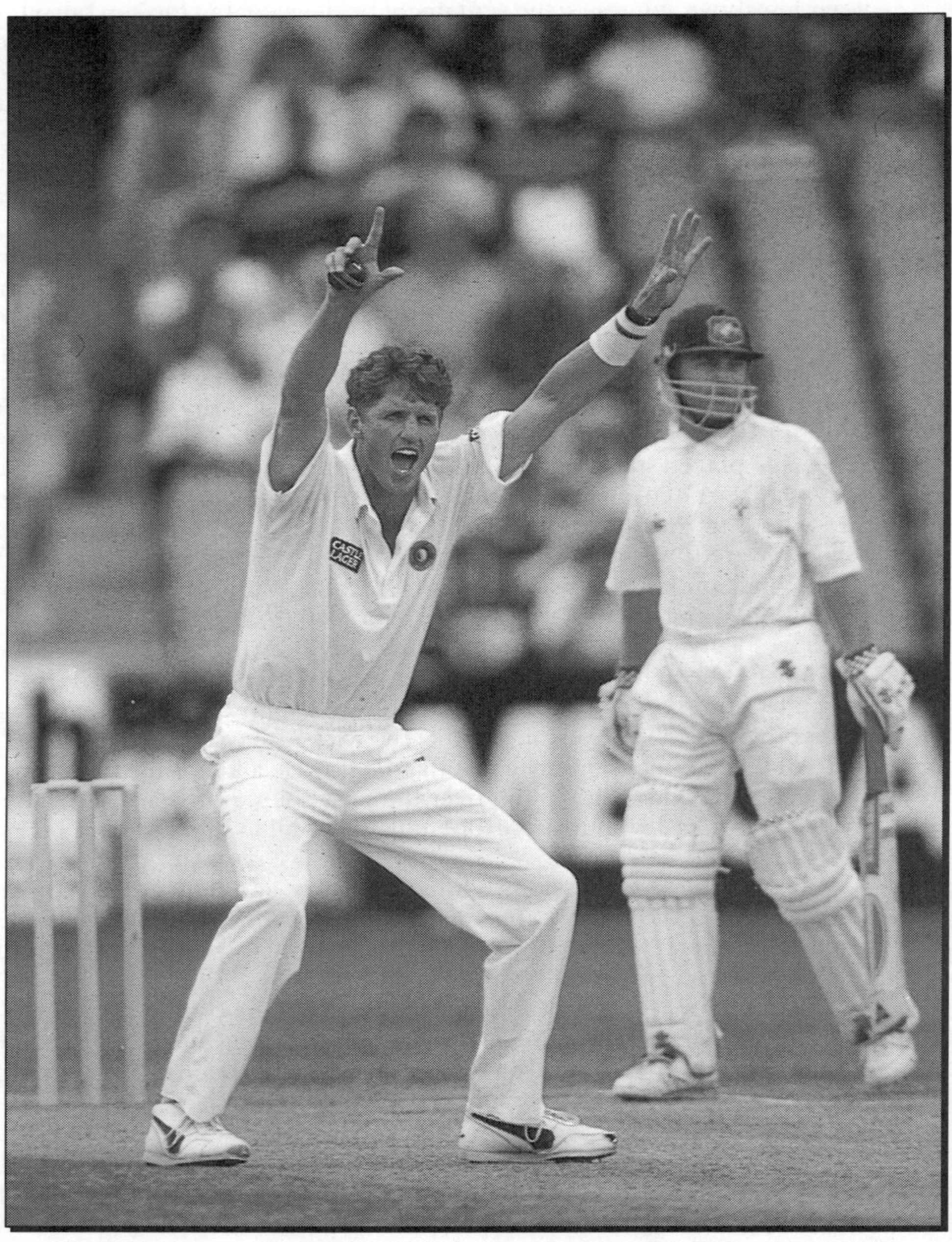

Fanie de Villiers appeals for lbw against Michael Slater. But this was a match becoming increasingly frustrating for bowlers.

During our match against Boland, at Stellenbosch, a pint-sized fan came onto the ground to organise an exchange of caps with Mark Taylor. I was given the responsibility of looking after the young bloke's bat.

Australian Picture Library — Mike Hewitt (All Sport)

Mark Waugh, with just a sample of the many amazing artefacts at Sun City.

Australian Picture Library — Tertius Pickard (Touchline Media)

Above: Shane Warne (in cap) and Jonty Rhodes, at a coaching clinic in a Cape Town township.
Below: Shane and Merv Hughes, with one of the locals at Sun City.

On the attack at Stellenbosch.
Australian Picture Library — Mike Hewitt (All Sport)

Ian Healy (left) and Craig McDermott, proving just how musical they can be, on the drums at Sun City.

Above: Dean Jones (left) and Michael Slater, in plush surroundings at Sun City.
Below: With Paul Reiffel in the water slides at Sun City.

Above: Tim May, the 'other' half of Australia's best spin-bowling partnership in years.

Below: A picture-postcard of the beautiful Newlands ground at Cape Town, with the imposing Table Mountain in the background.

Above and below: Australian Picture Library — Mike Hewitt (All Sport)

Above: Matt Hayden (left) and I look out over the extraordinary view from the top of Table Mountain.

Above and b
Australian Picture Libra
Mike Hewitt (All S

Below: We decided to wait on top of the mountain so we could experience the view at nightfall, and were rewarded with an absolutely breathtaking sunset. Left to right: myself, Ian Healy and Matt Hayden.

DAY 53 *March 29*

STRAIGHT TO the nets was the agenda for this morning and all the remaining batsmen had a good work-out, with the thought of saving the Test firmly in everyone's mind. Unbelievably for such an important day's cricket, the crowd was abysmal. Mind you, with the attitude the South Africans adopted for much of the game, I would not have wanted to be put through six more hours of such cricket either.

The home team began the day well by picking up Warney, who tried unsuccessfully to fend off a rising Donald delivery, for just 12. This dismissal illustrated a deficiency in Shane's batting technique which he should work on. With his natural batting ability, Warney has the capacity to score a lot of Test runs if his can improve his technique just a little. At the moment he doesn't put enough value on his wicket, which I suppose is understandable for a number nine. However, I'm sure that with a tougher attitude towards his batting he could end his career at number seven.

Fortunately, that early breakthrough proved to be an aberration. While Junior was finding his feet, Slats began to maul the opposition with a series of brutal strokes that gave the fieldsmen no chance of cutting them off. I keep getting the feeling that when Slats becomes more calculating in his choice of balls to tee off on he'll become unstoppable and post some massive scores in

Mark Waugh batting during the fifth day, when he scored the sole Australian century of the series.

Allan Border enters the Aussie dressing room after what we believed at the time was (and what was later confirmed to have been) his final innings in Test cricket. At right is Bob Simpson, who first became associated with the Australian team in 1986 and shared many a triumph – and the odd setback – with AB in the seasons that followed. Our captain's final Test innings was a typically gritty, fighting one that saved the match and ensured the series remained level at one Test all.

the future. With only five runs to go before reaching his third Test century he was adjudged to be lbw – Donald's third wicket of the innings and Slats' third Test score in the nineties. Our little opener was very unlucky – such was his domination and demolition of the South African attack everyone who watched his innings agreed he deserved a century.

Slater's dismissal left us 4-157, or more accurately 4-4 (after our first-innings deficit was considered) with still more than four hours play ahead of us. A steady partnership was needed and it was provided by Junior and AB. These two managed to hold South Africa's attack at bay for the following two hours, and by then we had reached a point where our defeat was more than highly unlikely. Our captain once again played the role for which he has become most renowned – fighting back – and, as he has done so often in the past, he won the battle. In doing so he was ably supported by Mark, who played a more subdued innings than we are accustomed to from him, but one vital to the team. A further 80 minutes of play after tea couldn't prise apart the partnership and a halt to proceedings was instigated by the umpires, who offered the batsmen the light 10 minutes before the scheduled finishing time. Their invitation was gladly accepted, and Junior remained unbeaten on 113 – a character-building knock for him – while the ultimate professional, Allan Border, was 42 not out.

As our captain made his way from the field it suddenly struck all of us we may never see such a sight during a Test match again, as he has hinted very strongly this will be his last Test. This is a fact that is hard to come to terms with. It was a strange situation, as we all gathered in the dressing room after the match, not knowing whether or not to say anything to AB. He hasn't officially retired yet, but we were almost 100 per cent certain he is going to. I guess that's what he wanted – an exit from the game on his terms, with as little fanfare and accolades as possible. He truly is a very humble man.

Perhaps the greatest hint that he will again never pull on the baggy green came when he began distributing his gear among his team-mates. I was lucky enough to grab a piece of history by claiming his helmet. At a brief presentation ceremony on the ground, Mark Waugh won the Man-of-the-Match award and I was handed the Man-of-the-Series trophy, which was a moment that didn't escape Merv and Maysie's quick wits, and we were hounded with comments such as: 'Gee whiz, what a moment for the Waugh family,' and, 'Won't Bev and Rodger be proud parents right now,' and then, 'What pedigree we have here.' And so on and so on. Then came a quick press conference, in front of about 30 journalists, where AB, Mark and I had to answer a series of questions. Ninety per cent were aimed at Allan, and most of those involved the retirement – which he deftly dodged.

As I look back on this series, I recall some really great cricket – an opinion shared by the legendary Richie Benaud, who is on record as saying that the first two Tests are in the top 20 Tests he's ever seen. But, unfortunately, the potentially series-deciding third Test was marred by the inexplicably negative tactics of the home captain, who payed it safe when he was in a position to push for victory. The net result of the six Tests between the two countries over the past few months is a two-all scoreline, which is something that could have been very different if the Sydney collapse hadn't occurred. But there was one reason it did – the 'never say die' attitude of the South Africans.

As the Australians wait on the field during the presentations, perhaps AB is contemplating his future. Next to him is Mark Taylor, the man who would eventually be named his successor as Australian captain.

Some people might say a deadlocked result is a major disappointment for us, but having played against these guys, I don't consider it such a bad effort. They're a high-class side who play tough, determined cricket and a team who will win more than they lose in the next couple of years.

As the bus drove away from the ground, I couldn't help but feel for AB. He was no doubt thinking – and it's a thought I would find very difficult to accept if I was in his position: 'Well that's it, my last Test.' But, whatever his emotions, he was with us for a 7pm cocktail function put on by the series sponsors, Castle Lager. The evening highlight was traditional dance performed by some Zulu dancers, and we also watched a packaged video which showed the highs and lows of the tour so far. A couple of relaxing ales were had, and then a couple more over the road at a popular bar. We were fully aware that the next two days are cricket free, and that knowledge was quite an enticement to 'let the hair down a bit'.

With the
Man-of-the-Match medal from
the second Test and the Player-of-the-Series award ...
I had absolutely no reason to complain about my form during the series.

THE DAY/NIGHT INTERNATIONALS

DAY 54 *March 30*

AN 8.15AM wake-up call came about six hours too early for my liking, but the thought of spending two days at a game reserve was enough incentive to drag my weary body out from between the sheets. Soon after, we boarded a 12-seater for a flight to Phinda Lodge, with the starting line-up featuring Taylor, Border, Slater, Healy, M. Waugh, C. Battersby, Johno, McGrath and S. Waugh, all of whom were very glad to find terra firma again despite a relatively smooth flight.

We were shown to our huts by a security guard, whose presence, we were quickly told, was a necessity ever since a guest, who had been making her way to her hut, was mauled to death nine months ago by a lion which had somehow managed to sidestep the electric safety fence. Then it was time for a bush walk, where we were guided by a local Zulu tribesman. He took us on an hour-long trip, and explained how their people use the native plants and trees for remedies, food, alcohol and domestic chores. A certain branch is used as a toothbrush, a plant's leaf can act as toilet paper, while other vegetation can stop you biting your finger nails or kill you if you eat it. Perhaps the most interesting of all was a tree that is commonly known as the 'wooden spoon' tree, because it is perfectly suited for domestic duties. The Blues contingent quickly renamed it 'The Queensland Sheffield Shield team tree'.

Junior stares in wonder as a Zulu tribesman explains how the leaves from this tree can help cure a bad nail-biting habit.

Back at the hotel, the boys were keen for a feed and the special of the day was ostrich pie which, while it didn't appear exactly mouth-watering when we saw it on the menu, was very tasty once we mustered up the courage to give the local bird a chance. After lunch, a 'siesta' was considered a must by the touring party, so a couple of hours of pushing zeds was squeezed into the schedule, before we set out on a 4pm river cruise.

The 30-minute drive by jeep to the river bank saw us cross the path of a few impala, kudu and warthog. For most of the journey, the jeep was full of very nervous passengers, because our host, a gentleman by the name of Mark, had informed us we were in an area were snakes are commonly found. The largest is the carpet python, which can grow to six metres in length and has been known to kill impala and springbok by latching onto their legs and then strangling them. This was an

THE NATAL
MERCURY

NATAL NEWSPAPERS •• WEDNESDAY MARCH 30, 1994 R1,00 (incl. VAT)

CITY COUNCIL
White House 'protected'
Council 'powerless' PAGE 3

RUGBY TICKETS
Answer - and win!
Season tickets up for grabs PAGE 3

TENNIS
SA Open
Fighting fire with fire PAGE 25

'War zone' Natal scares off tourists

By Kevin O'Grady

RISING violence in KwaZulu/Natal has had a devastating effect on the tourism industry and Durban hotels may have to start retrenching employees if the situation does not improve.

This was said yesterday by the Durban chairman of the Federated Hospitality Association of South Africa, Mr Alf Bodheim.

No Durban hotel could boast it was full for the coming, traditionally busy, Easter weekend which would "probably be the quietest Easter weekend Durban's ever had", he said.

"It's not a pretty picture at all. The little bit of overseas bookings we had have gone and we've had a lot of local cancellations as well," Mr Bodheim said.

The cancellations and drop-off in bookings were totally attributable to the violence raging through the province.

"We've been doing our budgets and working our positions out and are going to have to start retrenching people if things don't start going well," he warned.

People were viewing Natal as a "war zone" and were reluctant to travel to the province on holiday, he said.

It was too soon to tell what long-term effect Monday's violence in central Johannesburg would have on the tourism industry in general.

Mr John Tack, of the Natal South Coast publicity association, said hotels and self-catering establishments would be "nudging 80%" occupancy over the Easter weekend, dropping off to between 60% and 70% towards the end of the holiday.

Boy killed by car

WADE Rogers, six, was knocked down by a car and killed outside Funland in Beach Road, Amanzimtoti, yesterday afternoon. — (Mercury Reporter)

South African captain Kepler Wessels (left) and his Australian counterpart, Allan Border, pose with the trophy after their teams had shared the Test series 1-1 at Kingsmead yesterday. Picture by TERRY HAYWOOD

Wessels's Test tactics slammed

By Fred Forge
Sports Editor

SOUTH Africa's pedestrian batting against Australia came under fire yesterday as the final cricket Test at Kingsmead fizzled out into a draw leaving the series tied at 1-1.

General opinion was that Kepler Wessels, the home captain, was too negative and it would have been better had his batsmen adopted a more enterprising approach. This was particularly after SA had passed their opponents' score on Monday.

Former Springbok fast bowler Neil Adcock said: "SA were too slow and Wessels, rather than go for victory, seemed content to let his team plod along for a draw.

"It was difficult to fathom SA's tactics when, after passing the Aussie score on Monday, they continued to bat at a painfully slow rate instead of going for quick runs."

Former Springbok batting star Barry Richards echoed similar sentiments.

"I can understand SA not wanting to lose, but they needed to show a more positive attitude and try to win the game," he said.

Another ex-SA batsman, Billy Wade, said: "We don't have many stroke-makers at present and the Aussie bowlers with their accurate line made it hard to score quickly. They experienced a similar problem with our bowlers."

● See also Page 26

Natal state of emergency looming

Buthelezi warns of fight to the finish

Political Staff

KWAZULU chief minister Mangosuthu Buthelezi yesterday vowed to fight the ANC "to the finish" unless the elections were postponed — while the TEC recommended emergency security measures in KwaZulu/Natal.

A state of emergency encompassing the whole of Natal and KwaZulu would be proclaimed by President De Klerk within the next few days, the TEC agreed.

The declaration, accompanied by the deployment of more SADF troops, was intended to halt the recent surge in violence in the region as well as to ensure free and fair elections could be held next month.

However, a government spokesman warned that the TEC should not take precipitate action but "should rather wait for the outcome of the summit meeting between leaders that is definitely taking place next week".

The summit between President De Klerk, Mr Nelson Mandela, Dr Buthelezi and Zulu king Goodwill Zwelithini, due to start today, was postponed at the king's request and will now take place next week. This came after a flurry of telephone calls between the leaders yesterday following the mayhem in Johannesburg on Monday.

In a strong and uncompromising statement, Dr Buthelezi referred to the Johannesburg killings as the "Shell House (ANC HQ) massacre ... (which) was only paralleled by police action at Sharpeville".

"The Shell House massacre shows that we have now entered a final struggle to the finish between the ANC and the Zulu nation, unless there is an extension of the voting date deadline to enable a negotiated settlement regarding the question of Zulu sovereignty to be worked out before elections take place."

Dr Buthelezi said he could not stand before his king and report that he as chief minister and Inkatha leader had taken no action other than calling for an inquiry. "Enough is enough."

He had reports "of Zulus massing at hostels in Johannesburg and Zulus travelling up to Johannesburg to stand by their comrades". If the elected leaders of these people did not take action, "there is no saying what the people will do in taking the law into their own hands", he warned.

What had taken place in KwaZulu and Transvaal so far "are only precursors of what will yet come", he said, stating that, in pursuance of his demand for a postponement of the election, April 27 will be declared a "national Zulu day of mourning for those who died".

Failing the demand for the elections to be delayed being met, "the people of KwaZulu can only be driven to deeper anger and more determined attempts".

The government said it had been hoped the leaders could meet this week to deal with the tensions that had arisen. Mr De Klerk was "extremely concerned and would make every endeavour possible to bring the major two protagonists to some sort of agreement to prevent further violence" so that free and fair elections could proceed.

However, he said that to achieve this depended on leaders' ability to control their supporters, cease calls for mass action and stop making rash and inflammatory statements about war. An agreement at the summit meeting would prevent the necessity for the action envisaged by the TEC, he said.

ANC spokesman Carl Niehaus said: "The elections will proceed and the ANC will take whatever steps necessary to prevent a war."

In his letter to Mr De Klerk, King Goodwill referred to the events in Johannesburg on Monday, saying "the slaughter of the innocent ... will reverberate around Zulu society for a long time to come".

He suggested the meeting take place after the Easter weekend.

An Independent Electoral Commission spokesman said the organisation was legally bound to make preparations for an election in Natal, and Dr Buthelezi's comments did not alter that responsibility.

The TEC said it was "convinced and determined" that the elections would take place on April 26, 27 and 28 "throughout South Africa".

Government TEC delegate Roelf Meyer said the decision was not aimed at any organisation or political grouping, but to "ensure every person who wants to vote is allowed this right".

The state of emergency formed part of a "package" which allowed for negotiations to continue in an attempt to secure a political solution.

TEC joint executive secretary Mac Maharaj said regulations for the state of emergency were currently being drafted in conjunction with the TEC's sub-council on law and order.

The TEC agreed yesterday that "intensified security action" was necessary to ensure the safety of those who wanted to participate in the election.

No indication of the numbers of troops to be despatched to Natal was given, though Mr Maharaj said deployments had begun.

The special powers given to the security forces, including search and seizure and powers of arrest, would fall under constant review by the government, the TEC and the Independent Electoral Commission.

ANC delegate Cyril Ramaphosa said the steps had been taken to prevent Natal sliding into a "bottomless abyss of death and destruction".

R11m boost to storage

ISLAND View Storage, the Rennies group's bulk liquid storage division, is to undergo an R11 million expansion programme to increase its total national capacity to over by 350 000m³.

The new programme will be at the Durban harbour Bay V site, where contractors have just completed a R7 million contract for 12 tanks which added 12 000m³ capacity.

According to managing director Rodger Graham, the company's policy of keeping ahead of demand led them to building the 12 000m³ over the past year, but when, before completion, the economy showed signs of accelerating beyond the rate they had calculated, they considered it prudent to step up their capacity accordingly. — (Finance Reporter)

Breakthrough volkstaat accord set to be signed

Political Staff

JOHANNESBURG—The ANC, Freedom Front and the government are scheduled to sign an accord tomorrow on an Afrikaner volkstaat which will mean the Electoral Act will have to be changed.

This breakthrough, after months of on-off talks between the Afrikaner Volksfront and the ANC and government, will now lead to Gen Constand Viljoen's breakaway Freedom Front's full participation in the elections.

Gen Viljoen said after he had registered his party for the elections that participation would go ahead only if there was an accord on a volkstaat.

The accord sets out the conditions and the process under which a volkstaat may be established.

Freedom Front parliamentary candidate Corné Mulder said the Electoral Act would have to be changed by proclamation soon after the accord was signed.

The accord makes provision for a voters' second ballot — in the provincial elections — to be used to determine the volkstaters support-level, and where the support was, Mr Mulder said.

The volkstaat votes would be recorded separately at certain polling stations.

The ANC's Thabo Mbeki, who headed the ANC talks team, insisted that the accord specified non-racialism.

In your Mercury

CELLULAR phones are the new executive toy, but how do they work and what can consumers expect?

The Natal Mercury features a 12-page broadsheet supplement tomorrow giving all the answers.

● Banking by phone is the way to go. Read inside today how it has taken the market by storm.

See Pages 14 & 15

Cow on freeway

A SECTION of the southern freeway near Louis Botha airport was closed last night after a cow was killed by a car. The animal had been hit earlier by another vehicle. Earlier this week, a motorcyclist was killed in the same area when his machine also ploughed into a cow.

NewsScan

Tearful Di's pleas

LECH—A tearful Princess Diana asked photographers to leave her alone yesterday as she arrived for lunch at an Austrian restaurant.

"Why are you here?" she asked a group of British photographers, pointing out that she had already agreed to earlier photo calls. It was explained that no one had been taking pictures and she walked off with her head down.

She soon returned in tears. Pointing to her sons, she said: "You've upset these two."

Tourist sub for Loch Ness

LONDON—Tourists visiting Loch Ness will soon be able to join the ultimate monster hunt — in a submarine.

From April 1, a British company will be taking groups of visitors on an hour-long "underwater safari" to explore the dark waters that have inspired one of the world's greatest mysteries.

The former naval submarine will drop 180m to the loch bed which can be viewed through two portholes, at the bottom and in the front.

THE MARKET

Gold	Johannesburg Stock Exchange		
LON close $/oz	All Gold Index	Indust Index	All share Index
$ 386.25	2 123	5 763	[illegible]
$ 388.50	2 026	5 726	4 9[illegible]

JSE blue chip shift

JOHANNESBURG—Institutions came to the rescue of a beleaguered Diagonal Street yesterday as they shifted some of their burgeoning cash flows into blue chip industrial shares.

Good demand for index weighted shares after sharp recent declines restored a semblance of confidence to the market, but trading was cautious as Johannesburg remained tense because of fears of more violence.

The buying lifted the JSE industrial index 37 points to 5 763, but precious metal prices slid. The mining financial index fell 193 points to 6 231 and the all gold index slumped 97 points to 2 026.

Gran's teapot a treasure

LONDON—A 12cm high Victorian teapot which survived being used as a toy at children's tea parties was sold for R351 000 at auction in London yesterday.

The unadorned silverplate teapot, made in 1879, owes its value to its rarity and its unusual flat oval shape. Its simplicity anticipated the streamlined modernism fashionable in the 1920s and 1930s.

Car hijack backfires

QUICK action by a plucky driver prevented a bakkie hijack at Mariannhill, near Durban, yesterday.

The incident occurred about 1pm when Mr Bhekumusi Mchunu stopped his bakkie at an intersection in Recreation Road. Two men, one carrying a homemade gun, ordered him out of the car.

Mr Mchunu flung his door open and knocked the gunman over, upon which he and his accomplice fled.

Mr Mchunu and other witnesses chased and caught the gunman, who was severely beaten and handed to the police. He was later admitted to hospital under police guard.

The front page of the Natal Mercury *of March 30 contained its own epilogue to the final Test, but also offered some sobering reminders of the political storms that continued to torment the country.*

image still racing through my head as we made, with a degree of alacrity, the final 50-metre trip to the boat on foot.

Unfortunately, our river cruise was somewhat of a disappointment as the wildlife apparently boycotted our arrival. Finally we spotted a small crocodile sunning itself on the bank but, being a sceptical bunch, we believed this particular reptile was part of a set-up to keep the tourists happy. So we demanded a closer inspection, but still the croc wouldn't budge or show any sign of life. It was decided the only way to settle the argument was to hurl some unwanted cocktail frankfurters at the subject in question, and that soon resolved the issue as a barrage of missiles had the croc very agitated very quickly. Not long after, we were treated to the sight of the whole sky in front of us being crammed with European swallows. It was like a scene out of Alfred Hitchcock's *The Birds* – a stunning natural phenomenon.

After a thoroughly relaxing two hours cruising along the river, we made our way back to the jeeps to travel to our evening destination in the middle of the bush, where a traditional BBQ was already well in progress by the time we arrived. The site was set beneath the most magnificent umbrella tree you could ever see, and it provided shelter for all the people in attendance. The meal turned out to be one of the best of the tour, with the only drawback being all the insects that found their way into the food and drink. But I guess the night wouldn't have had an authentic African feeling without them. Glenn McGrath, in particular, seemed at home in this environment. The stick insects took a liking to him, and as they crawled all over his head someone was heard to comment: 'They've got two things in common – their physique and brain size.' A bit harsh on the insect I thought.

The trip home provided another opportunity for us to search for some wildlife, and the spotter at the front of the car used a high-powered light to try and find the animals, most of whom see very well at night and are, we were told, most active at this time. However, we could do no better than a number of impala. Once home, it was early to bed, as a 5.30am start is required for our early-morning drive through the game park.

Glenn McGrath, with a friendly stick insect perched atop his Australian cap.

DAY 55 *March 31*

I DIDN'T sleep too well last night as I was constantly distracted by the thunder and lighting that threatened to destroy my hut, and disturbed by the thought of a hungry lion waiting outside for me. Each of us was in a room on our own and, with no radio, TV or newspapers available, we felt a long way from civilisation, which is ideal for a quick getaway holiday. But we're also without phones or alarm clocks and needed a quick visit at the proposed wake-up time from a security guard to ensure we made our deadline.

As soon as I heard the knock on the door, I gathered my necessities for the day – suncream, camera and sunglasses – and raced to the door from where, in semi-darkness, I would be escorted to the foyer. However, when I opened the door, to my horror my chaperone had vanished and I was left with the task of making it to the reception area on my own, without suffering a heart attack as I thought of the ravenous lions lurking in the bushes. It took a while to summon enough courage to make the short journey and the mission was not completed before some frightful thoughts had entered my head. And I soon found out I was not alone in having to cope with such terror. Each of the lads made the foyer with a spring in his step and decidedly short of breath. Such was Junior's fear, he refused to make the journey back to his room to fetch a jumper he'd forgotten – he figured one trip a day was more than enough.

Once we were aboard our jeep, all our efforts were channelled into tracking down some cheetahs which had been spotted last evening about an hour away from our hotel. As we approached the area in question, our tracker found on a mud track two sets of footprints and for the next 30 minutes we followed this trail, which was a tough ask even for the locals as the footprints disappear once the animals head into the bush. However, our patience was eventually rewarded when out of nowhere a mother cheetah and four cubs materialised from the camouflage of metre-high grasses. No sooner had we laid eyes on these majestic animals, when the mother spotted a potential kill for the cubs in the form of a steenbuck. But, unfortunately for the mother, the potential victim had enough start to avoid even the fastest of all living animals mowing it down. Our guide informed us the cheetah could have caught the steenbuck had she really wanted to, but when she engages in a chase she weighs up how much effort is needed to catch her prey and how big a feed it will be for the cubs. If this criteria isn't met, the cheetah will only put in an effort for a short while before giving up – which is what happened on this occasion.

However, moments later the chase was on again, as a red darkar appeared. But again the effort required wasn't worth the end result and the chase was abandoned shortly after it began. Although it would have been memorable to see a 'kill' live, it was still an experience just to see the gracefulness and turn of speed a cheetah possesses. The next 90 minutes were spent following the mother and her family as they continued on their search for an unsuspecting prey. We were able to get as close as five metres from the cheetahs – we were told predators such as cheetahs, leopards and lions only see the vehicle you are in, not the people in it, and consequently do not perceive a threat. But if you break the profile of the jeep, by standing up or moving around too much, then they see you as a danger and that can mean trouble. So, needless to say, we stayed fairly still, even when taking photos.

One of the sights of our sight-seeing tour – a female cheetah with her family.

A call was received on the radio that two lions had been sighted about 30 minutes away, which was enough for us to join in on the search. When we reached the area in which the sighting had occurred we had to listen for the sound of the other vehicle on the prowl. The only way to do this was to stop our jeep and then radio through to the driver of the other vehicle, who then revved his engine to give us a rough idea as to where he was. Once we'd worked out in which direction to head, we had to make our own path through the virgin bush to try and find, first, the other jeep and, ultimately, the lions.

As luck would have it, we stumbled upon the king of the jungle before the other vehicle came in sight. Just seeing the creatures in their natural habitat made all the hard work of finding them worthwhile. We soon realised the lion and lioness we had stumbled upon were not the same ones that had been sighted earlier. That duo had both been males, who, our guides told us, were more than likely on the trail of our two with the plan of mating with the female. But before they turned up, and within minutes of our cautious arrival, the lion and lioness began their mating ritual, a sight that had the cameras clicking frantically. But once the formalities were over, our guides decided to get out of the area. The two males would soon catch up to our couple, and a fight for the right to mate would ensue. While that battle was on, we were told, the immediate vicinity wouldn't be a real safe place to be, so we all agreed to head back to camp.

However, halfway home our vehicle packed it in, which left the occupants feeling more than a little uncomfortable. Thankfully, our tracker was also a very handy mechanic and shortly afterwards we were mobile again, in time for our attention to be captured by a group of zebras and then a six-metre tall giraffe, which capped off an unforgettable adventure.

After we had safely arrived back at our base, we received flying instructions for our trip back to Durban and they were enough to send poor Tubs into a cold sweat. The journey would be via two five-seater planes – a concept that sent ominous shivers through the unashamed coward of the skies. However, Mark shouldn't have worried, as a pleasant flight was the end result and we touched down at five o'clock, in plenty of time to prepare for a cocktail party hosted by the Australian press contingent, which commenced at 7pm.

DAY 56 *April 1*

THIS MORNING we copped another 5am wake-up call. Five in the morning is a time of the day when all activities, with the possible exception of fishing, should be banned. Definitely out should be catching planes to East London. The hour-long trip from Durban wasn't too bad, but the 50 minutes spent trying to locate where our bags were wasn't pleasant, and even more difficult was the battle to get through the crowd to try and secure them. The East London airport was really little more than a small country town-style airport, with facilities to match.

Not for the first time, the airport was crammed with hordes of autograph hunters all intent of gaining that seemingly priceless scribble from the players. Even Johno was in high demand! Training was originally scheduled for 9am, but AB insisted on a 2pm session instead, so a quick breakfast was devoured before all lights were extinguished and a couple of hours' valuable sleep enjoyed.

Down at the ground, a huge Good Friday crowd gathered to watch us go through our paces. Tomorrow we face the South Africans in the fifth of the one-day internationals, and the first to be played under lights. Most of the guys are looking a little flat as some niggling injuries and the extremely heavy workload of recent times have begun to take their toll. Sensing this, Simmo made it a relatively light session, and I was excluded from fielding practice to have some ice and massage treatment on an extremely tender left shin. The freshest player of all was Damien Fleming, who joined the tour this morning. If Damien's recent Sheffield Shield form is any indication, he'll prove to be an asset.

Tonight, the team accepted an invitation to enjoy the hospitality of a local Irish restaurant called 'O'Hagan's'. The meal was good and the setting fabulous, as we dined with the ocean crashing below us. The team for tomorrow's game has been amended. Originally, AB wasn't going to play but now he's changed his mind, which means Tubs, Matty H., Fleming and Hughes have been left out. In the context of the one-day series, the game shapes as a crucial one for us. Having fallen behind three matches to one, a loss here would put a series victory out of our reach and could lead to an embarrassing scoreline for us to take home.

DAY 57 *April 2*

THE OPPORTUNITY of having a sleep in was not missed in room 139, and McGrath and S. Waugh did not stir until a sports fan broke the silence with a call to wish us all the best for today's game. Moments later came a hollow knocking noise from the door which bore all the trademarks of Johno – for obvious reasons he belts the door well below the usual height.

Johno has been an instant hit with the team, who all think he's a champion of a bloke and an inspiration to us all. And he'll tell you so as well. He joined us for breakfast, in our tastefully decorated room which features light fittings with shirts hanging off them and shoes lined up on top of the TV, features designed to give the room that 'lived in' feeling. As noon arrived my roomie with the lightweight frame decided he was hungry again and, as I didn't want him feeling like a glutton, I put my hand up for a burger and fries to go with his order. But we shouldn't have wasted our time, as the efforts of the chef on this occasion were abysmal – it wouldn't surprise me to see a bout of food poisoning take us down in the near future.

As was the case in the earlier one-day games, there were huge queues of people waiting to be let into the ground when we arrived. This venue has a country-type atmosphere, with no huge grandstands and a large grass embankment on one side. Such a 'hill' is a rarity these days, but a welcome sight as a contrast to many of the concrete jungles that can lack atmosphere.

Kepler Wessels won the toss and, as has become predictable, decided to bat first. The success of the team batting first, both in the World Series in Australia and then over here, has been remarkable. Nine of the 11 Australia-South Africa one-day internationals in 1993-94 before today have been won by the team batting first.

Within four overs it had become clear the wicket was extremely slow and therefore hard to score quickly on. Such a pitch can make it very difficult for many of the players. Timing the ball becomes more difficult under these conditions, while from the pace bowlers' point of view, there is no point trying to bowl as quickly as they can. Their speed is neutralised to the point of being just quick enough to be easily timed by the batsman. Such a wicket is much easier for a bowler of my style, as the batsman has to make all the running, by taking undue risks such as hitting over the infield or advancing down the pitch. There's no easy glides down to third man, or drives through the covers on the up. Consequently, my figures were my best of the tournament – 1-25 off nine overs – while AB's slow left-armers brought him the excellent return of 3-27 off 7.5 overs.

The South Africans looked very lethargic in accumulating their unimpressive total of 158 – they appeared to be feeling the effects of their demanding schedule of the past few months. As injuries and fatigue are very evident in both parties, the winners of the remaining games will be the side who can lift themselves above their weariness and want victory more than the other side. Peter Kirsten was the only player to spend much time at the crease, but he was far too slow in making his 53, off more than 100 balls, which is not satisfactory in this shortened form of the game.

Our quest for victory began well enough, as we raced to 0-57, but then we lost three wickets in a hurry – two to lousy shots and one to a dodgy decision.

I came to wicket to join my brother, with the total on 3-71, and from the moment I walked in to bat I felt relaxed and confident, and it showed in my results. I ended up scoring 67 not out from 60 balls – a fair effort under the conditions – and with Mark, who ended up unbeaten on 21, secured a much needed victory, by seven wickets. AB won the Man-of-the-Match award, for which he was slightly embarrassed as he thought I should have won, but the main thing is an Australian player won it and that means the cash goes into the team fund which we split up at the end of the tour.

This win took Johno's recent record as a cricket fan to 12 games without a loss (including matches involving NSW, who he supports with a passion). Afterwards, he declared he was going to have a few drinks and get 'legless', which I guess is a distinct possibility.

Heals, meanwhile was proudly displaying his Brisbane Broncos rugby league jersey for the first time on tour. He only wears it when the Brisbane lads manage a victory, and that finally happened last night when they thrashed Easts. Most of the guys like to keep in touch with all the sports scores from home and particularly the fortunes of the different teams we follow. Inevitably, supporting a certain team can often lead to arguments ... and to ridicule if results don't go the right way.

John Coutis – or 'Johno' as we all know him – a good friend to the Australian team.

A Day in the Life of a Touring Cricket Journalist

April 2 – East London

By Patrick Keane *(Australian Associated Press)*

THE FINISH of the Test series saw most of the media interest in the team's tour of South Africa reduced in Australia. The day-night games mean big money for the South African Board but they won't get a lot of attention at home because the rugby league and AFL seasons are in full swing.

For the travelling Australian journos, that means that last night was a chance for most of us to have an end-of-tour blow out, especially as the game tomorrow doesn't start until around 2.15pm. So most of the group didn't get in until around 3am with a few kicking on until dawn at a local nightclub, 'Numbers'.

The Australian media travelling with the Team are Malcolm Conn (*The Australian*), Phil Wilkins (*The Sydney Morning Herald*), Ron Reed (News Ltd), Nick Castellaro (Channel 7), Neville Oliver (ABC), Tony Jones and Paul Webb (Channel 9), and myself.

I got out of bed around midday, packed, and headed for the ground. First thing to do is to get the XII from Bob Simpson and file a short story for use on Saturday evening radio bulletins at home. Simpson informed me that Merv Hughes is out injured, while Hayden and Fleming are not picked. We had expected Fleming to play but the XII includes two spinners.

For this game, the newspaper guys have very small work requirements. The time difference means the game doesn't start until 10:15pm Sydney time and most Sunday newspapers are printing by then. Conn doesn't have to work because *The Australian* has no Sunday edition while Reed has been told his paper won't need anything either. Wilkins will do the first innings of the match for the *Sun Herald* while I will do the same for papers in Adelaide and Perth. I also do hourly bulletins for the radio and regular scores, as well as sending the full scoreboards at the end of each innings.

We have not been to East London before, and it's a nice enough ground, holding around 19,000. Wessels won the toss and the local journos predicted a total around the 220 mark.

South Africa started well enough but got into trouble when Warne and May bowled together. May took the big wickets of Cronje and Rhodes, who are the guys who can score at a good rate. During the 33rd over, Paul Reiffel fielded a ball at fine leg and it was a close decision whether he got it before it touched the boundary rope. Reiffel didn't know if it touched the rope and the crowd started booing him. Someone threw a

Continued over page

A Day in the Life of a Touring Cricket Journalist

continued from previous page

half-full beer can at him, which sent the members of the press room into a mild frenzy. The can didn't hit him but it was close.

That incident was enough for Wilkins and I to write a story. Crowd abuse has been a lingering issue for most of the tour because of what happened to Hughes and Warne in the first Test. Added to that, armed policemen have travelled with the team at all times. If a player has something thrown at him, it's news and rates highly in my story at the end of the innings, alongside positive comments on the bowling of Steve Waugh, May and Border. Border took 3-27 and a total of 158 doesn't look to be enough. By the time the Australian reply begins it's too late to file again, so the Sunday papers throughout Australia will have a story that Border's team is likely to win and that Reiffel had a can thrown at him.

In the Australian innings, Dean Jones received a shocking lbw decision that made the score 3-71 and there was still some work needed before the match was won. Jones was batting outside his crease and the inswinger hits him high just in front of leg stump, which made it likely it would go both over the stumps and down the leg side. However, any chance of a loss is eradicated by the Waughs. Steve bats particularly well for 67 not out and it's not often that Mark gets outscored three to one.

At the end of the game, the scorers can't agree on several details and that holds up filing the result of the match. Scorers who don't know what they are doing are the bane of an AAP cricket reporter's life. Radio and newspapers want the result as quick as possible but you can't do anything until everything adds up. A slow scorer also means you can miss the end-of-match press conference. On this tour, South African scorers have ranged from the very good to the decidedly poor. In my five years following the Australian team, Australian scorers are the best, just ahead of those from New Zealand. The West Indians are comfortably the worst – it was amazing how often two people sitting next to each other in the Caribbean can disagree by six or seven runs on the score. It was lucky there were no close matches on Australia's 1991 tour.

In the rooms, the Australian press hold a separate conference with Border. He's a bit embarrassed about winning Man of the Match. The next story we write is for Monday's paper in Australia, to be read some 24 hours after the game has finished. A wrap-up is out of date so my story will have to look forward to the sixth match, in Port Elizabeth on Tuesday. I also have to do a story for the afternoon papers, so I always have to talk to someone different. In this case it's Steve Waugh, asking him how a player can maintain form in the one-dayers when you can't play a normal game.

I was out of the ground tonight by 10:30pm, and went back to the hotel to work on Monday's story, which I wasn't happy with until 1am. Because there's a 7am departure for Port Elizabeth tomorrow, I didn't go out tonight. In fact, all I did before heading to bed was pack and check out so I don't have to do it in the morning.

DAY 58 *April 3*

INSTEAD OF using flying from East London to Port Elizabeth, where the sixth one-dayer will be contested tomorrow, we decided to take a leisurely drive by coach along the coast and stop off somewhere for lunch. The journey would have taken an hour in the air, but when you add on time to get to the airport, to wait in the departure lounge, to collect bags and finally to get to the new hotel, the entire 'flight' would have taken the best part of three and a half hours. So we travelled by road, and what a scenic drive it turned out to be.

The first half of the trip, which took two hours, gave us an opportunity to admire a coastline very similar to the North Coast of NSW, with rolling hills and superb beaches, before we reached our lunch-time destination of the Fish River casino. Lunch, unfortunately, was a major let-down, with the staff either struggling to come to terms with our accents or deliberately sabotaging our orders – the variety of meals that eventually arrived bore no resemblance to the ordered fare. However, this wasn't seen as much of a problem for the lads, as the sole objective for quite a few of our desperate punters was to walk out of the casino with a bag full of Rand. Warney headed straight for the roulette wheel to back his favourite number – 23 Red; Junior attempted the impossible – to beat a computerised machine at blackjack; while Jonesy had visions of a fortune as he tried his hand at poker. I quickly lost my cash on the poker machines.

As we relaxed during the second half of our journey, everyone was congratulating each other on our choice of transport until the driver realised he may have miscalculated the amount of fuel needed to reach our target. While the bus limped its way along the highway for at least 10 minutes, we were having visions of the Australian cricket team pushing the thing the rest of the way. We seemed to be in the middle of nowhere. But a miracle materialised, and the coach finally ran out of gas just three metres short of a bowser at a little petrol station about half an hour from Port Elizabeth.

The team finally checked into the Holiday Inn at 4.30pm and, while Slats and Matty headed straight for the beach directly opposite our hotel, most of the other lads caught up on some shut-eye. A little later on, Johno was feeling restless in his room and decided to come down and annoy the still sleeping McGrath and S. Waugh, which was handy because we were due in the foyer in 10 minutes time for a dinner appointment at The Ranch. It was lucky we made it, because the seafood buffet that was put on turned out to be the best feed of the tour to date.

DAY 59 *April 4*

WE DIDN'T leave the hotel until 12.15pm, for a five-minute drive to yet another ground overflowing with people desperate for a good vantage point. Inevitably, a full house was expected – the response of the South African fans to the limited-overs internationals has been remarkable. Our warm-up lap was greeted with generous applause – a rarity for visiting sides anywhere in the world. Except for the treatment we copped from the 'fans' during the first Test in Johannesburg, the crowds have been very good to us, which is a reflection on the extensive and excellent coverage the cricket has received, from the opening matches in Australia though to the fixtures over here.

Jonesy threw a scare into the camp when he damaged his ring finger taking a high catch off Simmo just before the line-ups were announced, but he declared himself available even though it was suspected a fracture may have occurred. AB then took his win/loss ratio in the Tests and one-day internationals on tour to two/seven by again calling incorrectly, which gave the home team the chance to bat first on a ground we have been told is notorious for the wicket playing a few tricks at night-time after a dew appears on the surface.

The first 15 overs went along according to plan for us, as the scoreline was restricted to 2-48. McGrath and Reiffel were doing an excellent job on a ground so small that 250 looked a very gettable total. However, what turned out to be the key point of the game happened shortly, when Jonesy was unable to hold onto a difficult chance off my bowling while fielding on the fence. Instead the ball went for six, and signalled a change in attitude from Hudson and Rhodes. From that point, as if sensing our disappointment, they picked up the tempo.

It's the sign of a good side and a good player when they/he can use or turn a good piece of fortune to their advantage, which is exactly what happened as Hudson and Rhodes both reached 60 and guided their team to a reasonable score of 6-227 from their 50 overs. McGrath, although he went wicketless, was once again our best bowler. The fact he didn't have even one wicket to show for his efforts is something that can happen in this shortened form of the game, but there will no doubt be a day when fate will even things up by handing him three or four wickets on an occasion when he bowls poorly. The only worry for the team is that Glenn might read too much into his figures of recent times, instead of saying to himself: 'I know I'm bowling well and if I keep bowling as I am now, the returns will come eventually.'

Our innings was scheduled to begin at 6:30pm but that was impossible as the light towers had only a small percentage of their globes working. The ground was in semi-darkness, while officials scurried around trying to find a solution. Fifteen minutes later, the umpire deemed the playing surface sufficiently lit for the game to resume even though a couple of rows of lights on each of the four pylons were still out of order. Without doubt, we were at a disadvantage, and the combination of the inadequate lighting, the now seaming wicket, and some quality bowling knocked us out of the game. We collapsed to be 7-77, at which point the few Aussie supporters in the crowd made their way towards the exits.

The two not out batsmen were the Victorians, Pistol and Warney. Such was our plight that this conversation took place in mid-pitch not long after the pair had come together. Pistol was on 15, Warney on 8, and Pistol had just played and missed at three consecutive deliveries.

'We may as well start slogging, Pistol,' said Shane. 'What do you reckon?'

'No, not yet,' Paul replied, 'I only need three more to be the top scorer for Australia.'

In fact, Pistol did end up being top scorer in the innings, but he managed a lot more than 18. Such is the fighting spirit in the side that from this hopeless situation Warney (55) and Pistol (58) both played outstanding knocks and created a new world record one-day eighth-wicket partnership of 119.

Their fightback was never quite going to take us to victory, although the losing margin of 26 runs was much closer than we had anticipated after our disastrous start. In the dressing room after the match, Johno was a shell of a man, having lost his first game since he began following NSW and Australia over two years ago. He put it down to the unlucky 13th game syndrome, but a more believable excuse came to light when Maysie admitted to not consuming his lucky pre-match meal of a rack of ribs.

Craig Matthews, who took the most wickets for South Africa in both the Tests and the limited-overs internationals during the Australian tour.

DAY 60 *April 5*

WITH OUR hectic schedule of four one-day games over seven days plus the travelling in between firmly in his mind, Simmo decided rest was our best preparation for tomorrow's fixture in Cape Town. Both teams travelled on the same 8.30am South African Airways flight and we were in good spirits as we mixed together on the plane. This a process that is much easier during the one-day series than during a more intense Test match, when the players are more intent on worrying about the state of the game. One exception to this rule has been the friendship struck up between Jonty Rhodes and Shane Warne, who have become very good mates and always shared a drink at the end of each day's play during the Tests.

We checked into the Vineyard Hotel and unpacked our bags for what seemed like the 100th time on tour. My bags are in a sorry state of disarray, full of clothes that haven't seen an iron for quite a while. Then it was down to Kentucky Fried Chicken for a quick fix. KFC is a team favourite over here, especially as there are no McDonald's in South Africa, a situation that makes touring life a little tougher for this team of devoted Golden Arches fans. My afternoon was spent lazing around the hotel, as my shin is too sore to walk the 18 holes of golf that most of the other lads enjoyed.

Dinner was once again courtesy of the O'Hagan's chain of Irish pub/restaurants, with the only catch being the 45-minute drive there, which we weren't aware of when we set out. Another hidden trap that quickly came to light was the dangerous stretch of road we had to travel along to get to our dinner destination. We were obliged to go straight through black townships reportedly notorious for their sniper attacks on innocent motorists. However, after some worrying thoughts had crossed our minds, an enjoyable evening was had by all as the locals served up some fine hospitality.

Our fears as we travelled through the townships were yet another reminder of the fragile state of the country. It has been impossible not to notice the increasing media reports of violence of late, even if we have not come into direct contact with any disturbances. But as the April 27 election draws closer the potential for a bloody confrontation between the major parties grows by the day. As recently as the final day of the third Test, a massacre occurred after a Zulu march was met by supporters of the ANC. At least 15 people died in the battle. Most of the team have the feeling that something dreadful will happen shortly, and, to be honest, we cannot wait to get out of the country before such carnage erupts.

DAY 61 *April 6*

THESE DAY/NIGHT fixtures are a godsend for the players, as they allow you the luxury of a sleep-in. Being fond of my sleep, I rarely let such an opportunity slip and it was 10.30am before I felt the urge to become vertical. When I finally ventured down to the hotel foyer, I heard that Slats would miss today's game as he is struggling with vomiting and diarrhoea.

We were greeted at the ground by – you guessed it – another sell-out crowd, and they were probably as stunned as us when AB won the toss. Batting first in the day/night matches is much more important over here than in Australia, as the lighting isn't quite as good as at home, so our captain's success was very welcome. Even a minor deterioration in lighting conditions, which may appear innocuous to the spectator, can make things enormously difficult for a batsman, as that extra split second it takes to adjust can cost you your wicket.

With Slats unavailable, Matt Hayden was called into the team. This was a difficult assignment for him as he hasn't played for nearly a month, but Matt has kept active at practice and by surfing the local beaches at every opportunity. Our main concern was whether he would remember to wear spikes instead of sandals and creams in preference to board shorts. In such a situation, you invariably manage a low score (because you're not prepared) or a big one (because you have nothing to lose) but this occasion the former applied as Matt was trapped lbw to a shooter from the under-rated Matthews. Matt's opening partner in this match was Mark Taylor, who came in because Boonie's knee has been causing havoc of late. With Hayden gone, Jonesy came in but he fell victim to an umpiring error for the third time in the series, which has made it hard for him to impart his normal stamp of authority on the matches.

Jonesy's misfortune left the score at a sorry 2-10, but Junior and Tubs stead-

This guy looks so much like Boonie it's scary, and he didn't seem to mind the fact at all. We'd first seen this bloke during the second Test, and he quickly developed almost folk hero status within the Australian team, and especially with Boonie, who for some reason took something of a liking to the guy.

Dean Jones' run of luck in the one-dayers had been less than ordinary, and it continued at Newlands, when he was given out caught behind when few thought he hit the ball.

ied the ship and gradually grew in confidence – to the point where we were in command after 30 overs at 2-120. But then Taylor fell in freakish circumstances. Junior should have been caught at cover, but the simple chance was spilt, only for the ball to be regathered quickly and thrown to the non-striker's end, where Tubs was stranded out of his ground. Junior followed soon after for 71, but AB came out to smash 40 off just 17 balls in an innings where he swung more like a baseballer than a cricketer and used his strong forearms to muscle the ball to all parts of the ground.

We looked upon our total of 6-242 as being enough, as we generally defend totals much more successfully than we chase targets. And so it proved. Through some consistent bowling and keen fielding the South Africans found themselves behind the required run-rate from the very first over and were never in a position from which victory looked likely. Warne and May tied the opposition up with subtle changes in flight and there was enough turn to have the batsmen doubting their ability to be aggressive and get away with it. The only South African to look at ease was Hudson, who is enjoying a 'hot streak' at the moment, and he combined a little bit of luck with quality strokemaking for 62, before his downfall snuffed out the flicker of hope he was providing for his team. Kepler Wessels looked all at sea in his quest for quick runs – a task that seems to be very much against his natural game. He is an accumulator of runs rather than a thrasher of the ball, a fact the crowd didn't appreciate, and they continually jeered his efforts before giving an enormous cheer when he was finally dismissed. South Africa ended up 36 runs short of our total, with Warney returning the best figures (3-31 from 10 overs).

The series now stands at 4-3 in favour of the locals, but the way we are playing at the moment we must be a good thing to level the series in the last game at Bloemfontein. It appears the South African team is now even more jaded than we are, a change that has really only emerged in the past few days. The weariness of the two teams is not surprising, considering the amount of cricket we have played over the past five months. We have played six Tests against each other (for two wins, two losses and two draws) and 14 one-day internationals (for seven wins each). Such even returns are no fluke – there really is very little between the two teams.

DAY 62 *April 7*

THANKFULLY SIMMO and Cam Battersby didn't make us catch the 7.30am flight the South Africans were on. Instead we boarded a late-afternoon flight – a decision by management that was much appreciated. The whole touring party, including Chips (who has been under the care of Merv for the past week), were dreading the thought of the journey to Bloemfontein, as it involved a stopover at Kimberley and a total time of two and a half hours from airport to airport. It's a pity our fines committee dissolved midway through the tour – due to the exemplary behaviour of the party and the consequent lack of penalties to be handed out – or there might have been some penalties being handed today to the people responsible for our schedule. Actually that was not the real reason the fines committee went out of existence. I think it was either because the meetings were just forgotten, or perhaps the boys lost interest and wanted to save their money instead.

Another nightmare awaited us at the airport at Bloemfontein, as hordes of autograph hunters swarmed all over us and the usual bedlam of bags going missing and officials and porters running around like headless chickens occurred. By the time we finally set off for the hotel 45 minutes later, we were all a little bit hot under the collar.

During the course of the tour the team has received many hundreds of letters, cards and faxes from supporters and critics in South Africa and Australia. One letter, which was addressed to the entire team, was passed on to me today from a lady who lives here in Cape Town, made me realise just how significant this tour has been for many people. I won't reproduce the entire letter, but here are a few paragraphs:

Just a few lines, firstly to welcome you all back to Cape Town. Secondly, writing to total strangers is a first for me, but I wanted to let you know how much we have enjoyed your visit. As one of the faceless thousands who would never get to tell you face to face, it seemed one way to do it.

At a very difficult time for those of us living in this country, you have provided us with outstanding entertainment that has had us riveted to either radio or television sets for days at a time. Our minds have had a break from the tensions around us, with nothing more important than the next ball to be bowled. Some days we feel that maybe, just maybe, with a great big dose of luck, with our faith in human nature, that we may have a chance at building a great new nation, only to have such naive notions dashed the following day by some senseless carnage.

I'm sure it hasn't been easy on you all either, not knowing whether you should be here or not. Well know this, that we do appreciate it and have loved every minute. Your professionalism and enthusiasm have shown through your games and we have learned a great deal from you ...

We wish you Godspeed as you leave us in a few days time. We shall follow your careers with interest and would love to have you back sometime for some more lovely cricket.

Tonight I enjoyed a quick hotel feed, called home, and finally had a brief view of Matt H. and Slats dancing in the corridors to the music of Jimmy Barnes, which was filtering, via their portable CD player, through the whole floor.

Ian Healy, aggressive as ever, during Australia's match-winning 6-242 in the third day/night international.

DAY 63 *April 8*

WITH ONLY two days of the tour left many of us have, because of the generous hospitality shown to us by the people of South Africa, quite a few Rand left over. This currency is just about worthless outside the Republic, but fortunately a banking representative came in this morning to enable us to exchange our Rand for $US travellers' cheques. Then it was down to the ground, where another full house was expected for what we saw as a vital game – as far as we were concerned a four-all result would be a good effort after being three-one down at the halfway point.

Our selectors sprang somewhat of a surprise by leaving Jonesy out of the side. The fully recovered Slater slotted back into the opening spot, while Junior was moved up to number three and Boonie came back in at number four. In addition, because the pitch looked like it would favour the seamers rather than the spinners, Damien Fleming made his first appearance of the series, replacing Maysie, who had played in the previous three one-dayers.

AB called correctly, in what will be almost certainly his last international (the fact this was his farewell in itself represented more than enough motivation for us to win tonight). Needless to say, we elected to bat first, but Taylor was out with the total on seven, and M. Waugh and Slater had joined him by the time the score had reached 69. However, the last 20 overs were quite profitable. Boonie finished with 45, I scored 42 at better than a run a ball, and Heals displayed great skill in reaching 41 off just 30 balls – the type of knock we have now come to expect from one of the best players in the world in the last five overs of a one-day innings. We finished with a very competitive total of 6-203, which set the scene for an exciting climax to our tour.

With *True Blue* blaring from the music box, the boys looked fired up for a big performance as we stepped out onto the field for our last outing in South Africa. The combination of having a chance to level the series and to be able to give AB a fitting farewell had me fired up for a huge effort, as I am sure it did the other players as well.

However, despite our best intentions, things looked shaky for much of the evening. Hudson once again proved to be a stumbling block, and he punished anything slightly off line for runs, usually boundaries. After 40 overs he appeared to have steered his side in a winning position at 2-143. But then McGrath finally had a piece of luck as Cronje was clean bowled, and we had a chance. The ball that dismissed the South African vice-captain just clipped the top of one bail, a welcome change of fortune for Glenn, who had appeared cursed right through the one-day series. Before the Cronje wicket, he had just three wickets to his name for the entire series, despite being arguably our best bowler.

Fifteen runs later came the vital breakthrough, when the miserly Reiffel removed Hudson, caught by Border. This wicket completely changed the nature of the game. From here on in we gained momentum, using a mixture of desperation and skill such as when Healy got rid of McMillan with a back flick that ran him out. Once again only a single bail came off.

With two overs to go, South Africa needed 17 runs with 4 wickets standing. Yours truly and Fleming were the bowlers left to be heroes or villains. I had the easier job of the two, in bowling the penultimate over, and things went according to plan (three runs off the first two balls) until an attempted yorker fell

Mark Waugh, during his innings of 71 in the third day/night international at Newlands, which won him the Man-of-the-Match award.

short of the intended mark and was picked up for six by Eric Simons. As the white ball sailed over the boundary, the crowd went into a frenzy ... while I went looking for a hole to crawl into. However, my next delivery found it's mark and had the desired result – Simons bowled Waugh. Then the final two balls cost just two singles, which left Fleming with the difficult situation of six needed by the locals, three wickets remaining, and the odds very much against an Aussie victory.

However, the determination and fight we had showed all day was still very much in evidence and Flem bowled a magnificent over under huge pressure to see us to a memorable victory by just one run – as good a win as I've been associated with. Our victory meant that, in a way, justice had been done, as neither side deserved to lose the series. The cricket was very evenly contested throughout, and was also played in a good and competitive spirit.

The end-of-the-series awards were presented on the field at the conclusion of the game, and, to my surprise, I was presented with the Man-of-the-Series award to sit alongside the Man-of-the-Series trophy I won after the Tests. This was a dual recognition I didn't really expect, but was very pleased to accept. Back in the dressing room, the emotions were mixed with the jubilation at our fantastic fighting win countered by the sadness we all felt at the thought of AB not playing with us again. And there was disbelief at the sudden and unexpected announcement from Jonesy that he would be retiring from international cricket, effective tonight. Jonesy explained his frustration at not being able to force his way back into the Test team, even though he was still a one-day regular. Having played with and against him, I know how he desperately wanted to wear the baggy green cap again and when he thought that was an impossibility he didn't want to keep torturing himself. At times like these, you feel for your fellow player – and from a selfish point of view you're sad because you know you'll never have the chance to play alongside that bloke again.

Allan Border, during his cavalier 40 not out at Cape Town on April 6.

DAY 64 *April 9*

IT'S ALWAYS a strange feeling the morning after the last day's cricket on tour. It's as if you're on remote control – you're ready to go to training or play again even though you're aware it's time to relax and forget about cricket for a while. A short flight back to Jo'burg was required, as the four players not going to Sharjah – Border, Jonesy (Matt Hayden is now going instead), Healy and Hughes – are due to leave from here early tomorrow morning, while the remainder fly to the Middle East the following day. After checking back into our home away from home, the Sandton Sun Hotel, we had one last duty to perform – the purchase of a present for our manager, Cam Battersby, who has been tremendous throughout the tour, supporting the team in every possible way. Another to offer great assistance to the team has been our liaison officer, Doug Russell, whose job it has been to organise buses, plane tickets, baggage, functions and defuse any travelling problems that have risen from time to time, which he has done without ever once complaining. This duo, plus physio Lindsay Tregar and coach Bob Simpson have provided a solid base for the side and played a significant part in the success of the team.

Late in the afternoon the squad gathered in a room at the hotel to have a 'signing session', where items such as team photos, bats, souvenir stumps, balls and clothing are passed from player to player to be autographed. This took the best part of an hour. Then it was on to Mulligan's Irish pub, the owners of which had foolishly volunteered their establishment as the venue for our farewell party. The lads were keen to let their hair down and immediately began to dismantle the upper shelf of the liquor cabinet with a series of exotic concoctions that included a Springbok, a Pickled Brain, B52s and Mudslides – just to kick the evening off. The boys were in good spirits by the time the karaoke machine was put into operation, and Slats' arm was sufficiently twisted for him to be the first lamb to the slaughter.

Much to everyone's amazement, Slater proved to be a revelation behind the microphone and sent the audience into a frenzy with a rendition of Elvis Presley that featured a dance routine the King himself would have been proud of. But sadly, from here on in the performances were a little shoddy. I graced the stage with Tubs, Matt and Slats and tried to sing *Khe Sanh* without the help of the karaoke machine, and the result was inevitable – one that belonged in a shower recess not on a stage in front of a stunned gathering. If the crowd thought this effort was below par, they wouldn't have been converted by our next number, the Carly Simon classic *You're So Vain*, which wasn't a good choice for the questionable singing talents of M. Taylor and S. Waugh.

Next morning ....

Everyone managed to wake up – a relief to those who had seen us during our celebrations last evening and farewells were bid to those departing, which signalled the end of a tour that will be long remembered by all those who were a part of it. Hopefully I will be back for the next one, and the team will go one step better and return home as winners. I believe we put in a fine effort through the tour, and have a lot to be proud of, but I must admit there wasn't the same totally satisfied feeling you have when you board the flying kangaroo for the long trip home victorious.

FAREWELL
TO A
CHAMPION
V500
V500

Allan Border, during his farewell Test innings, in Australia's second innings of the third Test, in Durban.

Australian Picture Library — Tertius Pickard (All Sport)

Above: Paul Reiffel keeps the autograph hunters happy in Durban.
Below: The Kingsmead ground at Durban, during the third Test.

Above and belo
Australian Picture Library
Thomas Turck (All Spo

Mark Taylor (in white hat) congratulates Shane Warne on a wicket at Kingsmead. Shane finished with 4-92 from a marathon 55 overs, as South Africa ground out a big first-innings lead at funereal speed.

Australian Picture Library — Tertius Pickard (All Sport)

Michael Slater, during his second-innings 95 in the final Test.

Australian Picture Library — Thomas Turck (All Sport)

South African all-rounder Brian McMillan plays a rare attacking shot during his long innings in the third Test. He finished with 84.

Australian Picture Library — Thomas Turck (All Sport)

Hansie Cronje, the South African batting star of the series, during the third Test.
Australian Picture Library — Tertius Pickard (All Sport)

Mark Waugh acknowledges the Durban crowd after scoring the only Australian century of the Test series.

Australian Picture Library — Tertius Pickard (All Sport)

Above: Australian captain Allan Border, a hero and inspiration to a complete generation of Australian Test cricketers, walks onto the Durban ground to begin what proved to be his final innings in Test cricket.

Below: Allan Border (left) and South African captain Kepler Wessels, sharing the spoils after the drawn third Test.

Above and belo
Australian Picture Library — Tertius Pickard (All Spo

EPILOGUE *June 1994*

BY THE TIME the entire Australian touring squad were safely back on Aussie soil, the much talked about South African election had produced a new President ... Mr Nelson Mandela. Fortunately, our worst fears of mass sabotage and murder during this tumultuous changeover period did not materialise. In fact, almost the complete reverse occurred. A few of my newly made friends in South Africa expressed to me a feeling of relief – it was as if a heavy weight had been lifted from their shoulders. The days of the dreaded *apartheid* regime were now gone forever. These people spoke positively about the future of their 'new' country.

This optimism came as a great relief to all those who had toured with the Australian team. The pre-election mood had been nervy, with the belief that widespread trouble was imminent. And even though we did not come across any trouble first-hand, there was always a feeling that something ugly could erupt at any time. To know that this did not happen in the weeks after Mr Mandela's triumph augurs well for the future of the country.

Not long after Mr Mandela's victory was confirmed, the uncertainty over the top position in Australian cricket was resolved as well. On May 11, Allan Border announced he had decided to retire from international cricket. Not long after, Mark Taylor was confirmed as his successor, with Ian Healy his deputy. The period that led up to AB's decision must have been an agonising one for him, especially as he was still playing to a level that would have seen him continue to be successful for many years to come. Without doubt, there would have been many reasons behind his decision but, in the end, I believe he made the right choice because he went out with his form sky-high, like every champion should.

If you asked me to nominate one moment in AB's career that summed up the man, I would think back to the typically cold, overcast Yorkshire morning that greeted the players as we alighted off the team coach at Headingley on morning three of the Fourth Test of the 1993 Ashes series. At that point we led the best-of-six series 2-0. The general consensus in the media that morning was that we had more than enough runs and would declare before the morning's play began. At the end of play the previous evening, we were in the impregnable position of 4-613. AB was 175 not out, while I was unbeaten on 144, and our stand had brought 292 runs.

The media, however, hadn't counted on the ruthlessness of AB. He had been on the wrong end of too many hidings during the early and mid-1980s while wearing his baggy green cap, could still recall the helplessness of such a situation, and could still remember the mental state his players were in at the time. Our captain announced we would be batting on for 30 or 40 more minutes ... 'to cause further mental and physical disintegration of the opposition.' That one statement sums up for me the killer instinct that has made Allan Border such a champion player and competitor throughout his career.

As long as I have known him, he was tough on the cricket field, but always fair. I first came into contact with Allan Border during the 1984-85 Sheffield Shield final. I had been fortunate enough to get a last-minute call-up into the Blues line-up after Geoff Lawson, our Test fast bowler, had failed a fitness test. This was only my fifth Shield game and it developed into one of the greatest contests I have ever been involved in. After a titanic struggle over five days NSW scraped home over Queensland by a solitary wicket, but my most vivid memory of that game is not the sweet taste of victory ... it is the unexpected sportsmanship of one of the opposition players.

In NSW's first innings, I managed to score 71. When I was dismissed, I was making my way back to the pavilion when I caught sight, out of the corner of my eye, of a figure racing towards me. It turned out to be Allan Border. He shook my hand and said: 'Well played.' It was a gesture that surprised me, and meant a great deal to me. Allan was the Australian captain, a position he had been given earlier that season, after the shock resignation of Kim Hughes.

This brief acquaintance left a lasting impression. His recognition of a fine performance by an opposition player was never forgotten and always respected.

My career began to merge with AB's when I won my first Test cap in late 1985. My first two years as an international cricketer proved to be testing ones, not only for myself but also for our leader as the team struggled to become a successful unit. I believe there were many reasons behind our ordinary performances. Players were looking after their own interests and not those of the team. Some team members were simply not up to Test standard, having been selected only because 15 Australian players were taking part in a 'rebel' tour of South Africa. And many of the team had adopted an amateurish attitude. In addition, the knowledge that AB had taken over the captaincy by default – he had apparently not been overly keen on the job, and was seen at the time as being somewhat of a 'least worst' candidate – had led to an unstable environment in which the team was trying to function.

The whole situation came to a head during a rather infamous press conference during our tour of New Zealand in early 1986, when AB poured his heart out and demanded a better performance from the Australian team or else he'd resign. In hindsight, I'm sure he would have preferred to have tackled the problems differently, but this was his way of telling the players they weren't showing the necessary pride and professionalism expected of an Australian cricketer. If we didn't change .... he couldn't continue playing in a team that was performing well below the standards he expected of himself and his Australian team.

Motivation within a team can be inspired by words or actions by individual members. AB definitely preferred the latter method, especially in his early years as captain. His attitude and commitment had quickly become legendary, and he combined these characteristics with a will to win and pride in playing for his country that was second to none. He expected his colleagues to follow suit.

Just being in the same side made me feel if I gave anything less than my very best I was letting down not only my captain and myself but also the people of Australia, who we were representing. I never saw AB not give 100 per cent while wearing the fabled baggy green cap, even if the game was petering out to a boring draw or we were involved in a minor tour game. His every action on the cricket field suggested he realised how fortunate he was to have the chance of playing cricket for his country.

Many people over the years have labelled AB as 'Captain Grumpy'. Which only goes to prove he's human! The position of leader of the Australian cricket team is the ultimate in Australian sport and consequently has many unseen pressures associated with it. AB's 'grumpy' reputation has also been enhanced because of his nature, which is to keep his emotions locked away until it becomes all too much. Then someone would cop the lot in one swift barrage.

Allan Border, batting in the third Day/Night International at Newlands.

And the truth was that his 'dark' days normally only occurred when he believed the team was not giving enough of themselves and when individuals were not doing everything in their power to perform at their peak.

During the second half of his Test career (which had begun in 1978) Allan blossomed as a captain. As he developed a belief in his own leadership abilities he became a supremely confident skipper who plotted and schemed the downfall of opposition teams and began to motivate his side by words as well as actions. The turning point for his Australian team came when we won the 1987 World Cup in India. We went into that tournament as rank outsiders but captured the ultimate prize thanks to the expertise and wisdom of captain Allan Border and coach Bob Simpson, who had devised a plan before the competition that deliberately intended to separate our style of cricket from all the other cricket nations. That formula revolved around opening batsman Geoff Marsh occupying as many overs as possible to anchor the innings, while the more aggressive batsmen around him played higher risk shots to keep the run-rate moving. And we considered it essential that we retained six or seven wickets for an assault during the final 10 overs of the innings. We also adopted a more aggressive approach to running between wickets. As for the bowlers, we knew approximately at which point of the innings each one would be required, which helped us focus on when we would be needed. And we were supported by fielding that had improved out of sight after endless hours of hard work.

From virtually the moment we lifted the World Cup, the fortunes of Australian cricket changed for the better. Our rise culminated in the magnificent 4-0 Ashes victory in England in 1989, when, it should be remembered, we began the series as underdogs. We won that famous series because we believed in ourselves, while AB's confidence in his own leadership reached the point where he was plotting strategies on opposition players that were often less than conventional but were proved remarkably effective. He would place fieldsman in positions you wouldn't find in the coaching manual; positions that were questioned by many a good judge until the 'good' judges realised they were working.

A perfect example of this was the downfall during the series of Graham Gooch, who we saw as the linchpin of the English batting line-up. AB's plan was quite simple. He knew Gooch liked to play across the line and score heavily through mid-wicket, so he placed two fieldsman in catching positions at short mid-wicket – the intention being to make the batsman think he had to change his plan of attack. At first glance the field placements looked illogical, but Gooch was quickly doubting the value of a shot he would normally play without a second thought. Suddenly he was attempting to avoid the fieldsman and attempting shots he wasn't familiar with. His indecision more often than not led to him being dismissed lbw and by series' end he looked a shadow of the great player we all knew he could be – all because AB had upset the mental side of his game.

Allan could be as superstitious as the next cricketer, especially in tight situations. I remember the conclusion to the second Test of the '89 Ashes series, at Lord's, when we needed 118 in our second innings to win the match, but had lost 4-67 to create a potentially exciting finish. However, Boonie and I steadied the ship somewhat, to the point where the target had been reduced to around 30. When a partnership begins to blossom in a situation such as this, the other players will inevitably refuse to budge from their seats or whatever position they're occupying at the time, which for AB on this occasion was the bathroom area of our change room. There was no way he was going to risk breaking up a key partnership by changing his position, even if it meant he didn't see another ball bowled. So he stayed exactly where he was. Fortunately (for Australia) we didn't lose another wicket on our way to the win, which left AB having to shave a couple of times and shower for over an hour until he was told it was safe for him to come out an enjoy the victory.

That '89 tour was a 'lifetime' tour for the Aussie squad. Team morale and camaraderie were exceptional, and this spirit continued in the years that followed. We had only one real hiccup – in the Caribbean in 1991 when we lost a hard-fought series 2-1 – a setback that made us all the more determined to topple the Windies in Australia in 1992-93. This was what we always considered the ultimate test ... a full five-Test series against the West Indies for the unofficial title of the world's No. 1 team. We had all dreamed of reaching this pinnacle, but none more so than AB, who had always aspired to lead Australia back to the very top of the pile. The '92-93 rubber was the seventh time he had been part of an Australian team that had challenged the West Indies in a three- or five-Test series, and in the previous six he had never been part of the series-winning side

On the fourth day of the fourth Test, in Adelaide, it seemed as if we were finally going to achieve our goal, as we needed 186 for victory, with all 10 wickets in hand to take an unbeatable 2-0 lead in the series. However, the West Indies showed all their renowned fighting qualities and class to reduce us to 9-144, with tailenders Tim May and Craig McDermott the two batsmen still at the crease. The Test looked lost, but Tim and Craig refused to budge and dramatically edged us towards the target. They took the total to within 10 of victory, while the Australian players in the dressing room remained glued to their seats, playing each ball as if they were out in the middle. This was an atmosphere as nervous and tense as any we had ever experienced.

As always in tight situations, AB had a cricket ball in his possession, which he tossed from hand to hand. He calls it his 'worry ball'. The score edged to within two of victory, one for a tie, when Craig was given out caught behind off Courtney Walsh, leaving us all with a dreadful empty feeling ... as if we had been robbed of something that was rightfully ours. It was the cruellest loss in cricket I've ever had to accept. So hard did AB take the defeat that he stood up and threw his worry ball in to the ground so angrily it bounced up and hit the roof.

For the next 20 minutes not a word was said. We all knew how close we had come to being No. 1, and we were all feeling especially disappointed for AB, as we knew it was his last throw of the dice at the prize that meant so much to him.

In England in 1993, we again dominated, to eventually win by four Tests to one. That partnership I shared with AB at Headingley ended up being worth 332 before Allan finally declared, and we went on to win the Test by an innings and 148 runs, and take an unassailable 3-0 lead in the series. That partnership was the third stand of over 175 we had put together in Test cricket. I am very aware that a great deal of my success in international cricket has come while AB was at the other end. In trying to work out why, I keep coming back to the fact that every time I was at the non-striker's end I could look down the pitch and see a man who put an enormous value on his wicket, possessed great courage and pride (in fact, I never once saw him show any pain, even with broken fingers, torn muscles or, worst of all, a blow in the mid-region), loved batting for Australia and enjoyed the heat of the battle. All these values were passed on to his batting partners. I felt that if I didn't approach the game in the same way I would not only be letting myself down, but also the team and the Australian team's supporters.

Unfortunately for AB and Australia, we didn't manage to beat South Africa in South Africa in 1994. It was our captain's last series, and we all desperately wanted to win. It was, however, a dream come true for all of us as we had not thought it would be possible for Australia to play against South Africa in our lifetime. AB, of course, left on a high note, remaining unbeaten on 42 in his farewell Test innings, for one last time not giving an inch to the opposition. When he walked off the field at Durban that day, there was a feeling of sadness in all the members of the Australian team. We didn't like the thought of not being able to play alongside this champion in the baggy green cap again. He will be sorely missed by players and spectators, but his legacy and the memories of him will not be forgotten in our lifetime.

After the South African tour was over, I approached the guys in the Australian team and asked them what they would remember most about Allan Border, and if they had a favourite Allan Border story. Here, in no particular order, are their responses ...

Mark Taylor

I will always remember AB's competitive spirit and his 'never say die' attitude with the bat. This was perhaps never better illustrated than when he scored 200 not out at Headingley in 1993, when he batted as poorly as I've ever seen him for his first 50, but hung in there and ended up with his double century.

My favourite Allan Border story occurred in Sri Lanka in 1992. I was catching a motorised rickshaw with him from the Taj Sumatra Hotel to the Hilton Hotel for dinner, and we were racing three other rickshaws occupied by other members of the Australian team. AB offered our driver an extra 50 rupees if we reached the Hilton first ...

We'd just taken the lead when we were cut off at a roundabout by a large official car. The driver of our rickshaw swerved to miss the car, locked up the steering, and we flipped over onto our side, before sliding for about 30 metres as sparks flew and our petrol tank ruptured. I ended up as a sandwich between the road and my captain, and we clambered out shaken but none the worse for the experience.

But we hadn't won, and AB refused to pay the fare, on the grounds that the driver was unable to complete the journey.

Quite rightly so!

Merv Hughes

I'll always remember how AB led by example and the way he played in the tough situations the side sometimes got itself into. He always saved his best for when the team most needed it.

I'll never forget one blast I copped from the captain. In the sixth and final Test of the 1989 Ashes series at The Oval, I had bowled two bouncers at Robin Smith, and then a third was called a no-ball (for intimidatory bowling) by the umpire, Harold 'Dickie' Bird. AB came flying in from mid-wicket to discuss this with Dickie, and as I walked past I heard:

AB: 'What's going on, Harold?'

Dickie: 'That's three in a row!'

AB: 'Why didn't you say something to Merv last ball instead of just no-balling him?'

Dickie: 'I did.'

Then I copped the blast from AB.

Michael Slater

I feel privileged to have had the opportunity to play 15 Test matches with AB. It is hard to believe that I was eight years old when he played his first Test match and that, 15 years later, after idolising him throughout my school life, I was suddenly playing alongside him.

Because of his legendary status, it took me quite a while before I felt comfortable around him. However, it soon became apparent that, yes, he was a legend, but also a normal, down-to-earth bloke who had a lot of time for people and enjoyed an uncomplicated lifestyle. He was a fun bloke to tour with and enjoyed a good laugh. I learned a lot about the game by just listening to him and especially by watching the way he went about his batting

The highlight for me was batting with him last season in the Sydney Test against South Africa. Our partnership realised more than 100 in very tough conditions. His concentration, allied to his legendary determination, provided a magnificent learning experience – something I could only benefit from.

AB – it has been an enormous pleasure to have played with you, and I wish you every success in retirement.

Thanks for everything!

Craig McDermott

AB to me was the complete cricketer. He was a player with guts, and a passion for the game he had no problem proving to anyone. He is one of the best players I have ever seen – I don't think they come any better.

There are a few words that I think go well for Allan Border ...

'He dreamed, he believed, he created, he succeeded.'

Cam Battersby *(Manager)*

We were in New Zealand in 1990, and I was on my first tour and pretty wet behind the ears. Some might say: 'What's changed?' I enquired of AB what the dress was for internal air travel and he replied: 'Jeans.' So I turned up in team shirt and Levis – while everyone else, including AB, was wearing blazer and tie. Embarrassment!

On another occasion in Sri Lanka, we were listed to do a promotional appearance at a supermarket, and the boys were whingeing (as usual). AB was being particularly intransigent. I stuck to my guns. Eventually he said: 'You've made up your mind, Cam, haven't you?' 'Yes,' I replied, and he said: 'Okay, we'll go.' So we did and everyone seemed to enjoy it.

One of the most courageous decisions I've ever seen made on a cricket field was made on that Sri Lankan tour. In the first Test in Colombo, AB gave Shane the ball with Sri Lanka needing a handful of runs and four wickets in hand. Shane was playing in his third Test, and still didn't have even one Test wicket to his name. But half an hour later, we'd won an improbable victory.

David Boon

AB is a cricketer of great determination and courage and a man with an enormous pride in his own game. Throughout his career, as he represented his country so many times, it is these attributes that are the reason why he climbed to the pinnacle of world cricket. He leaves the playing arena with a record amount of runs, and a reputation as one of the most respected players in the game.

I'm sure all who have played with AB have found it a pleasure and an honour to have been associated with him.

Thanks mate!

Glenn McGrath

Since I haven't played too many games with AB, I don't have too many stories to tell. But there is one thing I remember about him.

Every now and then when we were in the field, I would be fielding on the boundary and in between balls would sometimes switch off and gaze around the crowd or sign some autographs. Occasionally, AB would pick this precise moment to try and get my attention to change my position in the field. Only after most of the team were screaming, yelling and signalling at me did I realise it was my attention they were after. Then, after AB had moved me less than a metre, I wondered whether it had all been worth it.

AB, however, tells it differently.

This was the only time that AB lost his temper, even slightly, with me. I found AB to be a great captain, and never found the nickname 'Grumpy' to be appropriate.

I remember listening to the cricket on the radio when I was nine or 10, and AB was batting for Australia. He has been one of the all-time greats of Test cricket, and a man the Australian team will sadly miss. To have played alongside him will remain one of my greatest achievements. I wish AB all the best for the future. It has been a great honour to have played with him.

Ian Healy

The thing I'll remember most about AB is his absolute love for the traditions of the game. His passion for cricket and his actions demonstrated this even more so than his words.

My favourite story concerning him is one I was told happened during the Australian tour of the West Indies in 1984. The Aussies struggled throughout this series against one of cricket's all-time great and dangerous pace attacks (Malcolm Marshall, Joel Garner and so on), with only AB able to score runs consistently against them. In the second Test in Trinidad, AB was batting (alone again) and mumbled to himself that he thought Garner was a 'big c—!'. Straightaway, Des Haynes at short leg informed Joel that AB had called him a 'BLACK c—!', and AB then had to weather until stumps one of the biggest storms of his career.

Happily, the two sorted things out the next day at warm-ups, and AB went on to score 98 not out.

AB and myself at the press conference after our second Test win in Cape Town.

Dean Jones

The two things I'll most remember about AB were that he never held a grudge against a team-mate, even after he given them a rocket and that he was always able to score well, even though he felt he was playing badly.

His best line came during the tied Test in Madras in 1986. I was 160-odd not out in our first innings and feeling bloody awful, so bad in fact that I told AB I wanted to go off. He just looked at me and said: 'Okay, let's get a tough Australian – a Queenslander, Greg Ritchie – out here.' No disrespect to Greg, who I like very much, but a 'QUEENSLANDER'! Nice one coming from a New South Welshman!

Tim May

AB's fame is such that there have been many people I have met in my travels who have known absolutely nothing about cricket, in some cases very little about Australia, but they've heard about Allan Border. I can remember one bloke in Sharjah who gave us a lift in his Volvo one day who told us time and again the only thing he knew about Australian cricket was Allan Border. What he didn't realise was that our captain was in the back seat at the time.

I'll always picture Allan Border, the Australian Test cricket captain, in pretty much the same way every Australian cricket fan saw him – as the anchor for the entire Australian side. I know the analogy has been used many times over the years, but when AB walked onto the cricket field you really could see the Australian flag flowing out behind him. And I will always appreciate the fact that he was never in it for the personal glory – all he wanted was what was best for his side.

Paul Reiffel

Allan Border's leadership was invaluable, but the one thing I will always remember is the loyalty he showed to the team. It was so obvious. He gave 100 per cent to the team and he expected 100 per cent back, and if you did that he was with you all the way.

I remember the fourth Test against India in Adelaide in 1991-92, when I was the Australian 12th man. I hadn't played a Test at that stage in my career. Before the start of the final day, in which Australia would be fielding, we found out that Geoff Marsh had been dropped for the fifth Test. Geoff was AB's vice-captain. AB told me to get my whites on and go out and field for him, while he went and rang the chairman of selectors to find out what was going on. He must have been off the field for the best part of an hour, fighting the case for his good friend. This incident displayed the extent of the loyalty AB could have for his team-mates.

He would do anything for them.

Bob Simpson *(Coach)*

No higher praise can be given to Allan than to say he was a players' player. While others may have had more style and dash, no player in my experience made more of his natural gifts than did the skipper. He learned early to play within his talents and this, I believe, is what made him such a great player for such a long time. It was also the key to his amazing consistency. Apart from Sir Donald Bradman, no other player in the history of the game has matched him in this area. Within the first two years of his career, Allan was averaging over 50 and it stayed that way for the next 14 years. And in his time, no-one matched his accuracy in throwing – I reckon he hit the stumps more than any other player in the sport.

One of the unknown facts about Allan's great career is that he is part of the team that holds the world grape-catching record. It happened 20 years ago – Allan was only 18 and happy to pick up any dollar that came along. I was running my own sports promotion business at the time, and was approached by the Wine Marketing Board to organise two challengers for the title. It was really quite simple. Two cricketers were needed, one to throw and one to catch. For me, the choices were obvious – Allan Border to throw and John Dyson to catch ... not with his hands but with his mouth. AB was outstanding, with throws of 50 metres raining in on that target. But Dyson was struggling. Finally, after five throws, the record was achieved, after John finally got one in his mouth rather than all over his face. This was the first of many records to fall Allan's way, but it was one that had little impact on him. Since that time, I have hardly seen him drink the grape – he usually prefers his beloved XXXX.

Mark Waugh

What I will most remember about AB is his great competitiveness. No matter what or where he was playing, or the situation of the game, AB gave nothing less than 100 per cent and expected the same from his players.

His commitment to the game was outstanding. The fact that he was able to stay at the top for so long and that he gave so much time to the things that go with being the Australian cricket captain – the media, the practice, the overseas tours and soon – is really quite remarkable.

Errol Alcott *(Physio)*

I WILL always remember AB as one of those true Aussie battlers. He's a gritty little fellow, who had an amazing ability throughout his career of being able to focus on the job at hand. He had his fair share of injuries – which weren't usually documented in the press – but he was able to distance himself from them. The injuries were usually broken bones in the fingers or hands, rather than a torn muscle, but even so, when his number came up to go out to the middle he would just go and do it, without any obvious show of discomfort.

He was one of those characters who was rarely on the physio's bench. He did work on his fitness over the years, but I would never call him a fitness maniac. Some people like to purge their frustrations on the road or in the gym, but AB wasn't a fan of that. However, on the occasions when we really cracked down on fitness he would inevitably lead the way.

Because he rarely suffered any of the little niggling type of injuries (and when he did his attitude was simply to shrug them off), he could take a slightly cynical attitude to anyone who headed for the bench. If a player, usually a bowler of some sort, was lying on the bench after a break in play he'd come up and say: 'What's wrong with him now?' or refer to the player as a 'pussycat'. He *would* show concern for the player – he'd come up later and ask if the injury was going to put him out or impact on that player's performance – but he did like to have a bit of a joke at their expense. However, his cynicism came back to haunt him in one match at the MCG.

It was a day/nighter with a full house in. AB was fielding in close to the wicket, and had to make a reflex save to stop a ball that was travelling at some velocity. Of course he did his job and stopped it, but instead of bouncing to his feet, he stayed down on the ground. A few of the other players ran in, because he didn't usually do that sort of thing. And then I was waved on. I looked down at him, and could tell straightaway he had a broken finger.

'AB,' I said, 'big crowd tonight ... there must be 60,000 people here.'

He just mumbled something at me, and I replied: 'Look, if you're going to stay down in this position I'll go and get a bowl of milk for you.'

He took that rather indignantly. I strapped the finger and said: 'It's probably broken – you can either come off and rest it, or do you want to stay out here?' The answer was obvious, because he was the type of guy who would always stay out there, so long as he knew the injury wasn't going to hurt the team's performance. The following day X-rays confirmed the break, but there was a Test match coming up, so on he went. It was just another example of his remarkable ability to forget about the pain and go out and do the job.

An injury is only significant if it is going to damage the player's performance. For example, a bowler will be limited in his performance if he has a groin strain. A batsman or fieldsman like AB can tend to compensate for broken fingers and the like, but it still takes a special character to ignore the pain.

It was only late in his career that he suffered an injury that really affected him – a hamstring strain that cost him a few one-day internationals. I know this frustrated him. He had suffered so few injuries during his career, and consequently didn't really appreciate the entire recovery process. When he first damaged the leg, I'm sure he believed it was going to cost him a short time out of the game. But when we tested him out a little bit after three days, without upsetting the injury too much, he knew it wasn't right and that he couldn't go out and do what he wanted to do.

The whole process infuriated him – he hated being in the sidelines and not being involved.

When he finally came back I said to him: 'When you get out there, try not to take that quick single for your first hit. Try and warm the muscle up first.' He nodded his head, but then went out and hit this little dinky shot and scrambled for his first run. That was the type of guy he was – whatever the situation required, he obliged, without ever thinking of himself.

Shane Warne

Allan Border has been an idol of mine since I started playing cricket at the age of nine. I remember when my brother, Jason, and I used to play Test matches in the backyard and we'd imitate AB; to then, a bit more than a decade later, have had the chance the play alongside one of the greatest sportsmen and blokes of all time is something I will cherish.

I will always remember AB and the inspirational things he did. I've learned a lot of things from Allan Border. After all, he's played the most Tests ever and, for a young bloke like myself, having him there as a guide has given me a huge advantage. I am grateful for the time he has spent with me and the help he has provided.

There have been many great innings AB has played, but the two that stick out in my mind are the hundred against the West Indies at the MCG in 1992-93, when it was a tough game and the wicket was a bit uneven (sorry, Tony, I love the MCG wicket!), and the 200 against England at Headingley in 1993 – it was a superb innings.

I'll also never forget the look on his face when we won the Ashes in '93. It was one of a very proud man.

Matthew Hayden

AB is one of the most complicated characters I have ever met. You could say, when it comes to cricket, he is 'King of the Jungle'. Ruthless, determined, pugnacious, courageous, aggressive – words making up his claws which have shredded through the competitors that dare to enter his jungle.

But, inconsistent with this fighting nature, there is a softness in AB; the love and respect for his wife and three children. I admire this part of his character the most, as success so often makes people forget about the fundamentals of life, which are, or course, the very lifeblood of what led to this success in the first place.

AB – you'll be missed.

TOUR RECORD

TOUR SUMMARY

Date	Opponent	Venue	Result
February 10	Nicky Oppenheimer XI	Randjesfontein	Match abandoned (rain)
February 12-14	Nth Transvaal	Verwoerdburg	Australians won by 249 runs
February 17	President's XI	Potchefstroom	Match abandoned (rain)
One-Day Internationals			
February 19	South Africa	Johannesburg	South Africa won by five runs
February 20	South Africa	Verwoerdburg	South Africa won by 56 runs
February 22	South Africa	Port Elizabeth	Australia won by 88 runs
February 24	South Africa	Durban	South Africa won by 7 wickets
Feb 26-Mar 1	Orange Free State	Bloemfontein	Australians won by 60 runs
First Test			
March 4-8	South Africa	Johannesburg	South Africa won by 197 runs
March 12-14	Boland	Stellenbosch	Match drawn
Second Test			
March 17-21	South Africa	Cape Town	Australia by nine wickets
Third Test			
March 25-29	South Africa	Durban	Match drawn
Day/Night Internationals			
April 2	South Africa	East London	Australia won by seven wickets
April 4	South Africa	Port Elizabeth	South Africa won by 26 runs
April 6	South Africa	Cape Town	Australia won by 36 runs
April 8	South Africa	Bloemfontein	Australia won by one run

MATCHES	PLAYED	WON	LOST	DRAWN
Tests	3	1	1	1
Other first-class matches	3	2	1	-
§ Limited-overs internationals	8	4	4	-
§ Other limited-overs matches	2	-	-	2

§ *Non first-class matches*

*Note: In the following match records * indicates captain and # indicates wicketkeeper.*

THE TEST MATCHES

THE FIRST TEST *at the Wanderers, Johannesburg*
March 4-8 (South Africa won toss)

South Africa – First Innings

AC Hudson c Healy b McDermott	17
G Kirsten b Hughes	47
WJ Cronje c Border b SR Waugh	21
*KC Wessels c Hayden b Hughes	18
PN Kirsten b May	12
JN Rhodes c ME Waugh b McDermott	69
BM McMillan c Boon b May	0
#DJ Richardson lbw Warne	31
CR Matthews c Boon b Hughes	6
PS de Villiers b McDermott	14
AA Donald not out	0
Extras (1b, 10lb, 3nb)	14
Total	251

Fall of Wicket: 1-21, 2-70, 3-103, 4-116, 5-126, 6-126, 7-194, 8-203, 9-249, 10-251.
Bowling: McDermott 15.2-3-63-3; Hughes 20-6-59-3; May 22-5-62-2; SR Waugh 9-2-14-1; Warne 14-4-42-1.
Batting time: 327 minutes
Overs: 80.2

Australia – First Innings

MJ Slater c Hudson b de Villiers	26
ML Hayden c Richardson b Donald	15
DC Boon c de Villiers b Donald	17
ME Waugh run out	42
*AR Border run out	34
SR Waugh not out	45
#IA Healy b Matthews	11
MG Hughes c G Kirsten b McMillan	7
SK Warne lbw Matthews	15
CJ McDermott lbw Donald	31
TBA May lbw de Villiers	2
Extras (1b, 1lb, 1nb)	3
Total	248

Fall of Wickets: 1-35, 2-56, 3-70, 4-136, 5-142, 6-169, 7-176, 8-201, 9-245, 10-248.
Bowling: Donald 19-0-86-3; de Villiers 19.3-1-74-2; McMillan 14-3-46-1; Matthews 15-4-40-2.
Batting time: 303 minutes
Overs: 67.3

Man of the Match: WJ Cronje.

South Africa – Second Innings

AC Hudson b Warne 60	
G Kirsten c Hughes b May	35
WJ Cronje c SR Waugh b Hughes	122
*KC Wessels c Border b Warne	50
PN Kirsten c Boon b May	53
JN Rhodes c Healy b SR Waugh	14
PS de Villiers b McDermott	4
BM McMillan b Warne	24
#DJ Richardson c Border b Warne	20
CR Matthews not out	31
AA Donald not out	15
Extras (13b, 4lb, 5nb)	22
Total (9 wkts, declared)	450

Fall of Wicket: 1-76, 2-123, 3-258, 4-289, 5-324, 6-343, 7-366, 8-403, 9-406.
Bowling: McDermott 35-3-112-1; Hughes 25-5-86-1; May 39-11-107-2; SR Waugh 10-3-28-1; Warne 44.5-14-86-4; ME Waugh 6-2-14-0.
Batting time: 622 minutes
Overs: 159.5

Australia – Second Innings

MJ Slater b de Villiers	41
ML Hayden b de Villiers	5
DC Boon b Matthews	83
ME Waugh c Richardson b Donald	28
*AR Border c G Kirsten b McMillan	14
SR Waugh c Richardson b Matthews	0
#IA Healy c&b Donald	30
MG Hughes not out	26
SK Warne lbw McMillan	1
CJ McDermott b McMillan	10
TBA May c G Kirsten b Cronje	11
Extras (5lb, 2nb)	7
Total	256

Fall of Wickets: 1-18, 2-95, 3-136, 4-164, 5-164, 6-194, 7-219, 8-225, 9-235, 10-256.
Bowling: Donald 23-3-71-2; de Villiers 30-11-70-2; McMillan 19-2-61-3; Matthews 20-6-42-2; G Kirsten 4-0-7-0; Cronje 0.3-0-0-1.
Batting time: 417 minutes
Overs: 96.3

SOUTH AFRICA WON BY 197 RUNS

THE SECOND TEST *at Newlands, Cape Town*
March 17-21 (South Africa won toss)

South Africa – First Innings

AC Hudson run out	102
G Kirsten run out	29
WJ Cronje b McGrath	2
*KC Wessels c ME Waugh b McDermott	11
PN Kirsten lbw Warne	70
JN Rhodes lbw McGrath	5
BM McMillan b Warne	74
#DJ Richardson lbw lbw McDermott	34
CR Matthews not out	7
PS de Villiers c Taylor b Warne	7
AA Donald c Healy b McGrath	7
Extras (6lb, 7nb)	13
Total	361

Fall of Wicket: 1-71, 2-78, 3-100, 4-189, 5-198, 6-260, 7-335, 8-339, 9-348, 10-361.
Bowling: McDermott 27-6-80-2; Hughes 20-1-80-0; McGrath 26.1-4-65-3; SR Waugh 9-3-20-0; Warne 47-18-78-3; ME Waugh 10-3-23-0; Border 5-2-9-0.
Batting time: 575 minutes
Overs: 144.1

Australia – First Innings

MJ Slater c PN Kirsten b de Villiers	26
MA Taylor c Richardson b de Villiers	70
DC Boon c Richardson b de Villiers	96
ME Waugh c PN Kirsten b McMillan	7
*AR Border c Richardson b Matthews	45
SR Waugh b Matthews	86
#IA Healy c de Villiers b Matthews	61
MG Hughes lbw Matthews	0
SK Warne c McMillan b de Villiers	11
CJ McDermott c PN Kirsten b Matthews	1
GD McGrath not out	1
Extras (6b, 17lb, 1w, 7nb)	31
Total	435

Fall of Wickets: 1-40, 2-145, 3-153, 4-244, 5-310, 6-418, 7-418, 8-430, 9-434, 10-435.
Bowling: Donald 35-10-111-0; de Villiers 44.4-11-117-4; Matthews 36-12-80-5: McMillan 29-8-82-1; G Kirsten 4-0-13-0; Cronje 11-4-9-0.
Batting time: 691 minutes
Overs: 159.4

South Africa – Second Innings

AC Hudson lbw SR Waugh	49
G Kirsten lbw Warne	10
WJ Cronje c&b SR Waugh	19
*KC Wessels run out	9
PN Kirsten c Taylor b Warne	3
JN Rhodes c Border b SR Waugh	27
PS de Villiers lbw Warne	0
BM McMillan lbw SR Waugh	3
#DJ Richardson c Healy b McGrath	31
CR Matthews not out	0
AA Donald b SR Waugh	0
Extras (4b, 6lb, 3nb)	13
Total	164

Fall of Wicket: 1-33, 2-69, 3-94, 4-97, 5-97, 6-97, 7-103, 8-164, 9-164, 10-164.
Bowling: McDermott 13-3-39-0; Hughes 5-1-12-0; McGrath 16-6-26-1; SR Waugh 22.3-9-28-5; Warne 30-13-38-3; ME Waugh 3-1-11-0; Border 1-1-0-0.
Batting time: 352 minutes
Overs: 90.3

Australia – Second Innings

MJ Slater not out	43
MA Taylor b Donald	14
DC Boon not out	42
Extras (1b, 2nb)	3
Total (1 wkt)	92

Fall of Wickets: 1-30.
Bowling: de Villiers 6-1-20-0; Matthews 6-1-14-0; Donald 5-0-20-1; McMillan 5-0-23-0; G Kirsten 1.1-0-10-0; Cronje 2-0-4-0.
Batting time: 107 minutes
Overs: 25.1

Man of the Match: SR Waugh

AUSTRALIA WON BY NINE WICKETS

THE THIRD TEST *at Kingsmead, Durban*
March 25-29 (South Africa won toss)

Australia – First Innings

MJ Slater c Rhodes b Matthews	20
MA Taylor lbw Donald	1
DC Boon c G Kirsten b Donald	57
ME Waugh c Richardson b Donald	43
*AR Border c Rhodes b McMillan	17
SR Waugh c Wessels b Matthews	64
#IA Healy b Matthews	55
PR Reiffel lbw de Villiers	13
SK Warne c Wessels b Matthews	2
CJ McDermott c Donald b de Villiers	6
GD McGrath not out	0
Extras (1lb, 1w, 9nb)	11
Total	269

Fall of Wickets: 1-7, 2-45, 3-81, 4-123, 5-123, 6-215, 7-250, 8-256, 9-269, 10-269.
Bowling: Donald 18-1-71-3; de Villiers 24.2-5-55-2; Matthews 29-9-65-4: McMillan 19-5-56-1; Cronje 5-1-8-0; G Kirsten 6-1-13-0.
Batting time: 442 minutes
Overs: 101.2

South Africa – First Innings

AC Hudson lbw Reiffel	65
G Kirsten c Healy b Reiffel	41
WJ Cronje c SR Waugh b Warne	26
*KC Wessels lbw McDermott	1
PN Kirsten lbw SR Waugh	49
JN Rhodes lbw Warne	78
BM McMillan c Slater b SR Waugh	84
#DJ Richardson c Reiffel b Warne	59
CR Matthews lbw Warne	1
PS de Villiers lbw SR Waugh	0
AA Donald not out	0
Extras (3b, 10lb, 5nb)	18
Total	422

Fall of Wicket: 1-100, 2-117, 3-118, 4-155, 5-256, 6-274, 7-417, 8-422, 9-422, 10-422.
Bowling: McDermott 38-11-76-1; Reiffel 30-7-77-2; McGrath 41-11-78-0; Warne 55-20-92-4; SR Waugh 27.2-12-40-3; ME Waugh 11-3-38-0; Border 3-0-8-0.
Batting time: 832 minutes
Overs: 205.2

Australia – Second Innings

MJ Slater lbw Donald	95
MA Taylor lbw de Villiers	12
DC Boon c PN Kirsten b Donald	12
SK Warne c McMillan b Donald	12
ME Waugh not out	113
*AR Border not out	42
Extras (6lb, 1w, 4nb)	11
Total (4 wkts)	297

Fall of Wickets: 1-55, 2-81, 3-109, 4-157.
Bowling: Donald 28-7-66-3; de Villiers 24-5-69-1; Matthews 28-12-56-0; McMillan 22-6-53-0; Cronje 18-5-40-0; G Kirsten 3-1-7-0; Rhodes 1-1-0-0.
Batting time: 501 minutes
Overs: 124

Man of the Match: ME Waugh
Man of the Series: SR Waugh

MATCH DRAWN

OTHER FIRST-CLASS MATCHES

v NORTHERN TRANSVAAL *at Centurion Park, Verwoerdberg*
February 12-14 (Northern Transvaal won toss)

Australians – First Innings

MJ Slater b van Noordwyk	51
*MA Taylor b van Noordwyk	28
DC Boon run out	48
ME Waugh c Rule b Elworthy	8
ML Hayden c Rule b Smith	50
DM Jones c Rule b Elworthy	85
#IA Healy c Vorster b Smith	12
PR Reiffel c Rule b Elworthy	22
MG Hughes c&b Elworthy	30
TBA May not out	1
GD McGrath b Bosch	4
Extras (7lb, 1w, 16nb)	24
Total	363

Fall of Wickets: 1-62, 2-99, 3-141, 4-147, 5-273, 6-298, 7-309, 8-350, 9-358, 10-363
Bowling: Elworthy 25-5-85-4; Smith 20-1-97-2; Bosch 18.2-4-48-1; van Noordwyk 19-4-70-2; Pienaar 7-1-39-0; van Zyl 5-0-17-0.
Batting time: 412 minutes
Overs: 94.5

Australians – Second Innings

MJ Slater b Smith	8
*MA Taylor c Smith b van Zyl	75
ME Waugh st Rule b Sommerville	134
#IA Healy not out	38
DC Boon lbw van Zyl	1
ML Hayden not out	4
Extras (4b, 2w, 5nb)	11
Total (4 wkts, declared)	281

Fall of Wickets: 1-19, 2-184, 3-244, 4-245.
Bowling: Elworthy 11-0-54-0; Smith 6-0-38-1; Bosch 4-0-23-0; van Noordwyk 8-1-42-0; van Zyl 21-4-83-2; Sommerville 12-0-37-1.
Batting time: 232 minutes
Overs: 62

Northern Transvaal – First Innings

BJ Sommerville c Healy b Reiffel	10
VF du Preez c Boon b McGrath	25
*RF Pienaar c Healy b Reiffel	0
JJ Strydom c ME Waugh b Reiffel	22
#KJ Rule b McGrath	1
LP Vorster c Healy b McGrath	25
DJ van Zyl not out	63
S Elworthy c Healy b Hughes	29
T Bosch lbw Hughes	0
C van Noordwyk c Healy b Hughes	0
G Smith c Hayden b Reiffel	4
Extras (6lb, 6w, 18nb)	30
Total	209

Fall of Wickets: 1-35, 2-35, 3-47, 4-49, 5-94, 6-113, 7-187, 8-187, 9-188, 10-209.
Bowling: McGrath 20-3-50-3; Hughes 20-1-72-3; Reiffel 12.1-4-27-4; ME Waugh 4-0-19-0; May 11-2-35-0.
Batting time: 304 minutes
Overs: 67.1

Northern Transvaal – Second Innings

BJ Sommerville lbw Reiffel	21
VF du Preez c Healy b Hughes	0
*RF Pienaar b Hughes	42
JJ Strydom c Taylor b Reiffel	0
#KJ Rule c Healy b Reiffel	13
LP Vorster c Healy b McGrath	12
DJ van Zyl st Healy b May	8
S Elworthy c Healy b May	31
T Bosch c Healy b Reiffel	4
C van Noordwyk not out	18
G Smith b Jones	21
Extras (2b, 6lb, 3w, 5nb)	16
Total	186

Fall of Wickets: 1-0, 2-31, 3-31, 4-82, 5-82, 6-96, 7-114, 8-142, 9-146, 10-186.
Bowling: McGrath 11-2-61-1; Hughes 8-1-30-2; Reiffel 11-0-57-4; May 10-2-24-2; Jones 2-0-6-1.
Batting time: 185 minutes *Overs:* 42

AUSTRALIANS WON BY 249 RUNS

v ORANGE FREE STATE *at Springbok Park, Bloemfontein*
February 26 – March 1 (Australians won toss)

Australians – First Innings

MJ Slater c Liebenberg b Player	65
*MA Taylor c Radley b van Zyl	35
DC Boon c Radley b Player	9
ME Waugh c Arthur b Player	154
SR Waugh c Player b Bakkes	102
ML Hayden c Cronje b van Zyl	31
#IA Healy c Radley b Player	38
PR Reiffel c Arthur b van Zyl	2
SK Warne not out	0
Extras (1b, 6lb, 1w, 6nb)	14
Total (8 wkts, declared)	450

Did Not Bat: MG Hughes, TBA May.
Fall of Wickets: 1-66, 2-86, 3-135, 4-367, 5-382, 6-443, 7-450, 8-450.
Bowling: Bakkes 18-3-73-1; Player 28.3-2-107-4; van Zyl 27-4-76-3; Boje 22-4-90-0; Venter 12-0-68-0; Cronje 10-2-29-0.
Batting time: 439 minutes
Overs: 117.3

Australians – Second Innings

MJ Slater c Arthur b Boje	105
*MA Taylor c sub (CF Craven) b Venter	54
DC Boon b Venter	5
ML Hayden c Arthur b Venter	36
SK Warne c Steyn b Venter	34
#IA Healy not out	23
MG Hughes c Liebenberg b Venter	8
Extras (4lb, 1nb)	5
Total (6 wkts, declared)	270

Fall of Wickets: 1-81, 2-107, 3-203, 4-204, 5-260, 6-270.
Bowling: Bakkes 8-1-24-0; van Zyl 13-1-34-0; Player 7-1-20-0; Boje 17-1-68-1; Venter 26-4-101-5; Cronje 4-1-19-0.
Batting time: 268 minutes
Overs: 75

Orange Free State – First Innings

JM Arthur b Warne	51
GFJ Liebenberg c Taylor b Hughes	28
*WJ Cronje c Hayden b May	44
LJ Wilkinson c Reiffel b May	53
PJR Steyn c SR Waugh b Hughes	5
K Venter c Boon b May	13
CJPG van Zyl c SR Waugh b May	22
BT Player lbw Warne	10
N Boje st Healy b Warne	7
#PJL Radley not out	16
H Bakkes c Boon b May	2
Extras (5b, 5lb, 1w, 2nb)	13
Total	264

Fall of Wickets: 1-52, 2-127, 3-133, 4-142, 5-174, 6-206, 7-219, 8-231, 9-247, 10-264.
Bowling: Hughes 18-5-47-2; Reiffel 10-1-36-0; May 35.1-9-98-5; Warne 23-5-73-3.
Batting time: 327 minutes
Overs: 86.1

Orange Free State – Second Innings

JM Arthur lbw Hughes	10
GFJ Liebenberg lbw Hughes	39
*WJ Cronje c Reiffel b May	251
LJ Wilkinson b Reiffel	5
PJR Steyn c Healy b SR Waugh	22
K Venter run out	16
CJPG van Zyl c Healy b Hughes	2
BT Player c Healy b Hughes	17
N Boje st Healy b Warne	6
#PJL Radley lbw Warne	4
H Bakkes not out	12
Extras (5b, 2lb, 2w, 3nb)	12
Total	396

Fall of Wickets: 1-19, 2-127, 3-150, 4-225, 5-271, 6-286, 7-314, 8-374, 9-384, 10-396.
Bowling: Hughes 25-2-127-4; Reiffel 23-3-60-1; May 26-4-111-1; Warne 28.2-6-70-2; SR Waugh 6-0-21-0.
Batting time: 455 minutes
Overs: 108.2

AUSTRALIANS WON BY 60 RUNS

v BOLAND *at Stellenbosch*
March 12-14 (Boland won toss)

Australians – First Innings

MJ Slater c Henderson b Erasmus	40
*MA Taylor c Erasmas b Smith	10
DC Boon lbw Drew	52
ME Waugh st Germishuys b Henderson	43
DM Jones b Drew	63
SR Waugh run out	32
#IA Healy c Roos b Drew	1
PR Reiffel not out	8
Extras (1lb, 1w, 3nb)	5
Total (7 wkts, declared)	254

Did Not Bat: SK Warne, MG Hughes, GD McGrath.
Fall of Wickets: 1-15, 2-88, 3-138, 4-156, 5-221, 6-229, 7-254.
Bowling: Smith 12-3-32-1; Roos 13-3-40-0; Henderson 15-2-49-1; Erasmus 21-4-64-1; Drew 16-2-68-3.
Batting time: 275 minutes
Overs: 77

Australians – Second Innings

MJ Slater c Germishuys b Erasmus	28
*MA Taylor st Germishuys b Drew	74
SR Waugh lbw Henderson	71
DM Jones c Jackson b Henderson	20
SK Warne st Germishuys b Henderson	9
PR Reiffel lbw Erasmus	8
#IA Healy not out	8
ME Waugh not out	1
Extras (7b, 2lb)	9
Total (6 wkts, declared)	228

Fall of Wickets: 1-68, 2-140, 3-199, 4-206, 5-215, 6-219.
Bowling: Smith 10-1-29-0; Erasmus 21-5-37-2; Roos 3-1-8-0; Henderson 20-1-73-3; Drew 15-4-72-1.
Batting time: 242 minutes
Overs: 69

Boland – First Innings

L Ferreira c Reiffel b Hughes	3
KC Jackson lbw Warne	27
*TN Lazard c Boon b Hughes	4
JB Commins lbw Reiffel	4
RI Dalrymple c Healy b McGrath	33
JS Roos lbw McGrath	40
#L Germishuys c Warne b McGrath	2
M Erasmus lbw McGrath	0
CW Henderson not out	19
B Drew c SR Waugh b Warne	4
P Smith lbw Warne	3
Extras (1b, 3lb, 12nb)	16
Total	155

Fall of Wickets: 1-5, 2-18, 3-30, 4-48, 5-123, 6-126, 7-126, 8-129, 9-141, 10-155.
Bowling: Hughes 9-2-21-2; Reiffel 18-6-40-1; McGrath 18-6-38-4; Warne 20.4-9-49-3; SR Waugh 4-1-3-0.
Batting time: 293 minutes
Overs: 69.4

Boland – Second Innings

*TN Lazard b Reiffel	44
KC Jackson c Healy b Reiffel	4
L Ferreira lbw McGrath	41
JB Commins b McGrath	0
RI Dalrymple not out	17
JS Roos c Reiffel b Warne	9
#L Germishuys not out	4
Extras (1b, 8lb, 2w, 2nb)	13
Total (5wkts)	132

Fall of Wickets: 1-11, 2-96, 3-96, 4-96, 5-120.
Bowling: Hughes 11-3-29-0; Reiffel 12-3-23-2; McGrath 13-2-30-2; Warne 15-7-24-1; SR Waugh 2-1-3-0; ME Waugh 5-0-14-0.
Batting time: 232 minutes
Overs: 58

MATCH DRAWN

THE LIMITED-OVERS INTERNATIONALS

THE FIRST ONE-DAY INTERNATIONAL *at the Wanderers, Johannesburg*
February 19 (South Africa won toss)

South Africa

PN Kirsten c Reiffel b McGrath	47
G Kirsten c Healy b Reiffel	12
WJ Cronje c Reiffel b McDermott	112
JN Rhodes not out	47
AP Kuiper not out	2
Extras (5lb, 2w, 5nb)	12
Total (3 wkts, 50 overs)	232

Did Not Bat: *KC Wessels, #DJ Richardson, RP Snell, EO. Simons, PS de Villiers, AA Donald.
Fall of Wickets: 1-39, 2-123, 3-229.
Bowling: McDermott 10-0-52-1; Reiffel 10-1-36-1; McGrath 10-1-29-1; SR Waugh 10-0-54-0; Warne 10-0-56-0.

Australia

MA Taylor b Snell	30
DC Boon c Rhodes b Kuiper	58
DM Jones c Cronje b Simons	42
ME Waugh c Richardson b Simons	14
SR Waugh not out	46
*AR Border b de Villiers	25
#IA Healy not out	4
Extras (4lb, 3w, 1nb)	8
Total (5 wkts, 50 overs)	227

Did Not Bat: PR Reiffel, CJ McDermott, SK Warne, GD McGrath.
Fall of Wickets: 1-61, 2-108, 3-143, 4-155, 5-209.
Bowling: Donald 9-1-46-0; de Villiers 10-0-43-1; Snell 10-0-55-1; Simons 10-0-29-2; Kuiper 7-0-30-1; Cronje 4-0-20-0.

Man of the Match: WJ Cronje
SOUTH AFRICA WON BY FIVE RUNS

THE SECOND ONE-DAY INTERNATIONAL *at Centurion Park, Verwoerdburg*
February 20 (South Africa won toss)

South Africa

PN Kirsten b ME Waugh	22
G Kirsten c SR Waugh b McGrath	18
WJ Cronje run out	97
JN Rhodes lbw Warne	44
*KC Wessels c Healy b McGrath	22
AP Kuiper not out	47
EO Simons not out	2
Extras (6lb, 3w, 4nb)	13
Total (5 wkts, 50 overs)	265

Did Not Bat: #DJ Richardson, RP Snell, CR Matthews, PS de Villiers.
Fall of Wickets: 1-45, 2-58, 3-152, 4-203, 5-229.
Bowling: McDermott 10-2-46-1; Reiffel 8-0-50-0; ME Waugh 9-1-52-1; McGrath 10-1-42-2; SR Waugh 5-0-28-0; Warne 8-1-41-1.

Australia

DC Boon c Cronje b Matthews	2
MA Taylor run out	21
DM Jones b Matthews	5
ME Waugh lbw Matthews	0
SR Waugh b Simons	86
*AR Border run out	41
#IA Healy c G Kirsten b Kuiper	4
PR Reiffel c Simons b de Villiers	10
SK Warne c Wessels b Cronje	9
CJ McDermott run out	16
GD McGrath not out	0
Extras (12lb, 3w)	15
Total (42.4 overs)	209

Fall of Wickets: 1-11, 2-19, 3-19, 4-34, 5-141, 6-145, 7-174, 8-189, 9-209, 10-209.
Bowling: de Villiers 8-2-20-1; Matthews 8-2-26-3; Simons 7.4-0-39-1; Snell 8-0-38-0; Kuiper 6-0-38-1; Cronje 5-0-36-1.

Man of the Match: WJ Cronje
SOUTH AFRICA WON BY 56 RUNS

THE THIRD ONE-DAY INTERNATIONAL *at St George's Park, Port Elizabeth*
February 22 (Australia won toss)

Australia

MA Taylor c Richardson b de Villiers	2
DC Boon b de Villiers	76
DM Jones run out	67
ME Waugh c Rhodes b Matthews	60
CJ McDermott run out	15
SR Waugh c Matthews b Donald	18
*AR Border not out	40
#IA Healy not out	1
Extras (1lb, 1w)	2
Total (6 wkts, 50 overs)	281

Did Not Bat: PR Reiffel, SK Warne, GD McGrath.
Fall of Wickets: 1-12, 2-135, 3-180, 4-198, 5-233, 6-276.
Bowling: de Villiers 10-1-55-2; Matthews 10-1-46-1; Donald 10-0-60-1; Cronje 10-1-62-0; Symcox 4-0-25-0; Kuiper 6-0-32-0.

South Africa

PN Kirsten c McGrath b Warne	27
G Kirsten b McDermott	6
WJ Cronje c McDermott b SR Waugh	45
JN Rhodes c Healy b ME Waugh	36
*KC Wessels run out	5
AP Kuiper b McDermott	33
#DJ Richardson not out	23
PL Symcox c Boon b Warne	4
CR Matthews b Warne	0
PS de Villiers b Warne	4
AA Donald b McDermott	0
Extras (6lb, 4nb)	10
Total (43 overs)	193

Fall of Wickets: 1-8, 2-49, 3-115, 4-125, 5-127, 6-165, 7-178, 8-181, 9-188, 10-193.
Bowling: McDermott 10-0-35-3; McGrath 7-2-17-0; Reiffel 8-0-40-0; Warne 10-0-36-4; SR Waugh 4-0-33-1; ME Waugh 4-0-26-1.

Man of the Match: ME Waugh
AUSTRALIA WON BY 88 RUNS

THE FOURTH ONE-DAY INTERNATIONAL *at Kingsmead, Durban*
February 24 (Australia won toss)

Australia

DC Boon c de Villiers b Simons	34
MJ Slater c Richardson b de Villiers	1
DM Jones lbw Matthews	8
ME Waugh c Hudson b Matthews	3
SR Waugh lbw Simons	2
*AR Border not out	69
#IA Healy c Richardson b Kuiper	0
PR Reiffel c Wessels b Kuiper	0
SK Warne b Matthews	22
CJ McDermott b Matthews	0
GD McGrath c Richardson b Cronje	0
Extras (7b, 4w, 3nb)	14
Total (43.2 overs)	154

Fall of Wickets: 1-3, 2-12, 3-18, 4-23, 5-91, 6-93, 7-100, 8-138, 9-138, 10-154.
Bowling: de Villiers 8-0-30-1; Matthews 8-5-10-4; Simons 10-4-22-2; Snell 9-1-42-0; Cronje 3.2-0-19-1; Kuiper 5-0-24-2.

South Africa

AC Hudson lbw Reiffel	37
PN Kirsten c Healy b Reiffel	15
WJ Cronje not out	50
JN Rhodes c ME Waugh b Warne	3
*KC Wessels not out	40
Extras (1lb, 8w, 3nb)	12
Total (3 wkts, 45 overs)	157

Did Not Bat: AP Kuiper, EO Simons, #DJ Richardson, RP Snell, CR Matthews, PS de Villiers.
Fall of Wickets: 1-51, 2-55, 3-69.
Bowling: McDermott 10-0-35-0; McGrath 10-4-20-0; SR Waugh 4-0-24-0; Reiffel 10-1-31-2; Warne 8-2-32-2; ME Waugh 3-0-14-0.

Man of the Match: CR Matthews
SOUTH AFRICA WON BY SEVEN WICKETS

THE FIRST DAY/NIGHT INTERNATIONAL *at Buffalo Park, East London*
April 2 (South Africa won toss)

South Africa

AC Hudson c Warne b Reiffel	14
PN Kirsten c ME Waugh b Warne	53
WJ Cronje c Warne b May	10
JN Rhodes st Healy b May	16
AP Kuiper run out	12
*KC Wessels run out	15
EO Simons st Healy b Border	6
BM McMillan b SR Waugh	17
#DJ Richardson not out	7
CR Matthews c Healy b Border	0
PS de Villiers st Healy b Border	0
Extras (4lb, 1w, 3nb)	8
Total (49.5 overs)	158

Fall of Wickets: 1-35, 2-62, 3-87, 4-109, 5-118, 6-129, 7-139, 8-155, 9-158, 10-158.
Bowling: McGrath 6-1-20-0; Reiffel 7-1-13-1; SR Waugh 9-1-25-1; May 10-0-35-2; Warne 10-0-34-1; Border 7.5-0-27-3.

Australia

MJ Slater c Kirsten b Simons	31
DC Boon run out	30
DM Jones lbw Simons	8
ME Waugh not out	21
SR Waugh not out	67
Extras (2lb)	2
Total (3 wkts, 40 overs)	159

Did Not Bat: *AR Border, #IA Healy, PR Reiffel, SK Warne, TBA May, GD McGrath.
Fall of Wickets: 1-57, 2-66, 3-71.
Bowling: de Villiers 8-0-31-1; Matthews 8-0-34-0; Simons 10-2-32-2; McMillan 6-0-21-0; Cronje 7-0-32-0; Kuiper 1-0-7-0.

Man of the Match: AR Border
AUSTRALIA WON BY SEVEN WICKETS

THE SECOND DAY/NIGHT INTERNATIONAL *at St George's Park, Port Elizabeth*
April 4 (South Africa won toss)

South Africa

AC Hudson c Warne b May	63
PN Kirsten b Reiffel	10
WJ Cronje c Healy b ME Waugh	11
JN Rhodes c Jones b SR Waugh	66
*KC Wessels b Reiffel	27
EO Simons run out	23
BM McMillan not out	2
#DJ Richardson not out	2
Extras (1b, 15lb, 5w, 2nb)	23
Total (6 wkts, 50 overs)	227

Did Not Bat: TG Shaw, CR Matthews, PS de Villiers.
Fall of Wickets: 1-18, 2-48, 3-153, 4-175, 5-216, 6-223.
Bowling: McGrath 10-1-41-0; Reiffel 10-1-33-2; ME Waugh 7-0-26-1; SR Waugh 10-1-48-1; May 10-0-45-1; Warne 3-0-18-0.

Australia

DC Boon c Wessels b de Villiers	4
MJ Slater c Richardson b Matthews	16
DM Jones b Simons	13
ME Waugh b Simons	17
SR Waugh lbw McMillan	7
*AR Border lbw Shaw	5
#IA Healy c Wessels b Shaw	5
PR Reiffel c Simons b Matthews	58
SK Warne run out	55
TBA May c&b de Villiers	4
GD McGrath not out	0
Extras (13lb, 4w)	17
Total (49.1 overs)	201

Fall of Wickets: 1-4, 2-35, 3-50, 4-59, 5-65, 6-68, 7-77, 8-196, 9-201, 10-201.
Bowling: de Villiers 9-1-42-2; Matthews 9.1-1-35-2; McMillan 8-0-38-1; Simons 10-3-24-2; Shaw 8-2-19-2; Cronje 5-1-30-0.

Man of the Match: JN Rhodes
SOUTH AFRICA WON BY 26 RUNS

THE THIRD DAY/NIGHT INTERNATIONAL *at Newlands, Cape Town*
April 6 (Australia won toss)

Australia

MA Taylor run out	63
ML Hayden lbw Matthews	0
DM Jones c Richardson b Matthews	8
ME Waugh b Matthews	71
SR Waugh b Simons	23
*AR Border not out	40
#IA Healy c Wessels b Matthews	26
Extras (8lb, 1w, 2nb)	11
Total (6 wkts, 50 overs)	242

Did Not Bat: PR Reiffel, SK Warne, TBA May, GD McGrath.
Fall of Wickets: 1-0, 2-10, 3-133, 4-163, 5-180, 6-242.
Bowling: de Villiers 10-1-52-0; Matthews 10-0-47-4; McMillan 10-0-46-0; Simons 10-0-31-1; Cronje 5-0-40-0; Kuiper 5-0-18-0.

South Africa

AC Hudson lbw Warne	62
G Kirsten c ME Waugh b Reiffel	3
WJ Cronje c Taylor b Warne	37
JN Rhodes st Healy b Warne	35
AP Kuiper not out	38
*KC Wessels c Border b ME Waugh	12
EO Simons not out	9
Extras (1b, 8lb, 1nb)	10
Total (5 wkts, 50 overs)	206

Did Not Bat: BM McMillan, #DJ Richardson, CR Matthews, PS de Villiers.
Fall of Wickets: 1-22, 2-101, 3-114, 4-163, 5-186.
Bowling: McGrath 10-1-38-0; Reiffel 7-2-18-1; May 10-0-38-0; SR Waugh 4-0-22-0; Warne 10-0-31-3; ME Waugh 9-0-50-1.

Man of the Match: ME Waugh
AUSTRALIA WON BY 36 RUNS

THE FOURTH DAY/NIGHT INTERNATIONAL *at Springbok Park, Bloemfontein*
April 8 (Australia won toss)

Australia

MJ Slater st Richardson b Shaw	34
MA Taylor c Wessels b Matthews	1
ME Waugh c Wessels b Simons	13
DC Boon c Wessels b Matthews	45
SR Waugh c McMillan b de Villiers	42
*AR Border c McMillan b Matthews	11
#IA Healy not out	41
PR Reiffel not out	8
Extras (6lb, 1w, 1nb)	8
Total (6 wkts, 50 overs)	203

Did Not Bat: SK Warne, DW Fleming, GD McGrath.
Fall of Wickets: 1-7, 2-31, 3-69, 4-140, 5-143, 6-184.
Bowling: de Villiers 10-1-44-1; Matthews 10-0-40-3; Simons 10-2-36-1; Shaw 10-0-30-1; McMillan 7-0-34-0; Kuiper 3-0-13-0.

South Africa

AC Hudson c Border b Reiffel	84
*KC Wessels b SR Waugh	28
WJ Cronje b McGrath	18
JN Rhodes c SR Waugh b Reiffel	13
AP Kuiper c ME Waugh b Warne	6
BM McMillan run out	4
#DJ Richardson run out	18
EO Simons b SR Waugh	18
TG Shaw not out	2
Extras (6lb, 4w, 1nb)	11
Total (8 wkts, 50 overs)	202

Did Not Bat: CR Matthews, PS de Villiers.
Fall of Wickets: 1-82, 2-111, 3-143, 4-158, 5-162, 6-164, 7-196, 8-202.
Bowling: McGrath 10-0-44-1; Fleming 10-2-33-0; Reiffel 10-0-34-2; Warne 10-0-37-1; SR Waugh 10-0-48-2.

Man of the Match: AC Hudson
Man of the Series: SR Waugh
AUSTRALIA WON BY ONE RUN

OTHER MATCHES

AUSTRALIANS V NICKY OPPENHEIMER XI *at Halfway House, Randjesfontein.* **February 10**

Australians 223 (55.5 overs: DM Jones 60, ML Hayden 40; EAE Baptiste 4-56, J Malao 3-59) drew with **Nicky Oppenheimer XI 4-121** (29 overs: AP Kuiper 56).
(Match abandoned due to rain – there was no limit on the number of overs per side)

AUSTRALIANS V PRESIDENT'S XI *at Fanie du Toit Stadium, Potchefstroom* **February 17**

Australians 5-141 (35 overs: ME Waugh 55, DC Boon 41) drew with **President's XI**
(Match abandoned due to rain)

AUSTRALIAN FIRST-CLASS TOUR AVERAGES

BATTING AND FIELDING

Batsman	Mat	Inn	NO	Runs	HS	100	50	Avge	Ct	St
ME Waugh	6	10	2	573	154	3	-	71.63	3	-
SR Waugh	5	7	1	400	102	1	3	66.67	6	-
DM Jones	2	3	-	168	85	-	2	56.00	-	-
MJ Slater	6	12	1	548	105	1	3	49.82	1	-
IA Healy	6	10	3	277	61	-	2	39.57	20	3
DC Boon	6	11	1	392	96	-	3	39.20	7	-
AR Border	3	5	1	152	45	-	-	38.00	4	-
MA Taylor	5	10	-	373	75	-	4	37.30	4	-
ML Hayden	3	6	1	151	50	-	1	30.20	3	-
MG Hughes	5	5	1	71	30	-	-	17.75	1	-
PR Reiffel	4	5	1	53	22	-	-	13.25	5	-
CJ McDermott	3	4	-	48	31	-	-	12.00	-	-
SK Warne	5	8	1	84	34	-	-	12.00	1	-
TBA May	3	3	1	14	11	-	-	7.00	-	-
GD McGrath	4	3	2	5	4	-	-	5.00	-	-

BOWLING

Bowler	Overs	Mdns	Runs	Wkts	Best	5w	10w	Ave
DM Jones	2	0	6	1	1-6	-	-	6.00
SR Waugh	89.5	31	157	11	5-28	1	-	14.27
PR Reiffel	116.1	24	320	14	4-27	-	-	22.86
SK Warne	277.5	96	552	24	4-86	-	-	23.00
GD McGrath	145.1	34	348	14	4-38	-	-	24.86
MG Hughes	161	27	563	17	4-127	-	-	33.12
TBA May	143.1	33	437	12	5-98	1	-	36.42
CJ McDermott	128.2	26	370	7	3-63	-	-	52.86
AR Border	9	4	17	0	0-0	-	-	-
ME Waugh	39	9	119	0	0-11	-	-	-

TEST AVERAGES

AUSTRALIA – BATTING AND FIELDING

Batsman	Mat	Inn	NO	Runs	HS	100	50	Avge	Ct	St
SR Waugh	3	4	1	195	86	-	2	65.00	3	-
ME Waugh	3	5	1	233	113*	1	-	58.25	2	-
DC Boon	3	6	1	277	96	-	2	55.40	3	-
MJ Slater	3	6	1	251	95	-	1	50.20	1	-
IA Healy	3	4	-	157	61	-	2	39.25	5	-
AR Border	3	5	1	152	45	-	-	38.00	4	-
MA Taylor	2	4	-	97	70	-	1	24.25	2	-
MG Hughes	2	3	1	33	26*	-	-	16.50	1	-
PR Reiffel	1	1	-	13	13	-	-	13.00	1	-
CJ McDermott	3	4	-	48	31	-	-	12.00	-	-
ML Hayden	1	2	-	20	15	-	-	10.00	1	-
SK Warne	3	5	-	41	15	-	-	8.20	-	-
TBA May	1	2	-	13	11	-	-	6.50	-	-
GD McGrath	2	2	2	1	1*	-	-	-	-	-

AUSTRALIA – BOWLING

Bowler	Overs	Mdns	Runs	Wkts	Best	5w	10w	Ave
SR Waugh	77.5	29	130	10	5-28	1	-	13.00
SK Warne	190.5	69	336	15	4-86	-	-	22.40
PR Reiffel	30	7	77	2	2-77	-	-	38.50
TBA May	61	16	169	4	2-62	-	-	42.25
GD McGrath	83.1	21	169	4	3-65	-	-	42.25
CJ McDermott	128.2	26	370	7	3-63	-	-	52.86
MG Hughes	70	13	237	4	3-59	-	-	59.25
AR Border	9	4	17	0	0-0	-	-	-
ME Waugh	30	9	86	0	0-11	-	-	-

SOUTH AFRICA – BATTING AND FIELDING

Batsman	Mat	Inn	NO	Runs	HS	100	50	Avge	Ct	St
AC Hudson	3	5	-	293	102	1	2	58.60	1	-
JN Rhodes	3	5	-	193	78	-	2	38.60	2	-
WJ Cronje	3	5	-	190	122	1	-	38.00	-	-
PN Kirsten	3	5	-	187	70	-	2	37.40	4	-
BM McMillan	3	5	-	185	84	-	2	37.00	2	-
DJ Richardson	3	5	-	175	59	-	1	35.00	7	-
G Kirsten	3	5	-	162	47	-	-	32.40	4	-
CR Matthews	3	5	3	45	31*	-	-	22.50	-	-
KC Wessels	3	5	-	89	50	-	1	17.80	2	-
AA Donald	3	5	3	22	15*	-	-	11.00	2	-
PS de Villiers	3	5	-	27	16	-	-	5.40	2	-

SOUTH AFRICA – BOWLING

Bowler	Overs	Mdns	Runs	Wkts	Best	5w	10w	Ave
CR Matthews	134	44	297	13	5-80	1	-	22.85
AA Donald	128	21	425	12	3-66	-	-	35.42
PS de Villiers	148.3	34	405	11	4-117	-	-	36.82
BM McMillan	108	24	321	6	3-61	-	-	53.50
WJ Cronje	36.3	10	61	1	1-0	-	-	61.00
JN Rhodes	1	1	0	0	0-0	-	-	-
G Kirsten	18.1	2	50	0	0-7	-	-	-

LIMITED-OVERS INTERNATIONALS AVERAGES

AUSTRALIA – BATTING AND FIELDING

Batsman	Mat	Inn	NO	Runs	HS	100	50	Avge	Ct	St
AR Border	8	7	3	231	69*	-	1	57.25	2	-
SR Waugh	8	8	2	291	86	-	2	48.50	-	-
DC Boon	7	7	-	249	76	-	2	35.57	1	-
SK Warne	8	3	-	87	55	-	1	29.00	3	-
ME Waugh	8	8	1	199	71	-	2	28.42	4	-
PR Reiffel	8	4	1	76	58	-	1	25.33	2	-
MA Taylor	5	5	-	117	63	-	1	23.40	1	-
DM Jones	7	7	-	151	67	-	1	21.57	1	-
MJ Slater	4	4	-	82	34	-	-	20.50	-	-
IA Healy	8	7	3	81	41*	-	-	20.25	6	3
CJ McDermott	4	3	-	31	16	-	-	10.33	1	-
TBA May	3	1	-	4	4	-	-	4.00	-	-
GD McGrath	8	3	2	0	0*	-	-	0.00	1	-
ML Hayden	1	1	-	0	0	-	-	0.00	-	-
DW Fleming	1	-	-	-	-	-	-	-	-	-

AUSTRALIA – BOWLING

Bowler	Overs	Mdns	Runs	Wkts	Best	Average	RPO
AR Border	7.5	0	27	3	3-27	9.00	3.45
SK Warne	69	3	285	11	4-36	25.91	4.13
PR Reiffel	70	6	255	9	2-32	28.33	3.66
TBA May	30	0	118	3	2-35	39.33	3.93
CJ McDermott	40	2	168	4	3-35	42.00	4.20
ME Waugh	32	1	168	4	1-26	42.00	5.25
SR Waugh	56	2	282	5	2-48	56.40	5.04
GD McGrath	73	11	251	4	2-42	62.75	3.44
DW Fleming	10	2	33	0	0-33	-	3.30

SOUTH AFRICA – BATTING AND FIELDING

Batsman	Mat	Inn	NO	Runs	HS	100	50	Avge	Ct	St
WJ Cronje	8	8	1	380	112	1	2	54.29	2	-
AC Hudson	5	5	-	260	84	-	3	52.00	1	-
DJ Richardson	8	4	3	50	23*	-	-	50.00	7	1
AP Kuiper	7	6	3	138	47*	-	-	46.00	-	-
JN Rhodes	8	8	1	260	66	-	1	37.14	2	-
PN Kirsten	6	6	-	174	53	-	1	29.00	1	-
KC Wessels	8	7	1	149	40*	-	-	24.83	8	-
EO Simons	7	5	2	58	23	-	-	19.33	2	-
BM McMillan	4	3	1	23	17	-	-	11.50	2	-
G Kirsten	4	4	-	39	18	-	-	9.75	1	-
PL Symcox	1	1	-	4	4	-	-	4.00	-	-
PS de Villiers	8	2	-	4	4	-	-	2.00	2	-
CR Matthews	7	2	-	0	0	-	-	0.00	1	-
AA Donald	2	1	-	0	0	-	-	0.00	-	-
TG Shaw	2	1	1	2	2*	-	-	-	-	-
RP Snell	3	-	-	-	-	-	-	-	-	

SOUTH AFRICA – BOWLING

Bowler	Overs	Mdns	Runs	Wkts	Best	Average	RPO
CR Matthews	63.1	9	238	17	4-10	14.00	3.77
TG Shaw	18	2	49	3	2-19	16.33	2.72
EO Simons	67.4	14	213	11	2-22	19.36	3.15
PS de Villiers	73	6	317	8	2-42	39.63	4.07
AP Kuiper	33	0	162	4	2-24	40.50	4.91
AA Donald	19	1	106	1	1-60	106.00	5.58
WJ Cronje	39.2	2	239	2	1-19	119.50	6.08
RP Snell	27	1	135	1	1-55	135.00	5.00
BM McMillan	31	0	139	1	1-38	139.00	4.48
PL Symcox	4	0	25	0	0-25	-	6.25

** indicates not out*
RPO indicates runs per over